MznLnx

Missing Links Exam Preps

Exam Prep for

Physical Geology Exploring The Earth

Monroe, Wicander, 5th Edition

The MznLnx Exam Prep is your link from the texbook and lecture to your exams.
The MznLnx Exam Preps are unauthorized and comprehensive reviews of your textbooks.

All material provided by MznLnx and Rico Publications (c) 2010
Textbook publishers and textbook authors do not particpate in or contribute to these reviews.

MznLnx

Rico Publications

Exam Prep for Physical Geology Exploring The Earth
5th Edition
Monroe, Wicander

Publisher: Raymond Houge
Assistant Editor: Michael Rouger
Text and Cover Designer: Lisa Buckner
Marketing Manager: Sara Swagger
Project Manager, Editorial Production: Jerry Emerson
Art Director: Vernon Lowerui

Product Manager: Dave Mason
Editorial Assitant: Rachel Guzmanji
Pedagogy: Debra Long
Cover Image: Jim Reed/Getty Images
Text and Cover Printer: City Printing, Inc.
Compositor: Media Mix, Inc.

(c) 2010 Rico Publications
ALL RIGHTS RESERVED. No part of this work covered by the copyright may be reproduced or used in any form or by an means--graphic, electronic, or mechanical, including photocopying, recording, taping, Web distribution, information storage, and retrieval systems, or in any other manner--without the written permission of the publisher.

Printed in the United States
ISBN:

For more information about our products, contact us at:
Dave.Mason@RicoPublications.com

For permission to use material from this text or product, submit a request online to:
Dave.Mason@RicoPublications.com

Contents

CHAPTER 1
Understanding Earth: A Dynamic and Evolving Planet — 1

CHAPTER 2
Minerals—The Building Blocks of Rocks — 11

CHAPTER 3
Igneous Rocks and Intrusive Igneous Activity — 25

CHAPTER 4
Volcanism and Volcanoes — 38

CHAPTER 5
Weathering, Erosion, and Soil — 50

CHAPTER 6
Sediment and Sedimentary Rocks — 61

CHAPTER 7
Metamorphism and Metamorphic Rocks — 79

CHAPTER 8
Geologic Time: Concepts and Principles — 92

CHAPTER 9
Earthquakes — 103

CHAPTER 10
Earth's Interior — 111

CHAPTER 11
The Seafloor — 120

CHAPTER 12
Plate Tectonics: A Unifying Theory — 133

CHAPTER 13
Deformation, Mountain Building, and the Evolution of Continents 362 — 148

CHAPTER 14
Mass Wasting — 163

CHAPTER 15
Running Water — 170

CHAPTER 16
Groundwater — 180

CHAPTER 17
Glaciers and Glaciation — 190

CHAPTER 18
The Work of Wind and Deserts — 203

CHAPTER 19
Shorelines and Shoreline Processes — 214

CHAPTER 20
Physical Geology in Perspective — 224

ANSWER KEY — 228

TO THE STUDENT

COMPREHENSIVE

The *MznLnx* Exam Prep series is designed to help you pass your exams. Editors at MznLnx review your textbooks and then prepare these practice exams to help you master the textbook material. Unlike study guides, workbooks, and practice tests provided by the texbook publisher and textbook authors, *MznLnx* gives you **all** of the material in each chapter in exam form, not just samples, so you can be sure to nail your exam.

MECHANICAL

The MznLnx Exam Prep series creates exams that will help you learn the subject matter as well as test you on your understanding. Each question is designed to help you master the concept. Just working through the exams, you gain an understanding of the subject--its a simple mechanical process that produces success.

INTEGRATED STUDY GUIDE AND REVIEW

MznLnx is not just a set of exams designed to test you, its also a comprehensive review of the subject content. Each exam question is also a review of the concept, making sure that you will get the answer correct without having to go to other sources of material. You learn as you go! Its the easiest way to pass an exam.

HUMOR

Studying can be tedious and dry. MznLnx's instructional design includes moderate humor within the exam questions on occassion, to break the tedium and revitalize the brain

Chapter 1. Understanding Earth: A Dynamic and Evolving Planet

1. The terms _____ and icehouse Earth refer to the prevailing global climate on a timescale of millions of years.

During a _____ Earth period, the planet's atmosphere contains sufficient _____ gases such as carbon dioxide and methane for ice to be entirely absent from the planet's surface.

During icehouse periods, glaciers are present in fluctuating amounts; variations in the Earth's orbit may result in many ice ages, glacials, and interglacials.

   a. 1703 Genroku earthquake
   c. 1700 Cascadia earthquake

   b. 1509 Istanbul earthquake
   d. Greenhouse

2. The _____ is the rigid outermost shell of a rocky planet.

In the Earth, the _____ includes the crust and the uppermost mantle, which constitute the hard and rigid outer layer of the planet. The _____ is underlain by the asthenosphere, the weaker, hotter, and deeper part of the upper mantle.

   a. Nappe
   c. Continental crust

   b. Copperbelt Province
   d. Lithosphere

3. The _____ is a fundamental concept in geology that describes the dynamic transitions through geologic time among the three main rock types: sedimentary, metamorphic, and igneous. Each type of rock is altered or destroyed when it is forced out of its equilibrium conditions. An igneous rock such as basalt may break down and dissolve when exposed to the atmosphere, or melt as it is subducted under a continent.

   a. Metamorphic zone
   c. Rock cycle

   b. Magma
   d. Petrology

4. A _____ is a type of mudflow or landslide composed of pyroclastic material and water that flows down from a volcano, typically along a river valley. The term '_____' originated in the Javanese language of Indonesia. They can be best described as volcanic mudflows. They may not necessarily be caused by volcanic activity, but at the very least do originate from some type of volcanism.

   a. 1700 Cascadia earthquake
   c. 1509 Istanbul earthquake

   b. 1703 Genroku earthquake
   d. Lahar

5. The _____ is the mechanically weak ductilly-deforming region of the upper mantle of the Earth. It lies below the lithosphere, at depths between 100 and 200 km (~ 62 and 124 miles) below the surface, but perhaps extending as deep as 400 km (~ 249 miles.)

The _____ is a portion of the upper mantle just below the lithosphere that is involved in plate movements and isostatic adjustments. In spite of its heat, pressures keep it plastic, and it has a relatively low density. Seismic waves pass relatively slowly through the _____, compared to the overlying lithospheric mantle, thus it has been called the low-velocity zone. This was the observation that originally alerted seismologists to its presence and gave some information about its physical properties, as the speed of seismic waves decreases with decreasing rigidity.

a. AL 333
b. AASHTO Soil Classification System
c. Asthenosphere
d. AL 129-1

6. A _____ is a large, slow-moving mass of ice, formed from compacted layers of snow, that slowly deforms and flows in response to gravity and high pressure.

_____ ice is the largest reservoir of fresh water on Earth, and second only to oceans as the largest reservoir of total water.

a. Glacier
b. Pacific Decadal Oscillation
c. Greenhouse gases
d. Little Ice Age

7. A _____ or mudslide is the most rapid (up to 80 km/h, or 50 mph) and fluid type of downhill mass wasting. It is a rapid movement of a large mass of mud formed from loose earth and water. Similar terms are mudslide (not very liquid), mud stream, debris flow (e.g. in high mountains), j>ökulhlaup, and lahar

a. 1509 Istanbul earthquake
b. 1700 Cascadia earthquake
c. Mudflow
d. 1703 Genroku earthquake

8. The _____ is a chronologic schema (or idealized model) relating stratigraphy to time that is used by geologists, paleontologists and other earth scientists to describe the timing and relationships between events that have occurred during the history of the Earth. The table of geologic time spans presented here agrees with the dates and nomenclature proposed by the International Commission on Stratigraphy, and uses the standard color codes of the United States Geological Survey.

Evidence from radiometric dating indicates that the Earth is about 4.570 billion years old.

a. 1700 Cascadia earthquake
b. Geologic time scale
c. 1703 Genroku earthquake
d. 1509 Istanbul earthquake

9. _____ is the use of the principles of geology to reconstruct and understand the history of the Earth . It focuses on geologic processes that change the Earth's surface and subsurface; and the use of stratigraphy, structural geology and paleontology to tell the sequence of these events. It also focuses on the evolution of plants and animals during different time periods in the geological timescale.

a. Rockall
b. Historical geology
c. Loihi Seamount
d. Strike-slip faults

10. _____ is the solid-state recrystallization of pre-existing rocks due to changes in physical and chemical conditions, primarily heat, pressure, and the introduction of chemically active fluids. Both mineralogical, chemical and crystallographic changes can occur during this process.

Three types of _____ exist: dynamic, contact and regional.

a. Dike
b. Cross-bedding
c. Gradualism
d. Metamorphism

11. The _____ is the zone of the ocean floor that separates the thin oceanic crust from thick continental crust. _____s constitute about 28% of the oceanic area.

The transition from continental to oceanic crust commonly occurs within the outer part of the margin, called continental rise.

   a. 1509 Istanbul earthquake
   b. Longshore drift
   c. Continental margin
   d. Cuspate forelands

12. _____ is the change in population over time, and can be quantified as the change in the number of individuals in a population using 'per unit time' for measurement. The term _____ can technically refer to any species, but almost always refers to humans, and it is often used informally for the more specific demographic term _____ rate , and is often used to refer specifically to the growth of the population of the world.

Simple models of _____ include the Malthusian Growth Model and the logistic model.

   a. 1509 Istanbul earthquake
   b. 1703 Genroku earthquake
   c. 1700 Cascadia earthquake
   d. Population growth

13. _____ is a pattern of resource use that aims to meet human needs while preserving the environment so that these needs can be met not only in the present, but also for future generations. The term was used by the Brundtland Commission which coined what has become the most often-quoted definition of _____ as development that 'meets the needs of the present without compromising the ability of future generations to meet their own needs.'

_____ ties together concern for the carrying capacity of natural systems with the social challenges facing humanity. As early as the 1970s 'sustainability' was employed to describe an economy 'in equilibrium with basic ecological support systems.' Ecologists have pointed to the 'limits of growth' and presented the alternative of a 'steady state economy' in order to address environmental concerns.

   a. 1509 Istanbul earthquake
   b. 1703 Genroku earthquake
   c. 1700 Cascadia earthquake
   d. Sustainable development

14. _____ is the geomorphic process by which soil, regolith, and rock move downslope under the force of gravity. Types of _____ include creep, slides, flows, topples, and falls, each with its own characteristic features, and taking place over timescales from seconds to years. _____ occurs on both terrestrial and submarine slopes, and has been observed on Earth, Mars, and Venus.

   a. 1700 Cascadia earthquake
   b. 1509 Istanbul earthquake
   c. Soil liquefaction
   d. Mass wasting

15. A _____ or sandstorm is a meteorological phenomenon common in arid and semi-arid regions and arises when a gust front passes or when the wind force exceeds the threshold value where loose sand and dust are removed from the dry surface. Particles are transported by saltation and suspension, causing soil erosion from one place and deposition in another. The Sahara and drylands around the Arabian peninsula are the main source of airborne dust, with some contributions from Iran, Pakistan and India into the Arabian Sea, and China's storms deposit dust in the Pacific.

   a. 1703 Genroku earthquake
   b. 1509 Istanbul earthquake
   c. Dust storm
   d. 1700 Cascadia earthquake

16. _____ is constantly present in the environment and is emitted from a variety of natural and artificial sources. Primary contributions come from:

- Sources in the earth. These include sources in food and water, which are incorporated in the body, and in building materials and other products that incorporate those radioactive sources;
- Sources from space, in the form of cosmic rays;
- Sources in the atmosphere. One significant contribution comes from the radon gas that is released from the Earth's crust and subsequently decays into radioactive atoms that become attached to airborne dust and particulates. Another contribution arises from the radioactive atoms produced in the bombardment of atoms in the upper atmosphere by high-energy cosmic rays.

About 3% of _____ comes from other man-made sources such as:

- Self-luminous dials and signs
- Global radioactive contamination due to historical nuclear weapons testing
- Nuclear power station or nuclear fuel reprocessing accidents (though these are rare)
- Normal operation of facilities used for nuclear power and scientific research
- Emissions from burning fossil fuels, such as coal fired power plants
- Emissions from nuclear medicine facilities and patients
- Emissions from the improper disposal or recycling of radioactive materials used in nuclear medicine

Accidental exposure to man-made radioactive substances can result in radiation exposure that is many times that received from background sources, whether natural or man-made. Additionally, radiation therapy can cause relatively high levels of exposure. However, when it comes to _____, naturally occurring sources are responsible for the vast majority of radiation exposure.

a. Background radiation
b. 1509 Istanbul earthquake
c. 1700 Cascadia earthquake
d. Radionuclide

17. The _____ is a cosmological model of the initial conditions and subsequent development of the universe. It is supported by the most comprehensive and accurate explanations from current scientific evidence and observation. As used by cosmologists, the term _____ generally refers to the idea that the universe has expanded from a primordial hot and dense initial condition at some finite time in the past, and continues to expand to this day.

a. 1700 Cascadia earthquake
b. 1509 Istanbul earthquake
c. 1703 Genroku earthquake
d. Big Bang

18. In particle physics, the _____ or color force, holds quarks and gluons together to form protons, neutrons and other particles. The _____ is one of the four fundamental interactions, along with gravitation, the electromagnetic force and the weak interaction. The word strong is used since the _____ is the most powerful of the four fundamental forces; its typical field strength is 100 times the strength of the electromagnetic force, some 10^{13} times as great as that of the weak force, and about 10^{38} times that of gravitation.

a. Power
b. 1509 Istanbul earthquake
c. Turbulent flow
d. Strong interaction

Chapter 1. Understanding Earth: A Dynamic and Evolving Planet   5

19. In physics, _____ describes any process in which energy emitted by one body travels through a medium or through space, ultimately to be absorbed by another body. Non-physicists often associate the word with ionizing _____, but it can also refer to electromagnetic _____ (i.e., radio waves, infrared light, visible light, ultraviolet light, and X-rays) which can also be ionizing _____, to acoustic _____, or to other more obscure processes. What makes it _____ is that the energy radiates (i.e., it travels outward in straight lines in all directions) from the source.
- a. Radiation
- b. 1703 Genroku earthquake
- c. 1509 Istanbul earthquake
- d. 1700 Cascadia earthquake

20. _____s, sometimes called minor planets or planetoids, are small Solar System bodies in orbit around the Sun, especially in the inner Solar System; they are smaller than planets but larger than meteoroids. The term '_____' has historically been applied primarily to bodies in the inner Solar System since the outer Solar System was poorly known when it came into common usage. The distinction between _____s and comets is made on visual appearance: Comets show a perceptible coma while _____s do not.
- a. AL 333
- b. Asteroid
- c. AL 129-1
- d. AASHTO Soil Classification System

21. A _____ is a sand- to boulder-sized particle of debris in the Solar System. The visible path of a _____ that enters Earth's (or another body's) atmosphere is called a meteor, or commonly a 'shooting star' or 'falling star.' If a _____ reaches the ground, it is then called a meteorite. Many meteors are part of a meteor shower.
- a. 1509 Istanbul earthquake
- b. 1703 Genroku earthquake
- c. 1700 Cascadia earthquake
- d. Meteoroid

22.

A widely accepted theory of planet formation, the so-called _____ hypothesis of Viktor Safronov, states that planets form out of dust grains that collide and stick to form larger and larger bodies. When the bodies reach sizes of approximately one kilometer, then they can attract each other directly through their mutual gravity, aiding further growth into moon-sized protoplanets enormously.

- a. 1509 Istanbul earthquake
- b. 1700 Cascadia earthquake
- c. 1703 Genroku earthquake
- d. Planetesimal

23. The _____ is the layer of igneous, sedimentary, and metamorphic rocks which form the continents and the areas of shallow seabed close to their shores, known as continental shelves. This layer is sometimes called sial due to more felsic, or granitic, bulk composition, which lies in contrast to the oceanic crust, called sima due to its mafic, or basaltic rock. (Based on the change in velocity of seismic waves, it is believed that at a certain depth sial becomes close in its physical properties to sima.
- a. Mirovia
- b. Divergent boundary
- c. Continental crust
- d. Plate tectonics

24. _____ is the part of Earth's lithosphere that surfaces in the ocean basins. _____ is primarily composed of mafic rocks, or sima. It is thinner than continental crust, or sial, generally less than 10 kilometers thick, however it is denser, having a mean density of about 3.3 grams per cubic centimeter.
- a. Oceanic crust
- b. AASHTO Soil Classification System
- c. AL 333
- d. AL 129-1

25. The lithosphere is broken up into what are called _____. In the case of Earth, there are eight major and many minor plates The lithospheric plates ride on the asthenosphere. These plates move in relation to one another at one of three types of plate boundaries: convergent, or collisional boundaries; divergent boundaries, also called spreading centers; and transform boundaries.
   a. Tectonic plates
   b. Subduction
   c. Juan de Fuca Ridge
   d. Lithosphere

26. _____, is the process of coastal sediments returning to the visible portion of a beach or foreshore following a submersion event. A sustainable beach or foreshore often goes through a cycle of submersion during rough weather then _____ during calmer periods. If a coastline is not in a healthy sustainable condition, then erosion can be more serious and _____ does not fully restore the original volume of the visible beach or foreshore leading to permanent beach or foreshore loss.
   a. AL 129-1
   b. AL 333
   c. AASHTO Soil Classification System
   d. Accretion

27. A _____ is a large emplacement of igneous intrusive rock that forms from cooled magma deep in the Earth's crust. they are almost always made mostly of felsic or intermediate rock-types, such as granite, quartz monzonite, or diorite

   Although they may appear uniform, _____s are in fact structures with complex histories and compositions.

   a. Scoria
   b. Tuff
   c. Great Dyke
   d. Batholith

28. _____ is molten rock that is found beneath the surface of the Earth, and may also exist on other terrestrial planets. Besides molten rock, _____ may also contain suspended crystals and gas bubbles. _____ often collects in a _____ chamber inside a volcano. _____ is capable of intrusion into adjacent rocks, extrusion onto the surface as lava, and explosive ejection as tephra to form pyroclastic rock.
   a. Rock cycle
   b. Vesicular texture
   c. Metavolcanic rock
   d. Magma

29. _____ is a common extrusive volcanic rock. It is usually grey to black and fine-grained due to rapid cooling of lava at the surface of a planet. It may be porphyritic containing larger crystals in a fine matrix, or vesicular, or frothy scoria.
   a. 1703 Genroku earthquake
   b. 1700 Cascadia earthquake
   c. 1509 Istanbul earthquake
   d. Basalt

30. A _____ is a phenomenon of fluid dynamics that occurs in situations where there are temperature differences within a body of liquid or gas.

Fluids are materials that exhibit the property of flow. Both gases and liquids have fluid properties, and in sufficient quantity, even particulate solids such as salt, grain, and gravel show some fluid properties. When a volume of fluid is heated, it expands and becomes less dense and thus more buoyant than the surrounding fluid. The colder, denser fluid settles underneath the warmer, less dense fluid and forces it to rise. Such movement is called convection, and the moving body of liquid is referred to as a _____.

Chapter 1. Understanding Earth: A Dynamic and Evolving Planet 7

a. 1703 Genroku earthquake
b. Convection cell
c. 1509 Istanbul earthquake
d. 1700 Cascadia earthquake

31. The _____ is a tectonic plate arising from the Juan de Fuca Ridge, and subducting under the northerly portion of the western side of the North American Plate at the Cascadia subduction zone. It is bounded on the south by the Blanco Fracture Zone, on the north by the Nootka Fault, and along the west by the Pacific Plate. The _____ was originally part of the once-vast Farallon Plate, now largely subducted under the North American Plate, and has since fractured into three pieces.

a. Banda Sea Plate
b. Juan de Fuca plate
c. Lhasa Plate
d. South Bismarck Plate

32. _____ refers to natural mountain building, and may be studied as a tectonic structural event, (b) as a geographical event, and (c) a chronological event. Orogenic events (a) cause distinctive structural phenomena and related tectonic activity, (b) affect certain regions of rocks and crust, and (c) happen within a specific period of time.

a. Antler orogeny
b. Alice Springs Orogeny
c. Orogenesis
d. Orogeny

33. A _____ is a dense, coarse-grained igneous rock, consisting mostly of the minerals olivine and pyroxene. _____ is ultramafic, as the rock contains less than 45% silica. It is high in magnesium, reflecting the high proportions of magnesium-rich olivine, with appreciable iron.

_____ is the dominant rock of the upper part of the Earth's mantle. The compositions of _____ nodules found in certain basalts and diamond pipes (kimberlites) are of special interest, because they provide samples of the Earth's Mantle roots of continents brought up from depths from about 30 km or so to depths at least as great as about 200 km.

a. 1700 Cascadia earthquake
b. 1509 Istanbul earthquake
c. Peridotite
d. 1703 Genroku earthquake

34. _____ describes the large scale motions of Earth's lithosphere. The theory encompasses the older concepts of continental drift, developed during the first decades of the 20th century by Alfred Wegener, and seafloor spreading, understood during the 1960s.

The outermost part of the Earth's interior is made up of two layers: the lithosphere and the asthenosphere.

a. Lithosphere
b. Copperbelt Province
c. Supercontinent cycle
d. Plate tectonics

35. _____ is the geological process by which material is added to a landform or land mass. Fluids such as wind and water, as well as sediment gravity flows, transport previously eroded sediment, which, at the loss of enough kinetic energy in the fluid, is deposited, building up layers of sediment.

_____ occurs when the forces responsible for sediment transportation are no longer sufficient to overcome the forces of particle weight and friction, which resist motion.

a. Hydrothermal circulation
b. Hydraulic action
c. Stoping
d. Deposition

36. _____ is one of the three main rock types (the others being sedimentary and metamorphic rock.) _____ is formed by magma (molten rock) being cooled and becoming solid . They may form with or without crystallization, either below the surface as intrusive (plutonic) rocks or on the surface as extrusive (volcanic) rocks. They make up approximately 95% of the upper part of the Earth's crust, but their great abundance is hidden on the Earth's surface by a relatively thin but widespread layer of sedimentary and metamorphic rocks.
    a. Igneous rock
    b. AL 333
    c. AASHTO Soil Classification System
    d. AL 129-1

37. _____ is the result of the transformation of an existing rock type, the protolith, in a process called metamorphism, which means 'change in form'. The protolith is subjected to heat and pressure (temperatures greater than 150 to 200 >°C and pressures of 1500 bars) causing profound physical and/or chemical change. The protolith may be sedimentary rock, igneous rock or another older _____.
    a. Phenocryst
    b. Metamorphic rock
    c. Volcanic rock
    d. Sedimentary rock

38. _____ is one of the three main rock types (the others being igneous and metamorphic rock.) _____ is formed by deposition and consolidation of mineral and organic material and from precipitation of minerals from solution. The processes that form _____ occur at the surface of the Earth and within bodies of water.
    a. Groundmass
    b. Sedimentary rock
    c. Migmatite
    d. Pluton

39. _____ is the decomposition of Earth rocks, soils and their minerals through direct contact with the planet's atmosphere. _____ occurs in situ, or 'with no movement', and thus should not be confused with erosion, which involves the movement of rocks and minerals by agents such as water, ice, wind and gravity.

Two important classifications of _____ processes exist -- physical and chemical _____.

    a. 1509 Istanbul earthquake
    b. Physical weathering
    c. Frost disintegration
    d. Weathering

40. _____ is the process of determining a specific date for an archaeological or palaeontological site or artifact. Some archaeologists prefer the terms chronometric or calendar dating, as use of the word 'absolute' implies a certainty and precision that is rarely possible in archaeology. _____ is usually based on the physical or chemical properties of the materials of artifacts, buildings, or other items that have been modified by humans.
    a. Uranium-lead dating
    b. Erathem
    c. AASHTO Soil Classification System
    d. Absolute dating

41. An _____ is the result of a sudden release of energy in the Earth's crust that creates seismic waves. They are recorded with a seismometer or the related and mostly obsolete Richter magnitude, with a magnitude 3 or lower _____ being mostly imperceptible and magnitude 7 causing serious damage over large areas.
    a. Earthquake
    b. AL 129-1
    c. AL 333
    d. AASHTO Soil Classification System

Chapter 1. Understanding Earth: A Dynamic and Evolving Planet

42. _____ was the supercontinent that is theorized to have existed during the Paleozoic and Mesozoic eras about 250 million years ago, before the component continents were separated into their current configuration.

The name was first used by the German originator of the continental drift theory, Alfred Wegener, in the 1920 edition of his book The Origin of Continents and Oceans , in which a postulated supercontinent _____ played a key role.

The single enormous ocean which surrounded Pangaea is known as Panthalassa.

- a. 1509 Istanbul earthquake
- b. 1700 Cascadia earthquake
- c. 1703 Genroku earthquake
- d. Pangea

43. _____ is any particulate matter that can be transported by fluid flow, and which eventually is deposited.

They are most often transported by water (fluvial processes) transported by wind (aeolian processes) and glaciers. Beach sands and river channel deposits are examples of fluvial transport and deposition, though _____ also often settles out of slow-moving or standing water in lakes and oceans.

- a. Sediment
- b. Salt glacier
- c. Quick clay
- d. Bovey Beds

44. _____ is the principle that the same scientific laws and processes are constant throughout space and time. It applies specifically to sciences that require a long timescale such as geology, astronomy, and paleontology. It was first defined by Charles Lyell (1797 - 1875), who incorporated James Hutton's gradualism into the idea of _____.
- a. AL 129-1
- b. AASHTO Soil Classification System
- c. AL 333
- d. Uniformitarianism

45. _____ is a common and widely distributed type of rock formed by high-grade regional metamorphic processes from pre-existing formations that were originally either igneous or sedimentary rocks. Gneissic rocks are usually medium to coarse foliated and largely recrystallized but do not carry large quantities of micas, chlorite or other platy minerals. _____es that are metamorphosed igneous rocks or their equivalent are termed granite _____es, diorite _____es, etc.
- a. 1703 Genroku earthquake
- b. 1509 Istanbul earthquake
- c. 1700 Cascadia earthquake
- d. Gneiss

46. _____ is a common and widely occurring type of intrusive, felsic, igneous rock. _____ has a medium to coarse texture, occasionally with some individual crystals larger than the groundmass forming a rock known as porphyry. _____s can be pink to dark gray or even black, depending on their chemistry and mineralogy.
- a. Granite
- b. 1700 Cascadia earthquake
- c. 1703 Genroku earthquake
- d. 1509 Istanbul earthquake

47. _____ is a hard metamorphic rock which was originally sandstone. Sandstone is converted into _____ through heating and pressure usually related to tectonic compression within orogenic belts. Pure _____ is usually white to grey, though _____s often occur in various shades of pink and red due to varying amounts of iron oxide .

a. Schist
c. Facies
b. Shock metamorphism
d. Quartzite

48. The general term '_____' or, more precisely, 'glacial age' denotes a geological period of long-term reduction in the temperature of the Earth's surface and atmosphere, resulting in an expansion of continental ice sheets, polar ice sheets and alpine glaciers. Within a long-term _____, individual pulses of extra cold climate are termed 'glaciations'. Glaciologically, _____ implies the presence of extensive ice sheets in the northern and southern hemispheres; by this definition we are still in an _____
   a. AL 333
   c. AASHTO Soil Classification System
   b. AL 129-1
   d. Ice Age

49. _____ is a technique used to date materials, usually based on a comparison between the observed abundance of a naturally occurring radioactive isotope and its decay products, using known decay rates. It is the principal source of information about the absolute age of rocks and other geological features, including the age of the Earth itself, and can be used to date a wide range of natural and man-made materials. Together with stratigraphic principles, _____ methods are used in geochronology to establish the geological time scale.
   a. Radiometric dating
   c. Milankovitch Theory
   b. Chronostratigraphy
   d. Paleomagnetism

Chapter 2. Minerals—The Building Blocks of Rocks

1. A _____ or gem is a piece of attractive mineral, which -- when cut and polished -- is used to make jewelry or other adornments. However certain rocks, and organic materials are not minerals, but are still used for jewelry, and are therefore often considered to be _____s as well. Most _____s are hard, but some soft minerals are used in jewelry because of their lustre or other physical properties that have aesthetic value.
   - a. 1700 Cascadia earthquake
   - b. 1703 Genroku earthquake
   - c. 1509 Istanbul earthquake
   - d. Gemstone

2. _____ is a common and widely occurring type of intrusive, felsic, igneous rock. _____ has a medium to coarse texture, occasionally with some individual crystals larger than the groundmass forming a rock known as porphyry. _____s can be pink to dark gray or even black, depending on their chemistry and mineralogy.
   - a. Granite
   - b. 1700 Cascadia earthquake
   - c. 1509 Istanbul earthquake
   - d. 1703 Genroku earthquake

3. _____ is the second most abundant mineral in the Earth's continental crust. It is made up of a framework of silicon-oxygen tetrahedra SiO_4, with each silicon shared between two oxygens to give the overall formula SiO_2. _____ has a hardness of 7 on the Mohs scale and a density of 2.65 g/cmÂ³.
   - a. Quartz
   - b. Shocked quartz
   - c. 1700 Cascadia earthquake
   - d. 1509 Istanbul earthquake

4. _____ is one of the three main rock types (the others being igneous and metamorphic rock.) _____ is formed by deposition and consolidation of mineral and organic material and from precipitation of minerals from solution. The processes that form _____ occur at the surface of the Earth and within bodies of water.
   - a. Migmatite
   - b. Pluton
   - c. Sedimentary rock
   - d. Groundmass

5. The _____ is the zone of the ocean floor that separates the thin oceanic crust from thick continental crust. _____s constitute about 28% of the oceanic area.

   The transition from continental to oceanic crust commonly occurs within the outer part of the margin, called continental rise.

   - a. Cuspate forelands
   - b. Longshore drift
   - c. 1509 Istanbul earthquake
   - d. Continental margin

6. _____ is fossil tree resin, which is appreciated for its color and beauty. Good quality _____ is used for the manufacture of ornamental objects and jewelry. Although not mineralized, it is often classified as a gemstone.

   A common misconception is that _____ is made of tree sap; it is not. Sap is the fluid that circulates through a plant's vascular system, while resin is the semi-solid amorphous organic substance secreted in pockets and canals through epithelial cells of the plant.

   - a. AASHTO Soil Classification System
   - b. AL 129-1
   - c. AL 333
   - d. Amber

Chapter 2. Minerals—The Building Blocks of Rocks

7. _____ is a soft, deep blue copper mineral produced by weathering of copper ore deposits. It is also known as Chessylite after the Chessy-les-Mines near Lyon, France, where striking specimens have been found. The mineral has been known since ancient times, and was mentioned in Pliny the Elder's Natural History under the Greek name kuanos and the Latin name caeruleum The blue of _____ is exceptionally deep and clear, and for that reason the mineral has tended to be associated since antiquity with the deep blue color of low-humidity desert and winter skies.
   a. AASHTO Soil Classification System
   b. AL 333
   c. Azurite
   d. AL 129-1

8. _____ is a carbonate mineral normally known as 'copper carbonate' with the formula $CuCO_3 \cdot Cu(OH)_2$. This green-colored mineral crystallizes in the monoclinic crystal system, and most often forms botryoidal, fibrous, or stalagmitic masses. Individual crystals are rare but do occur as slender to acicular prisms.
   a. 1509 Istanbul earthquake
   b. 1700 Cascadia earthquake
   c. 1703 Genroku earthquake
   d. Malachite

9. The _____ is the total number of protons and neutrons in an atomic nucleus. Because protons and neutrons both are baryons, the _____ A is identical with the baryon number B as of the nucleus as of the whole atom or ion. The _____ is different for each different isotope of a chemical element.
   a. 1703 Genroku earthquake
   b. Mass number
   c. 1509 Istanbul earthquake
   d. 1700 Cascadia earthquake

10. In chemistry and physics, the _____ is the number of protons found in the nucleus of an atom and therefore identical to the charge number of the nucleus. It is conventionally represented by the symbol Z. The _____ uniquely identifies a chemical element. In an atom of neutral charge, _____ is equal to the number of electrons.
    a. AASHTO Soil Classification System
    b. AL 333
    c. AL 129-1
    d. Atomic number

11. A _____ is a free neutron that is Boltzmann distributed with kT = 0.024 eV (4.0×10^{-21} J) at room temperature. This gives characteristic (not average, or median) speed of 2.2 km/s. The name 'thermal' comes from their energy being that of the room temperature gas or material they are permeating.
    a. 1700 Cascadia earthquake
    b. 1703 Genroku earthquake
    c. 1509 Istanbul earthquake
    d. Thermal neutron

12. A _____ is an atom with an unstable nucleus, which is a nucleus characterized by excess energy which is available to be imparted either to a newly-created radiation particle within the nucleus, or else to an atomic electron . The _____, in this process, undergoes radioactive decay, and emits a gamma ray(s) and/or subatomic particles. These particles constitute ionizing radiation.
    a. 1700 Cascadia earthquake
    b. Half-life
    c. 1509 Istanbul earthquake
    d. Radionuclide

13. A covalent bond is a form of chemical bonding that is characterized by the sharing of pairs of electrons between atoms, or between atoms and other covalent bonds. In short, attraction-to-repulsion stability that forms between atoms when they share electrons is known as _____.

_____ includes many kinds of interaction, including >σ-bonding, >π-bonding, metal to non-metal bonding, agostic interactions, and three-center two-electron bonds.

Chapter 2. Minerals—The Building Blocks of Rocks

a. Covalent bonding
b. Van der Waals force
c. 1700 Cascadia earthquake
d. 1509 Istanbul earthquake

14. An _____ is a type of chemical bond that involves a metal and a non-metal ion (or polyatomic ions such as ammonium) through electrostatic attraction. In short, it is a bond formed by the attraction between two oppositely charged ions. The metal donates one or more electrons, forming a positively charged ion or cation with a stable electron configuration.
   a. AL 333
   b. AL 129-1
   c. Ionic bond
   d. AASHTO Soil Classification System

15. _____ is the electromagnetic interaction between delocalized electrons, called conduction electrons, and the metallic nuclei within metals. Understood as the sharing of 'free' electrons among a lattice of positively-charged ions (cations), _____ is sometimes compared with that of molten salts; however, this simplistic view holds true for very few metals. In a more quantum-mechanical view, the conduction electrons divide their density equally over all atoms that function as neutral (non-charged) entities.
   a. Metallic bonding
   b. 1509 Istanbul earthquake
   c. 1700 Cascadia earthquake
   d. Van der Waals force

16. In physical chemistry, the _____ is the attractive or repulsive force between molecules (or between parts of the same molecule) other than those due to covalent bonds or to the electrostatic interaction of ions with one another or with neutral molecules. The term includes:

- permanent dipole-permanent dipole forces
- permanent dipole-induced dipole forces
- instantaneous induced dipole-induced dipole (London dispersion forces.)

It is also sometimes used loosely as a synonym for the totality of intermolecular forces. _____s are relatively weak compared to normal chemical bonds, but play a fundamental role in fields as diverse as supramolecular chemistry, structural biology, polymer science, nanotechnology, surface science, and condensed matter physics. _____s define the chemical character of many organic compounds.

   a. 1700 Cascadia earthquake
   b. Metallic bonding
   c. 1509 Istanbul earthquake
   d. Van der Waals force

17. Traditionally, _____ compounds are considered to be of a mineral, not biological, origin. Complementarily, most organic compounds are traditionally viewed as being of biological origin. Over the past century, the precise classification of _____ vs organic compounds has become less important to scientists, primarily because the majority of known compounds are synthetic and not of natural origin.

Minerals are mainly oxides and sulfides, which are strictly _____. In fact, most of the earth and the universe is _____. Although the components of the Earth's crust are well elucidated, the processes of mineralization and the composition of the deep mantle remain active areas of investigation, which are mainly covered in geology-oriented venues.

Chapter 2. Minerals—The Building Blocks of Rocks

    a. Inorganic
    c. AL 333
    b. AASHTO Soil Classification System
    d. AL 129-1

18. An _____ is a solid in which there is no long-range order of the positions of the atoms. (Solids in which there is long-range atomic order are called crystalline solids or morphous). Most classes of solid materials can be found or prepared in an amorphous form.
    a. AL 129-1
    c. Amorphous solid
    b. AASHTO Soil Classification System
    d. AL 333

19. _____, in structural geology and related disciplines, describes the tendency of a rock to break along preferred planes of weakness.

Rocks deformed under very low to low metamorphic grade often develop planes along which the rock can easily be split. Slates are an example of a rock with a penetrative _____ caused partly by the realignment of phyllosilicate minerals with increasing flattening strain.

    a. Combe
    c. Fault
    b. Depression
    d. Cleavage

20. In chemistry, the _____ of a chemical compound is a simple expression of the relative numbers of each type of atom in it, or the simplest whole number ratio of atoms of each element present in a compound. An _____ makes no reference to isomerism, structure, or absolute number of atoms. The _____ is used as standard for most ionic compounds, such as $CaCl_2$, and for macromolecules, such as SiO_2.
    a. AL 333
    c. Empirical formula
    b. AL 129-1
    d. AASHTO Soil Classification System

21. The mineral _____ is a magnesium iron silicate with the formula $(Mg,Fe)_2SiO_4$. It is one of the most common minerals on Earth, and has also been identified in meteorites and on the Moon, Mars, and comet Wild 2.

The ratio of magnesium and iron varies between the two endmembers of the solid solution series: forsterite (Mg-endmember) and fayalite (Fe-endmember.)

    a. Olivine
    c. AASHTO Soil Classification System
    b. AL 129-1
    d. AL 333

22. The _____ is the layer of igneous, sedimentary, and metamorphic rocks which form the continents and the areas of shallow seabed close to their shores, known as continental shelves. This layer is sometimes called sial due to more felsic, or granitic, bulk composition, which lies in contrast to the oceanic crust, called sima due to its mafic, or basaltic rock. (Based on the change in velocity of seismic waves, it is believed that at a certain depth sial becomes close in its physical properties to sima.
    a. Divergent boundary
    c. Mirovia
    b. Plate tectonics
    d. Continental crust

23. _____ is the part of Earth's lithosphere that surfaces in the ocean basins. _____ is primarily composed of mafic rocks, or sima. It is thinner than continental crust, or sial, generally less than 10 kilometers thick, however it is denser, having a mean density of about 3.3 grams per cubic centimeter.

Chapter 2. Minerals—The Building Blocks of Rocks

a. Oceanic crust
c. AL 333

b. AASHTO Soil Classification System
d. AL 129-1

24. A _____ is a large emplacement of igneous intrusive rock that forms from cooled magma deep in the Earth's crust. they are almost always made mostly of felsic or intermediate rock-types, such as granite, quartz monzonite, or diorite

Although they may appear uniform, _____s are in fact structures with complex histories and compositions.

a. Batholith
c. Tuff

b. Great Dyke
d. Scoria

25. In chemistry, a _____ is a salt or ester of carbonic acid.

To test for the presence of the _____ anion in a salt, the addition of dilute mineral acid (e.g. hydrochloric acid) will yield carbon dioxide gas.

_____-containing salts are industrially and mineralogically ubiquitous.

a. Carbonate
c. 1703 Genroku earthquake

b. 1509 Istanbul earthquake
d. 1700 Cascadia earthquake

26. A _____ is a binary compound, of which one part is a halogen atom and the other part is an element or radical that is less electronegative than the halogen, to make a fluoride, chloride, bromide, iodide, or astatide compound. Many salts are _____s. All Group 1 metals form _____s with the halogens and they are white solids.

a. Halide
c. 1703 Genroku earthquake

b. 1509 Istanbul earthquake
d. 1700 Cascadia earthquake

27. _____ is an important tectosilicate mineral which forms igneous rock. The name is from the Greek for 'straight fracture,' because its two cleavage planes are at right angles to each other. An alternate name is alkali feldspar.

_____ is a common constituent of most granites and other felsic igneous rocks and often forms huge crystals and masses in pegmatite.

a. AASHTO Soil Classification System
c. Orthoclase

b. AL 129-1
d. AL 333

28. _____ are those minerals that contain the tetrahedrally coordinated phosphate (PO_4^{3-}) anion along with the freely substituting arsenate (AsO_4^{3-}) and vanadate (VO_4^{3-}.) Chlorine (Cl^-), fluorine (F^-), and hydroxide (OH^-) anions also fit into the crystal structure.

The phosphate class of minerals is a large and diverse group, however, only a few species are relatively common.

a. 1509 Istanbul earthquake
c. 1700 Cascadia earthquake

b. 1703 Genroku earthquake
d. Phosphate minerals

Chapter 2. Minerals—The Building Blocks of Rocks

29. The chemical compound silicon dioxide, also known as _____ , is an oxide of silicon with a chemical formula of SiO_2 and has been known for its hardness since antiquity. _____ is most commonly found in nature as sand or quartz, as well as in the cell walls of diatoms. It is a principal component of most types of glass and substances such as concrete.
    a. 1703 Genroku earthquake
    b. 1509 Istanbul earthquake
    c. 1700 Cascadia earthquake
    d. Silica

30. A _____ is a compound containing an anion in which one or more central silicon atoms are surrounded by electronegative ligands. This definition is broad enough to include species such as hexafluorosilicate ('fluorosilicate'), $[SiF_6]^{2-}$, but the _____ species that are encountered most often consist of silicon with oxygen as the ligand. _____ anions, with a negative net electrical charge, must have that charge balanced by other cations to make an electrically neutral compound.
    a. 1509 Istanbul earthquake
    b. 1700 Cascadia earthquake
    c. 1703 Genroku earthquake
    d. Silicate

31. In inorganic chemistry, a _____ is a salt of sulfuric acid.

    The _____ ion is a polyatomic anion with the empirical formula SO_4^{2-} and a molecular mass of 96.06 daltons; it consists of a central sulfur atom surrounded by four equivalent oxygen atoms in a tetrahedral arrangement. The sulfur atom is in the +6 oxidation state while the four oxygen atoms are each in the -2 state.

    a. 1509 Istanbul earthquake
    b. Sulfate
    c. 1703 Genroku earthquake
    d. 1700 Cascadia earthquake

32. The _____ make up the largest and most important class of rock-forming minerals, comprising approximately 90 percent of the crust of the Earth. They are classified based on the structure of their silicate group. _____ all contain silicon and oxygen.
    a. 1700 Cascadia earthquake
    b. Silicate minerals
    c. 1509 Istanbul earthquake
    d. Mineraloid

33. _____ is a common phyllosilicate mineral within the mica group, with the approximate chemical formula $K(Mg, Fe)_3AlSi_3O_{10}(F, OH)_2$. More generally, it refers to the dark mica series, primarily a solid-solution series between the iron-endmember annite, and the magnesium-endmember phlogopite; more aluminous endmembers include siderophyllite.
    a. Biotite
    b. Magnesium
    c. Pyrope
    d. 1509 Istanbul earthquake

34. _____ is a naturally occurring material composed primarily of fine-grained minerals, which show plasticity through a variable range of water content, and which can be hardened when dried and/or fired. _____ deposits are mostly composed of _____ minerals (phyllosilicate minerals), minerals which impart plasticity and harden when fired and/or dried, and variable amounts of water trapped in the mineral structure by polar attraction. Organic materials which do not impart plasticity may also be a part of _____ deposits.
    a. Clay
    b. 1509 Istanbul earthquake
    c. 1703 Genroku earthquake
    d. 1700 Cascadia earthquake

Chapter 2. Minerals—The Building Blocks of Rocks 17

35. _____ are hydrous aluminium phyllosilicates, sometimes with variable amounts of iron, magnesium, alkali metals, alkaline earths and other cations. Clays have structures similar to the micas and therefore form flat hexagonal sheets. _____ are common weathering products (including weathering of feldspar) and low temperature hydrothermal alteration products.
  a. 1509 Istanbul earthquake
  b. Glauconite
  c. Clay minerals
  d. Kaolinite

36. Two important classifications of weathering processes exist -- physical and _____. Mechanical or physical weathering involves the breakdown of rocks and soils through direct contact with atmospheric conditions, such as heat, water, ice and pressure. The second classification, _____, involves the direct effect of atmospheric chemicals or biologically produced chemicals (also known as biological weathering) in the breakdown of rocks, soils and minerals.
  a. Frost disintegration
  b. Physical weathering
  c. Chemical weathering
  d. 1509 Istanbul earthquake

37. _____ is the decomposition of Earth rocks, soils and their minerals through direct contact with the planet's atmosphere. _____ occurs in situ, or 'with no movement', and thus should not be confused with erosion, which involves the movement of rocks and minerals by agents such as water, ice, wind and gravity.

Two important classifications of _____ processes exist -- physical and chemical _____.

  a. Weathering
  b. Physical weathering
  c. 1509 Istanbul earthquake
  d. Frost disintegration

38. _____ is a carbonate mineral, one of the two common, naturally occurring polymorphs of calcium carbonate, $CaCO_3$. The other polymorph is the mineral calcite. _____'s crystal lattice differs from that of calcite, resulting in a different crystal shape, an orthorhombic system with acicular crystals.
  a. AASHTO Soil Classification System
  b. AL 333
  c. AL 129-1
  d. Aragonite

39. _____ is a carbonate mineral and the most stable polymorph of calcium carbonate ($CaCO_3$.) The other polymorphs are the minerals aragonite and vaterite. Aragonite will change to _____ at 470>°C, and vaterite is even less stable.

_____ is a common constituent of sedimentary rocks, limestone in particular, much of which is formed from the shells of dead marine organisms. Approximately 10% of sedimentary rock is limestone.

  a. Calcite
  b. 1703 Genroku earthquake
  c. 1509 Istanbul earthquake
  d. 1700 Cascadia earthquake

40. _____ is the name of a sedimentary carbonate rock and a mineral, both composed of calcium magnesium carbonate $CaMg_2$ found in crystals.

_____ rock (also dolostone) is composed predominantly of the mineral _____. Limestone that is partially replaced by _____ is referred to as dolomitic limestone, or in old U.S. geologic literature as magnesian limestone.

a. Sandstone
b. Dolomite
c. Keystone
d. Diatomaceous earth

41. _____ or dolomite rock is a sedimentary carbonate rock that contains a high percentage of the mineral dolomite. In old U.S.G.S. publications it was referred to as magnesian limestone. Most _____ formed as a magnesium replacement of limestone or lime mud prior to lithification.
   a. Sandstone
   b. Dolostone
   c. Pelagic sediments
   d. Metasediment

42. _____ are a group of rock-forming tectosilicate minerals which make up as much as 60% of the Earth's crust.

_____ crystallize from magma in both intrusive and extrusive igneous rocks, as veins, and are also present in many types of metamorphic rock. Rock formed entirely of plagioclase feldspar is known as anorthosite.
   a. 1703 Genroku earthquake
   b. Feldspars
   c. 1509 Istanbul earthquake
   d. 1700 Cascadia earthquake

43. _____ is a common and widely distributed type of rock formed by high-grade regional metamorphic processes from pre-existing formations that were originally either igneous or sedimentary rocks. Gneissic rocks are usually medium to coarse foliated and largely recrystallized but do not carry large quantities of micas, chlorite or other platy minerals. _____es that are metamorphosed igneous rocks or their equivalent are termed granite _____es, diorite _____es, etc.
   a. Gneiss
   b. 1700 Cascadia earthquake
   c. 1509 Istanbul earthquake
   d. 1703 Genroku earthquake

44. _____ is a sedimentary rock composed largely of the mineral calcite (calcium carbonate: $CaCO_3$.) The deposition of _____ strata is often a by-product and indicator of biological activity in the geologic record. Calcium (along with nitrogen, phosphorus, and potassium) is a key mineral to plant nutrition: soils overlying _____ bedrock tend to be pre-fertilized with calcium.
   a. Limestone
   b. 1703 Genroku earthquake
   c. 1509 Istanbul earthquake
   d. 1700 Cascadia earthquake

45. _____ is a chemical element. It has the symbol K, atomic number 19, and atomic mass 39.0983. _____ was first isolated from potash.
   a. Potassium
   b. 1509 Istanbul earthquake
   c. 1703 Genroku earthquake
   d. 1700 Cascadia earthquake

46. _____ is a sedimentary rock composed mainly of sand-size mineral or rock grains. Most _____ is composed of quartz and/or feldspar because these are the most common minerals in the Earth's crust. Like sand, _____ may be any color, but the most common colors are tan, brown, yellow, red, gray and white.
   a. Dolomite
   b. Porcellanite
   c. Dolostone
   d. Sandstone

Chapter 2. Minerals—The Building Blocks of Rocks

47. The _____ are a small, isolated mountain range rising from the Great Plains of North America in western South Dakota and extending into Wyoming, USA. Set off from the main body of the Rocky Mountains, the region is something of a geological anomaly--accurately described as an 'island of trees in a sea of grass'. The _____ encompass the _____ National Forest and are home to the tallest peaks of continental North America east of the Rockies.
   a. Rano Kau
   b. Black Hills
   c. Monument Valley
   d. Paleorrota

48. The _____ was the first major U.S. deposit of silver ore, discovered under what is now Virginia City, Nevada on the eastern slope of Mt. Davidson, a peak in the Virginia range. After the discovery was made public in 1859, prospectors rushed to the area and scrambled to stake their claims.
   a. 1703 Genroku earthquake
   b. Comstock Lode
   c. 1509 Istanbul earthquake
   d. 1700 Cascadia earthquake

49. _____ is a form of mining that employs water to dislodge rock material or move sediment. Previously, the use of a large volume of water had been developed by the Romans to remove overburden and then gold-bearing debris as in Las M>édulas of Spain, and Dolaucothi in Britain. The method was also used in Elizabethan Britain for developing lead, tin and copper mines, and became known as hushing.
   a. 1703 Genroku earthquake
   b. 1509 Istanbul earthquake
   c. 1700 Cascadia earthquake
   d. Hydraulic mining

50. _____ is a mineral composed of calcium fluoride, CaF_2. It is an isometric mineral with a cubic habit, though octahedral and more complex isometric forms are not uncommon. Cubic crystals up to 20 cm across have been found at Dalnegorsk, Russia.

   _____ may occur as a vein deposit, especially with metallic minerals, where it often forms a part of the gangue (the worthless 'host-rock' in which valuable minerals occur) and may be associated with galena, sphalerite, barite, quartz, and calcite. It is a common mineral in deposits of hydrothermal origin and has been noted as a primary mineral in granites and other igneous rocks and as a common minor constituent of dolostone and limestone.

   a. 1509 Istanbul earthquake
   b. 1703 Genroku earthquake
   c. 1700 Cascadia earthquake
   d. Fluorite

51. _____ is a very coarse-grained igneous rock that has a grain size of 20 mm or more; such rocks are referred to as pegmatitic.

   Most _____ is composed of quartz, feldspar and mica; in essence a 'granite'. Rarer 'intermediate' and 'mafic' _____ containing amphibole, Ca-plagioclase feldspar, pyroxene and other minerals are known, found in recrystallised zones and apophyses associated with large layered intrusions.

   a. 1509 Istanbul earthquake
   b. Pegmatite
   c. 1700 Cascadia earthquake
   d. 1703 Genroku earthquake

52. A _____ is a pink to blood-red gemstone, a variety of the mineral corundum (aluminium oxide.) The red color is caused mainly by the presence of the element chromium. Its name comes from ruber, Latin for red.

Chapter 2. Minerals—The Building Blocks of Rocks

a. 1509 Istanbul earthquake
b. 1703 Genroku earthquake
c. 1700 Cascadia earthquake
d. Ruby

53. In geology, a _____ or _____ line is a planar fracture in rock in which the rock on one side of the fracture has moved with respect to the rock on the other side. Large _____s within the Earth's crust are the result of differential or shear motion and active _____ zones are the causal locations of most earthquakes. Earthquakes are caused by energy release during rapid slippage along a _____.
   a. Cohesion
   b. Combe
   c. Geothermal
   d. Fault

54. In geology the term _____ refers to a fracture in rock where there has been no lateral movement in the plane of the fracture (up, down or sideways) of one side relative to the other. This makes it different from a fault which is defined as a fracture in rock where one side slides laterally past to the other. _____s normally have a regular spacing related to either the mechanical properties of the individual rock or the thickness of the layer involved.
   a. Joint
   b. 1703 Genroku earthquake
   c. 1700 Cascadia earthquake
   d. 1509 Istanbul earthquake

55. The _____ is a cosmological model of the initial conditions and subsequent development of the universe. It is supported by the most comprehensive and accurate explanations from current scientific evidence and observation. As used by cosmologists, the term _____ generally refers to the idea that the universe has expanded from a primordial hot and dense initial condition at some finite time in the past, and continues to expand to this day.
   a. 1509 Istanbul earthquake
   b. 1703 Genroku earthquake
   c. Big Bang
   d. 1700 Cascadia earthquake

56. The _____ characterizes the scratch resistance of various minerals through the ability of a harder material to scratch a softer material. It was created in 1812 by the German mineralogist Friedrich Mohs and is one of several definitions of hardness in materials science. The method, however, is of great antiquity, having first been mentioned by Theophrastus in his treatise On Stones in ca 300 BC, followed by Pliny the Elder in his Naturalis Historia circa A.D.
   a. Mohs scale of mineral hardness
   b. 1509 Istanbul earthquake
   c. 1703 Genroku earthquake
   d. 1700 Cascadia earthquake

57. _____ is defined as the ratio of the density of a given solid or liquid substance to the density of water at a specific temperature and pressure, typically at 4 >°C (39 >°F) and 1 atm (760.00 mmHg) , making it a dimensionless quantity Substances with a _____ greater than one are denser than water, and so (ignoring surface tension effects) will sink in it, and those with a _____ of less than one are less dense than water, and so will float in it. _____ is a special case of, or in some usages synonymous with, relative density, with the latter term often preferred in modern scientific writing.
   a. 1700 Cascadia earthquake
   b. 1509 Istanbul earthquake
   c. 1703 Genroku earthquake
   d. Specific gravity

58. _____ is a common extrusive volcanic rock. It is usually grey to black and fine-grained due to rapid cooling of lava at the surface of a planet. It may be porphyritic containing larger crystals in a fine matrix, or vesicular, or frothy scoria.
   a. 1703 Genroku earthquake
   b. Basalt
   c. 1509 Istanbul earthquake
   d. 1700 Cascadia earthquake

Chapter 2. Minerals—The Building Blocks of Rocks

59. A _____ or sea vent, is a type of hydrothermal vent found on the ocean floor. They are formed in fields hundreds of meters wide when superheated water from below Earth's crust comes through the ocean floor. This water is rich in dissolved minerals from the crust, most notably sulfides.
   a. 1703 Genroku earthquake
   b. 1509 Istanbul earthquake
   c. 1700 Cascadia earthquake
   d. Black smoker

60. _____ is molten rock expelled by a volcano during eruption. When first expelled from a volcanic vent, it is a liquid at temperatures from 700 >°C to 1,200 >°C (1,300 >°F to 2,200 >°F.) Although _____ is quite viscous, with about 100,000 times the viscosity of water, it can flow great distances before cooling and solidifying, because of both its thixotropic and shear thinning properties.
   a. Pumice
   b. Pyroclastic flow
   c. Cinder
   d. Lava

61. _____ is the solid-state recrystallization of pre-existing rocks due to changes in physical and chemical conditions, primarily heat, pressure, and the introduction of chemically active fluids. Both mineralogical, chemical and crystallographic changes can occur during this process.

Three types of _____ exist: dynamic, contact and regional.

   a. Metamorphism
   b. Cross-bedding
   c. Gradualism
   d. Dike

62. _____ is a naturally occurring glass formed as an extrusive igneous rock. It is produced when felsic lava extruded from a volcano cools without crystal growth. _____ is commonly found within the margins of rhyolitic lava flows known as _____ flows, where the chemical composition (high silica content) induces a high viscosity and polymerization degree of the lava.
   a. AL 333
   b. AL 129-1
   c. Obsidian
   d. AASHTO Soil Classification System

63. The chemical compound _____, also known as silica, is an oxide of silicon with a chemical formula of SiO_2 and has been known for its hardness since antiquity. Silica is most commonly found in nature as sand or quartz, as well as in the cell walls of diatoms. It is a principal component of most types of glass and substances such as concrete.
   a. 1703 Genroku earthquake
   b. 1700 Cascadia earthquake
   c. Silicon dioxide
   d. 1509 Istanbul earthquake

64. _____ are common features on the ocean floor. Some are active and, in shallow water, disclose their presence by blasting steam and rocky debris high above the surface of the sea. Many others lie at such great depths that the tremendous weight of the water above them prevents the explosive release of steam and gases, although they can be detected by hydrophones and discoloration of water because of volcanic gases.
   a. 1703 Genroku earthquake
   b. 1700 Cascadia earthquake
   c. 1509 Istanbul earthquake
   d. Submarine volcanoes

65. A _____ is a fissure in a planet's surface from which geothermally heated water issues. they are commonly found near volcanically active places, areas where tectonic plates are moving apart, ocean basins, and hotspots.

They are locally very common because the earth is both geologically active and has large amounts of water on its surface and within its crust. Common land types include hot springs, fumaroles and geysers. The most famous _____ system on land is probably within Yellowstone National Park in the United States.

a. 1509 Istanbul earthquake
b. Hydrothermal vent
c. 1703 Genroku earthquake
d. 1700 Cascadia earthquake

66. _____ is a silvery white and ductile member of the boron group of chemical elements. It has the symbol Al; its atomic number is 13. It is not soluble in water under normal circumstances. _____ is the most abundant metal in the Earth's crust, and the third most abundant element therein, after oxygen and silicon. It makes up about 8% by weight of the Earth'e;s solid surface.

a. AL 129-1
b. AL 333
c. Aluminum
d. AASHTO Soil Classification System

67. The term _____ can be used to describe both the conduct of a survey for geological purposes and an institution holding geological information.

A _____ is the systematic investigation of the subsurface of a given piece of ground for the purpose of creating a geological map or model. A _____ employs techniques from the traditional walk-over survey, studying outcrops and landforms, to intrusive methods, such as hand augering and machine driven boreholes, to the use of geophysical techniques and remote sensing methods, such as aerial photography and satellite imagery.

a. Geological Survey
b. Reading Prong
c. Leaverite
d. Paralithic

68. _____ is a gas consisting primarily of methane. It is found associated with fossil fuels, in coal beds, as methane clathrates, and is created by methanogenic organisms in marshes, bogs, and landfills. It is an important fuel source, a major feedstock for fertilizers, and a potent greenhouse gas.

a. 1509 Istanbul earthquake
b. 1703 Genroku earthquake
c. Natural gas
d. 1700 Cascadia earthquake

69. The _____ is the extended perimeter of each continent and associated coastal plain, and was part of the continent during the glacial periods, but is undersea during interglacial periods such as the current epoch by relatively shallow seas (known as shelf seas) and gulfs.

The continental rise is below the slope, but landward of the abyssal plains. Its gradient is intermediate between the slope and the shelf, on the order of 0.5-1°.

a. Continental slope
b. Mud
c. Surface runoff
d. Continental shelf

70. An _____ is the result of a sudden release of energy in the Earth's crust that creates seismic waves. They are recorded with a seismometer or the related and mostly obsolete Richter magnitude, with a magnitude 3 or lower _____ being mostly imperceptible and magnitude 7 causing serious damage over large areas.

Chapter 2. Minerals—The Building Blocks of Rocks

a. AASHTO Soil Classification System
b. AL 129-1
c. AL 333
d. Earthquake

71. An _____ is a type of rock that contains minerals such as gemstones and metals that can be extracted through mining and refined for use. Samples of _____ in the form of exceptionally beautiful crystals, exotic layering visible when sectioned or polished or metallic presentations such as large nuggets or crystalline formations of metals such as gold or copper may command a value far beyond their value as mere _____ or raw metal for subsequent reduction to utilitarian purposes.

The grade or concentration of an _____ mineral, or metal, as well as its form of occurrence, will directly affect the costs associated with mining the _____.

a. Iron ores
b. Ore
c. Ore genesis
d. AASHTO Soil Classification System

72. A _____ or sandstorm is a meteorological phenomenon common in arid and semi-arid regions and arises when a gust front passes or when the wind force exceeds the threshold value where loose sand and dust are removed from the dry surface. Particles are transported by saltation and suspension, causing soil erosion from one place and deposition in another. The Sahara and drylands around the Arabian peninsula are the main source of airborne dust, with some contributions from Iran, Pakistan and India into the Arabian Sea, and China's storms deposit dust in the Pacific.

a. 1509 Istanbul earthquake
b. 1703 Genroku earthquake
c. Dust storm
d. 1700 Cascadia earthquake

73. _____ is a hard, lustrous, grey metal, a chemical element with symbol Co and atomic number 27. Although _____-based colors and pigments have been used since ancient times for making jewelry and paints, and miners have long used the name kobold ore for some minerals, the free metalic _____ was not prepared and discovered until 1735 by Georg Brandt.

_____ is found in various metallic-lustred ores for example cobaltite , but it is produced as a by-product of copper and nickel mining.

a. 1703 Genroku earthquake
b. 1700 Cascadia earthquake
c. 1509 Istanbul earthquake
d. Cobalt

74. _____ are rocks and minerals from which metallic iron can be economically extracted. The ores are usually rich in iron oxides and vary in color from dark grey, bright yellow, deep purple, to rusty red. The iron itself is usually found in the form of magnetite (Fe_3O_4), haematite (Fe_2O_3), goethite, limonite or siderite.

a. Iron ores
b. AASHTO Soil Classification System
c. Ore
d. Ore genesis

75. _____ is a naturally occurring granular material composed of finely divided rock and mineral particles.

As the term is used by geologists, _____ particles range in diameter from 0.0625 (or $>^1\!/_{16}$ mm, or 62.5 micrometers) to 2 millimeters. An individual particle in this range size is termed a _____ grain.

a. 1509 Istanbul earthquake
b. 1700 Cascadia earthquake
c. 1703 Genroku earthquake
d. Sand

Chapter 3. Igneous Rocks and Intrusive Igneous Activity

1. _____ is the removal of solids (sediment, soil, rock and other particles) in the natural environment. It usually occurs due to transport by wind, water, or ice; by down-slope creep of soil and other material under the force of gravity; or by living organisms, such as burrowing animals, in the case of bioerosion.

   _____ is distinguished from weathering, which is the process of chemical or physical breakdown of the minerals in the rocks, although the two processes may occur concurrently.

   a. AL 333
   b. AL 129-1
   c. AASHTO Soil Classification System
   d. Erosion

2. _____ is a common and widely occurring type of intrusive, felsic, igneous rock. _____ has a medium to coarse texture, occasionally with some individual crystals larger than the groundmass forming a rock known as porphyry. _____s can be pink to dark gray or even black, depending on their chemistry and mineralogy.
   a. 1700 Cascadia earthquake
   b. Granite
   c. 1509 Istanbul earthquake
   d. 1703 Genroku earthquake

3. _____ is one of the three main rock types (the others being sedimentary and metamorphic rock.) _____ is formed by magma (molten rock) being cooled and becoming solid . They may form with or without crystallization, either below the surface as intrusive (plutonic) rocks or on the surface as extrusive (volcanic) rocks. They make up approximately 95% of the upper part of the Earth's crust, but their great abundance is hidden on the Earth's surface by a relatively thin but widespread layer of sedimentary and metamorphic rocks.
   a. AL 129-1
   b. AASHTO Soil Classification System
   c. AL 333
   d. Igneous rock

4. _____ is molten rock expelled by a volcano during eruption. When first expelled from a volcanic vent, it is a liquid at temperatures from 700 >°C to 1,200 >°C (1,300 >°F to 2,200 >°F.) Although _____ is quite viscous, with about 100,000 times the viscosity of water, it can flow great distances before cooling and solidifying, because of both its thixotropic and shear thinning properties.
   a. Pyroclastic flow
   b. Lava
   c. Cinder
   d. Pumice

5. _____ refers to natural mountain building, and may be studied as a tectonic structural event, (b) as a geographical event, and (c) a chronological event. Orogenic events (a) cause distinctive structural phenomena and related tectonic activity, (b) affect certain regions of rocks and crust, and (c) happen within a specific period of time.
   a. Orogeny
   b. Antler orogeny
   c. Alice Springs Orogeny
   d. Orogenesis

6. _____ is the part of Earth's lithosphere that surfaces in the ocean basins. _____ is primarily composed of mafic rocks, or sima. It is thinner than continental crust, or sial, generally less than 10 kilometers thick, however it is denser, having a mean density of about 3.3 grams per cubic centimeter.
   a. AL 129-1
   b. AL 333
   c. Oceanic crust
   d. AASHTO Soil Classification System

7. A _____ in geology is an intrusive igneous rock body that crystallized from a magma slowly cooling below the surface of the Earth. _____s include batholiths, dikes, sills, laccoliths, lopoliths, and other igneous bodies. In practice, '_____' usually refers to a distinctive mass of igneous rock, typically kilometers in dimension, without a tabular shape like those of dikes and sills.

a. Metamorphic rock
c. Metavolcanic rock
b. Petrology
d. Pluton

8. _____ is one of the three main rock types (the others being igneous and metamorphic rock.) _____ is formed by deposition and consolidation of mineral and organic material and from precipitation of minerals from solution. The processes that form _____ occur at the surface of the Earth and within bodies of water.
   a. Groundmass
   b. Pluton
   c. Migmatite
   d. Sedimentary rock

9. A _____ is a large emplacement of igneous intrusive rock that forms from cooled magma deep in the Earth's crust. they are almost always made mostly of felsic or intermediate rock-types, such as granite, quartz monzonite, or diorite

Although they may appear uniform, _____ s are in fact structures with complex histories and compositions.

   a. Batholith
   b. Great Dyke
   c. Tuff
   d. Scoria

10. The _____ is the zone of the ocean floor that separates the thin oceanic crust from thick continental crust. _____ s constitute about 28% of the oceanic area.

The transition from continental to oceanic crust commonly occurs within the outer part of the margin, called continental rise.

   a. 1509 Istanbul earthquake
   b. Longshore drift
   c. Continental margin
   d. Cuspate forelands

11. An _____ is a type of rock that contains minerals such as gemstones and metals that can be extracted through mining and refined for use. Samples of _____ in the form of exceptionally beautiful crystals, exotic layering visible when sectioned or polished or metallic presentations such as large nuggets or crystalline formations of metals such as gold or copper may command a value far beyond their value as mere _____ or raw metal for subsequent reduction to utilitarian purposes.

The grade or concentration of an _____ mineral, or metal, as well as its form of occurrence, will directly affect the costs associated with mining the _____.

   a. Ore
   b. AASHTO Soil Classification System
   c. Iron ores
   d. Ore genesis

12. The lithosphere is broken up into what are called _____. In the case of Earth, there are eight major and many minor plates The lithospheric plates ride on the asthenosphere. These plates move in relation to one another at one of three types of plate boundaries: convergent, or collisional boundaries; divergent boundaries, also called spreading centers; and transform boundaries.
   a. Lithosphere
   b. Juan de Fuca Ridge
   c. Subduction
   d. Tectonic plates

13. _____ are a group of rock-forming tectosilicate minerals which make up as much as 60% of the Earth's crust.

Chapter 3. Igneous Rocks and Intrusive Igneous Activity

_____ crystallize from magma in both intrusive and extrusive igneous rocks, as veins, and are also present in many types of metamorphic rock. Rock formed entirely of plagioclase feldspar is known as anorthosite.

- a. 1700 Cascadia earthquake
- b. 1509 Istanbul earthquake
- c. 1703 Genroku earthquake
- d. Feldspars

14. _____ is a term used in geology to refer to silicate minerals, magma, and rocks which are enriched in the lighter elements such as silicon, oxygen, aluminium, sodium, and potassium. _____ minerals are usually light in color and have specific gravities less than 3. Common _____ minerals include quartz, muscovite, orthoclase, and the sodium-rich plagioclase feldspars.
- a. Phenocryst
- b. Sedimentary rock
- c. Laccolith
- d. Felsic

15. In volcanology, a _____ is a roughly circular mound-shaped protrusion resulting from the slow extrusion of viscous lava from a volcano. The geochemistry of _____s can vary from basalt to rhyolite although most preserved domes tend to have high silica content.

The characteristic dome shape is attributed to high viscosity that prevents the lava from flowing very far. This high viscosity can be obtained in two ways: by high levels of silica in the magma, or by degassing of fluid magma.

- a. 1700 Cascadia earthquake
- b. 1703 Genroku earthquake
- c. Lava dome
- d. 1509 Istanbul earthquake

16. _____ is an adjective describing a silicate mineral or rock that is rich in magnesium and iron; the term was derived by contracting 'magnesium' and 'ferric'. Most _____ minerals are dark in color and the specific gravity is greater than 3. Common rock-forming _____ minerals include olivine, pyroxene, amphibole, and biotite.

_____ lava, before cooling, has a low viscosity, in comparison to felsic lava, due to the lower silica content in _____ magma. Water and other volatiles can more easily and gradually escape from _____ lava, so eruptions of volcanoes made of _____ lavas are less explosively violent than felsic lava eruptions.

- a. 1703 Genroku earthquake
- b. 1700 Cascadia earthquake
- c. Mafic
- d. 1509 Istanbul earthquake

17. _____ is the second most abundant mineral in the Earth's continental crust. It is made up of a framework of silicon-oxygen tetrahedra SiO_4, with each silicon shared between two oxygens to give the overall formula SiO_2. _____ has a hardness of 7 on the Mohs scale and a density of 2.65 g/cmÂ³.
- a. Shocked quartz
- b. Quartz
- c. 1700 Cascadia earthquake
- d. 1509 Istanbul earthquake

18. The chemical compound silicon dioxide, also known as _____ , is an oxide of silicon with a chemical formula of SiO_2 and has been known for its hardness since antiquity. _____ is most commonly found in nature as sand or quartz, as well as in the cell walls of diatoms. It is a principal component of most types of glass and substances such as concrete.

Chapter 3. Igneous Rocks and Intrusive Igneous Activity

   a. 1700 Cascadia earthquake
   c. 1703 Genroku earthquake
   b. 1509 Istanbul earthquake
   d. Silica

19. A _____ is a compound containing an anion in which one or more central silicon atoms are surrounded by electronegative ligands. This definition is broad enough to include species such as hexafluorosilicate ('fluorosilicate'), $[SiF_6]^{2-}$, but the _____ species that are encountered most often consist of silicon with oxygen as the ligand. _____ anions, with a negative net electrical charge, must have that charge balanced by other cations to make an electrically neutral compound.
   a. Silicate
   c. 1509 Istanbul earthquake
   b. 1700 Cascadia earthquake
   d. 1703 Genroku earthquake

20. _____ is an igneous rock of volcanic origin.

They are usually fine-grained or aphanitic to glassy in texture. They often contain clasts of other rocks and phenocrysts.
   a. Laccolith
   c. Metamorphic rock
   b. Serpentinite
   d. Volcanic rock

21. _____ is molten rock that is found beneath the surface of the Earth, and may also exist on other terrestrial planets. Besides molten rock, _____ may also contain suspended crystals and gas bubbles. _____ often collects in a _____ chamber inside a volcano. _____ is capable of intrusion into adjacent rocks, extrusion onto the surface as lava, and explosive ejection as tephra to form pyroclastic rock.
   a. Vesicular texture
   c. Rock cycle
   b. Metavolcanic rock
   d. Magma

22. A _____ is an opening in a planet's surface or crust, which allows hot, molten rock, ash, and gases to escape from below the surface. Volcanic activity involving the extrusion of rock tends to form mountains or features like mountains over a period of time.
   a. 1509 Istanbul earthquake
   c. 1700 Cascadia earthquake
   b. 1703 Genroku earthquake
   d. Volcano

23. _____ is a measure of the resistance of a fluid which is being deformed by either shear stress or extensional stress. In everyday terms (and for fluids only), _____ is 'thickness'. Thus, water is 'thin', having a lower _____, while honey is 'thick' having a higher _____.
   a. Shear stress
   c. Tensile stress
   b. Thixotropy
   d. Viscosity

24. The _____ is the layer of igneous, sedimentary, and metamorphic rocks which form the continents and the areas of shallow seabed close to their shores, known as continental shelves. This layer is sometimes called sial due to more felsic, or granitic, bulk composition, which lies in contrast to the oceanic crust, called sima due to its mafic, or basaltic rock. (Based on the change in velocity of seismic waves, it is believed that at a certain depth sial becomes close in its physical properties to sima.
   a. Mirovia
   c. Divergent boundary
   b. Plate tectonics
   d. Continental crust

Chapter 3. Igneous Rocks and Intrusive Igneous Activity

25. The _____ is the rigid outermost shell of a rocky planet.

In the Earth, the _____ includes the crust and the uppermost mantle, which constitute the hard and rigid outer layer of the planet. The _____ is underlain by the asthenosphere, the weaker, hotter, and deeper part of the upper mantle.

a. Lithosphere
b. Continental crust
c. Copperbelt Province
d. Nappe

26. The mineral _____ is a magnesium iron silicate with the formula $(Mg,Fe)_2SiO_4$. It is one of the most common minerals on Earth, and has also been identified in meteorites and on the Moon, Mars, and comet Wild 2.

The ratio of magnesium and iron varies between the two endmembers of the solid solution series: forsterite (Mg-endmember) and fayalite (Fe-endmember.)

a. Olivine
b. AASHTO Soil Classification System
c. AL 333
d. AL 129-1

27. The _____ is the mechanically weak ductily-deforming region of the upper mantle of the Earth. It lies below the lithosphere, at depths between 100 and 200 km (~ 62 and 124 miles) below the surface, but perhaps extending as deep as 400 km (~ 249 miles.)

The _____ is a portion of the upper mantle just below the lithosphere that is involved in plate movements and isostatic adjustments. In spite of its heat, pressures keep it plastic, and it has a relatively low density. Seismic waves pass relatively slowly through the _____, compared to the overlying lithospheric mantle, thus it has been called the low-velocity zone. This was the observation that originally alerted seismologists to its presence and gave some information about its physical properties, as the speed of seismic waves decreases with decreasing rigidity.

a. AL 129-1
b. AL 333
c. AASHTO Soil Classification System
d. Asthenosphere

28. _____ is a common phyllosilicate mineral within the mica group, with the approximate chemical formula $K(Mg, Fe)_3AlSi_3O_{10}(F, OH)_2$. More generally, it refers to the dark mica series, primarily a solid-solution series between the iron-endmember annite, and the magnesium-endmember phlogopite; more aluminous endmembers include siderophyllite.

a. Biotite
b. Magnesium
c. 1509 Istanbul earthquake
d. Pyrope

29. In geology, _____ refers to heat sources within the planet. _____ is technically an adjective (e.g., _____ energy) but in U.S. English the word has attained frequent use as a noun.

The planet's internal heat was originally generated during its accretion, due to gravitational binding energy, and since then additional heat has continued to be generated by decay heat from the radioactive decay of elements.

| a. Cleavage | b. Stratification |
| c. Geothermal | d. Combe |

30. The _____ is the rate of increase in temperature per unit depth in the Earth. It varies with location and is typically measured by determining the bottom open-hole temperature after borehole drilling. To achieve accuracy the drilling fluid needs time to reach the ambient temperature.

    a. Geothermal power
    c. Geothermal heat pump
    b. Hot Dry Rock Geothermal Energy
    d. Geothermal gradient

31. A _____ is an upwelling of abnormally hot rock within the Earth's mantle. As the heads of _____s can partly melt when they reach shallow depths, they are thought to be the cause of volcanic centers known as hotspots and probably also to have caused flood basalts. It is a secondary way that Earth loses heat, much less important in this regard than is heat loss at plate margins.

    a. Seismic refraction
    c. Strainmeter
    b. Mazuku
    d. Mantle plume

32. _____ is an important tectosilicate mineral which forms igneous rock. The name is from the Greek for 'straight fracture,' because its two cleavage planes are at right angles to each other. An alternate name is alkali feldspar.

    _____ is a common constituent of most granites and other felsic igneous rocks and often forms huge crystals and masses in pegmatite.

    a. AL 333
    c. Orthoclase
    b. AASHTO Soil Classification System
    d. AL 129-1

33. _____ is a process of melting that takes place in the Earth's mantle. The melting temperatures are unlikely high enough to melt the entire source rock, and only portions of or some of the minerals they contain melt.

    a. Raton hotspot
    c. Submarine eruption
    b. Volcanic blocks
    d. Partial melting

34. In geology, _____ is the process that takes place at convergent boundaries by which one tectonic plate moves under another tectonic plate, sinking into the Earth's mantle, as the plates converge. A _____ zone is an area on Earth where two tectonic plates move towards one another and _____ occurs. Rates of _____ are typically measured in centimeters per year, with the average rate of convergence being approximately 2 to 8 centimeters per year (about the rate a fingernail grows.)

    a. Thrust fault
    c. Forearc
    b. Panthalassa
    d. Subduction

35. _____ is any particulate matter that can be transported by fluid flow, and which eventually is deposited.

They are most often transported by water (fluvial processes) transported by wind (aeolian processes) and glaciers. Beach sands and river channel deposits are examples of fluvial transport and deposition, though _____ also often settles out of slow-moving or standing water in lakes and oceans.

Chapter 3. Igneous Rocks and Intrusive Igneous Activity

a. Bovey Beds
c. Sediment
b. Salt glacier
d. Quick clay

36. _____ is a geological term meaning the rock native to an area. It is similar and in many cases interchangeable with the terms basement and wall rocks.

The term is used to denote the usual strata of a region in relation to the rock which is being discussed or observed.

a. Country rock
c. Pyroclastic rocks
b. Great Dyke
d. Coldwell Complex

37. _____ are chemical substances that may or may not be present in a cell, depending on the cell type. _____ are stored nutrients, secretory products, and pigment granules. Examples of _____ are; glycogen granules in the liver and muscle cells; lipid droplets in fat cells; pigment granules in certain cells of skin and hair; water containing vacuoles; and crystals of various types.
a. Inclusions
c. AL 333
b. AL 129-1
d. AASHTO Soil Classification System

38. _____ is a common extrusive volcanic rock. It is usually grey to black and fine-grained due to rapid cooling of lava at the surface of a planet. It may be porphyritic containing larger crystals in a fine matrix, or vesicular, or frothy scoria.
a. Basalt
c. 1703 Genroku earthquake
b. 1509 Istanbul earthquake
d. 1700 Cascadia earthquake

39. The matrix or _____ of rock is the fine-grained mass of material in which larger grains or crystals are embedded.

The matrix of an igneous rock consists of fine-grained, often microscopic, crystals in which larger crystals (phenocrysts) are embedded. This porphyritic texture is indicative of multi-stage cooling of magma.

a. Metamorphic rock
c. Large igneous provinces
b. Groundmass
d. Magma

40. _____ is a naturally occurring glass formed as an extrusive igneous rock. It is produced when felsic lava extruded from a volcano cools without crystal growth. _____ is commonly found within the margins of rhyolitic lava flows known as _____ flows, where the chemical composition (high silica content) induces a high viscosity and polymerization degree of the lava.
a. AL 333
c. AASHTO Soil Classification System
b. AL 129-1
d. Obsidian

41. _____ is a term usually used to refer to igneous rock grain size. It means that the size of matrix grains in the rock are large enough to be distinguished with the unaided eye as opposed to aphanitic This texture forms by slow cooling of magma deep underground in the plutonic environment.
a. Petrified forest
c. Phaneritic
b. 1509 Istanbul earthquake
d. 1700 Cascadia earthquake

Chapter 3. Igneous Rocks and Intrusive Igneous Activity

42. A _____ is a relatively large and usually conspicuous crystal distinctly larger than the grains of the rock groundmass of a porphyritic igneous rock. _____s often have euhedral forms either due to early growth within a magma or by post-emplacement recrystallization.

Plagioclase _____s often exhibit zoning with a more calcic core surrounded by progressively more sodic rinds.

   a. Phenocryst
   b. Metavolcanic rock
   c. Volcanic rock
   d. Groundmass

43. _____ are igneous and meta-igneous rocks with very low silica content (less than 45%), generally >18% MgO, high FeO, low potassium, and are composed of usually greater than 90% mafic minerals (dark colored, high magnesium and iron content.) The Earth's mantle is considered to be composed of _____.
   a. AASHTO Soil Classification System
   b. AL 333
   c. Ultramafic rocks
   d. AL 129-1

44. _____ is a volcanic rock texture characterised by, or containing many vesicles. The texture is often found in extrusive aphanitic igneous rock. The vesicles are small cavities formed by the expansion of bubbles of gas or steam during the solidification of the rock.
   a. Phenocryst
   b. Vesicular texture
   c. Metamorphic zone
   d. Volcanic rock

45. In materials science, _____ is the distribution of crystallographic orientations of a polycrystalline sample. A sample in which these orientations are fully random is said to have no _____. If the crystallographic orientations are not random, but have some preferred orientation, then the sample has a weak, strong, or moderate _____.
   a. Streak
   b. Texture
   c. Melange
   d. Deformation

46. _____ is an igneous, volcanic rock, of intermediate composition, with aphanitic to porphyritic texture. The mineral assemblage is typically dominated by plagioclase plus pyroxene and/or hornblende. Magnetite, zircon, apatite, ilmenite, biotite, and garnet are common accessory minerals.
   a. Andesite
   b. AL 333
   c. AASHTO Soil Classification System
   d. AL 129-1

47. _____ refers to a large group of dark, coarse-grained, intrusive igneous rocks chemically equivalent to basalt. The rocks are plutonic, formed when molten magma is trapped beneath the Earth's surface and cools into a crystalline mass.

The vast majority of the Earth's surface is underlain by _____ within the oceanic crust, produced by basalt magmatism at mid-ocean ridges.

   a. Gabbro
   b. 1703 Genroku earthquake
   c. 1509 Istanbul earthquake
   d. 1700 Cascadia earthquake

Chapter 3. Igneous Rocks and Intrusive Igneous Activity

48. A _____ is a dense, coarse-grained igneous rock, consisting mostly of the minerals olivine and pyroxene. _____ is ultramafic, as the rock contains less than 45% silica. It is high in magnesium, reflecting the high proportions of magnesium-rich olivine, with appreciable iron.

_____ is the dominant rock of the upper part of the Earth's mantle. The compositions of _____ nodules found in certain basalts and diamond pipes (kimberlites) are of special interest, because they provide samples of the Earth's Mantle roots of continents brought up from depths from about 30 km or so to depths at least as great as about 200 km.

   a. 1703 Genroku earthquake
   b. 1700 Cascadia earthquake
   c. 1509 Istanbul earthquake
   d. Peridotite

49. _____ is an igneous, volcanic (extrusive) rock, of felsic (silicon-rich) composition. It may have any texture from aphanitic to porphyritic. The mineral assemblage is usually quartz, alkali feldspar and plagioclase. Biotite and hornblende are common accessory minerals.

_____ can be considered as the extrusive equivalent to the plutonic granite rock, and consequently, outcroppings of it often bear a resemblance to granite. Due to their high content of silica and low iron and magnesium contents, _____ melts are highly polymerized and form highly viscous lavas.

   a. 1700 Cascadia earthquake
   b. 1509 Istanbul earthquake
   c. 1703 Genroku earthquake
   d. Rhyolite

50. _____ is an intrusive igneous rock similar to granite, but contains more plagioclase than potassium feldspar. It usually contains abundant biotite mica and hornblende, giving it a darker appearance than true granite. Mica may be present in well-formed hexagonal crystals, and hornblende may appear as needle-like crystals.
   a. 1703 Genroku earthquake
   b. 1700 Cascadia earthquake
   c. 1509 Istanbul earthquake
   d. Granodiorite

51. _____ is a very coarse-grained igneous rock that has a grain size of 20 mm or more; such rocks are referred to as pegmatitic.

Most _____ is composed of quartz, feldspar and mica; in essence a 'granite'. Rarer 'intermediate' and 'mafic' _____ containing amphibole, Ca-plagioclase feldspar, pyroxene and other minerals are known, found in recrystallised zones and apophyses associated with large layered intrusions.

   a. 1703 Genroku earthquake
   b. Pegmatite
   c. 1509 Istanbul earthquake
   d. 1700 Cascadia earthquake

52. _____ is a textural term for a volcanic rock that is a solidified frothy lava typically created when super-heated, highly pressurized rock is violently ejected from a volcano. It can be formed when lava and water are mixed. This unusual formation is due to the simultaneous actions of rapid cooling and rapid depressurization.
   a. Pumice
   b. Volcanic ash
   c. Wadati-Benioff zone
   d. Pit crater

Chapter 3. Igneous Rocks and Intrusive Igneous Activity

53. _____ is a textural term for macrovesicular volcanic rock. It is commonly, but not exclusively, basaltic or andesitic in composition. _____ is light as a result of numerous macroscopic ellipsoidal vesicles, but most _____ has a specific gravity greater than 1, and sinks in water.

   a. Country rock
   b. Tuff
   c. Charnockite
   d. Scoria

54. _____ is a type of rock consisting of consolidated volcanic ash ejected from vents during a volcanic eruption. _____ is sometimes called tufa, particularly when used as construction material, although tufa also refers to a quite different rock.

The products of a volcanic eruption are volcanic gases, lava, steam, and tephra. Magma is blown apart when it interacts violently with volcanic gases and steam. Solid material produced and thrown into the air by such volcanic eruptions is called tephra, regardless of composition or fragment size. If the resulting pieces of ejecta are small enough, the material is called volcanic ash, defined as such particles less than 2 mm in diameter, sand-sized or smaller.

   a. Charnockite
   b. Country rock
   c. Tuff
   d. Scoria

55. _____ is a pyroclastic rock, of any origin, that was sufficiently hot at the time of deposition to weld together. Strictly speaking, if the rock contains scattered pea-sized fragments or fiamme in it, it is called a welded lapilli-tuff. They (and welded lapilli-tuffs) can be of fallout origin, or deposited from pyroclastic density currents, as in the case of ignimbrites.

   a. Litchfieldite
   b. Welded tuff
   c. Country rock
   d. Charnockite

56. _____ is a rock composed of angular fragments of minerals or rocks in a matrix (cementing material), that may be similar or different in composition to the fragments. A _____ may have a variety of different origins, as indicated by the named types including sedimentary _____, tectonic _____, igneous _____, impact _____ and hydrothermal _____.

Sedimentary _____s are a type of clastic sedimentary rock which are composed of angular to subangular, randomly oriented clasts of other sedimentary rocks.

   a. Coprolite
   b. 1509 Istanbul earthquake
   c. Ventifacts
   d. Breccia

57. The _____ was a great mountain building period that perhaps had the greatest overall effect on the geologic structure of basement rocks within the New York Bight region. The effects of this orogeny are most apparent throughout New England, but the sediments derived from mountainous areas formed in the northeast can be traced throughout the Appalachians and midcontinental North America.

Beginning in Cambrian time, about 550 million years ago, the Iapetus Ocean began to grow progressively narrower.

Chapter 3. Igneous Rocks and Intrusive Igneous Activity

a. Taconic orogeny
b. Trans-Hudson orogeny
c. Sevier orogeny
d. Nevadan orogeny

58. A _____ or dyke in geology is a type of sheet intrusion referring to any geologic body that cuts discordantly across

- planar wall rock structures, such as bedding or foliation
- massive rock formations, like igneous/magmatic intrusions and salt diapirs.

They can therefore be either intrusive or sedimentary in origin.

An intrusive _____ is an igneous body with a very high aspect ratio, which means that its thickness is usually much smaller than the other two dimensions. Thickness can vary from sub-centimeter scale to many meters and the lateral dimensions can extend over many kilometers. A _____ is an intrusion into an opening cross-cutting fissure, shouldering aside other pre-existing layers or bodies of rock; this implies that a _____ is always younger than the rocks that contain it.

a. Schmidt hammer
b. Haloclasty
c. Fabric
d. Dike

59. A _____ is an igneous intrusion (or concordant pluton) that has been injected between two layers of sedimentary rock. The pressure of the magma is high enough that the overlying strata are forced upward, giving the _____ a dome or mushroom-like form with a generally planar base.

They tend to form at relatively shallow depths and are typically formed by relatively viscous magmas, such as those that crystallize to diorite, granodiorite, and granite. Cooling underground takes place slowly, giving time for larger crystals to form in the cooling magma. The surface rock above the _____ often erodes away completely, leaving the core mound of igneous rock.

a. Laccolith
b. Sedimentary rock
c. Groundmass
d. Vesicular texture

60. The _____ was a major mountain building event that took place along the western edge of ancient North America between the Mid to Late Jurassic (between about 180 and 140 million years ago.) The _____ was the first of three major mountain building episodes to transform Western North America between the Late Mesozoic and Early Cenozoic Eras, the latter two being the Sevier and Laramide orogeny, chronologically. Much like the two orogenies that followed, the Nevadan was caused by the subduction of oceanic lithosphere at a subduction zone running along the edge of the North American continent.

a. Kaikoura Orogeny
b. Nevadan orogeny
c. Trans-Hudson orogeny
d. Sevier orogeny

61. A _____ is a volcanic landform created when magma hardens within a vent on an active volcano. When forming, a _____ can cause an extreme build-up of pressure if volatile-charged magma is trapped beneath it, and this can sometimes lead to an explosive eruption. If a plug is preserved, erosion may remove the surrounding rock while the erosion-resistant plug remains, producing a distinctive landform.

a. 1703 Genroku earthquake
b. 1700 Cascadia earthquake
c. 1509 Istanbul earthquake
d. Volcanic plug

62. _____ is a region of the Colorado Plateau characterized by a cluster of vast and iconic sandstone buttes, the largest reaching 1,000 ft (300 m) above the valley floor. It is located on the southern border of Utah with northern Arizona (around >>36>°59>'N 110>°6>'W'#20;/'#20;>36.983>°N 110.1>°W>'#20;/'#20;36.983; -110.1), near the Four Corners area. The valley lies within the range of the Navajo Nation Reservation, and is accessible from U.S. Highway 163.
a. Rano Kau
b. Thirtynine Mile volcanic field
c. Paleorrota
d. Monument Valley

63. _____ is a fine-grained sedimentary rock whose original constituents were clay minerals or muds. It is characterized by thin laminae breaking with an irregular curving fracture, often splintery and usually parallel to the often-indistinguishable bedding plane. This property is called fissility.
a. Diatomaceous earth
b. Siltstone
c. Sandstone
d. Shale

64. _____, (Navajo: >Ts>é Bit'a'>í, 'rock with wings' or 'winged rock') is a rock formation rising nearly 1,800 feet (550 m) above the high-desert plain on the Navajo Nation and in San Juan County, New Mexico.

_____ is composed of fractured volcanic breccia and black dikes of igneous rock called 'minette'. It is the erosional remnant of the throat of a volcano, and the volcanic breccia formed in a diatreme. The exposed rock probably was originally formed 2,500-3000 feet (750-1,000 meters) below the earth's surface, but it was exposed after millions of years of erosion. Wall-like sheets of minette, known as dikes, radiate away from the central formation. Radiometric age determinations of the minette establish that these volcanic rocks solidified about 27 million years ago.

a. 1509 Istanbul earthquake
b. 1703 Genroku earthquake
c. Shiprock
d. 1700 Cascadia earthquake

65. In geology the term _____ refers to a fracture in rock where there has been no lateral movement in the plane of the fracture (up, down or sideways) of one side relative to the other. This makes it different from a fault which is defined as a fracture in rock where one side slides laterally past to the other. _____s normally have a regular spacing related to either the mechanical properties of the individual rock or the thickness of the layer involved.
a. 1509 Istanbul earthquake
b. 1700 Cascadia earthquake
c. Joint
d. 1703 Genroku earthquake

66. _____ is the solid-state recrystallization of pre-existing rocks due to changes in physical and chemical conditions, primarily heat, pressure, and the introduction of chemically active fluids. Both mineralogical, chemical and crystallographic changes can occur during this process.

Three types of _____ exist: dynamic, contact and regional.

a. Gradualism
b. Metamorphism
c. Cross-bedding
d. Dike

67. A _____ is a type of structural dome formed when a thick bed of evaporite minerals found at depth intrudes vertically into surrounding rock strata, forming a diapir.

The salt that forms these domes was deposited within restricted marine basins. Due to restricted flow of water into a basin, evaporation occurs resulting in the precipitation of salts from solution, depositing evaporites.

a. 1509 Istanbul earthquake
b. 1703 Genroku earthquake
c. 1700 Cascadia earthquake
d. Salt dome

Chapter 4. Volcanism and Volcanoes

1. A _____ is a cauldron-like volcanic feature usually formed by the collapse of land following a volcanic eruption such as the one at Yellowstone National Park. They are sometimes confused with volcanic craters.
    a. 1509 Istanbul earthquake
    b. Caldera
    c. 1703 Genroku earthquake
    d. 1700 Cascadia earthquake

2. _____ is a term used in geology to refer to silicate minerals, magma, and rocks which are enriched in the lighter elements such as silicon, oxygen, aluminium, sodium, and potassium. _____ minerals are usually light in color and have specific gravities less than 3. Common _____ minerals include quartz, muscovite, orthoclase, and the sodium-rich plagioclase feldspars.
    a. Phenocryst
    b. Laccolith
    c. Sedimentary rock
    d. Felsic

3. _____ is an adjective describing a silicate mineral or rock that is rich in magnesium and iron; the term was derived by contracting 'magnesium' and 'ferric'. Most _____ minerals are dark in color and the specific gravity is greater than 3. Common rock-forming _____ minerals include olivine, pyroxene, amphibole, and biotite.

    _____ lava, before cooling, has a low viscosity, in comparison to felsic lava, due to the lower silica content in _____ magma. Water and other volatiles can more easily and gradually escape from _____ lava, so eruptions of volcanoes made of _____ lavas are less explosively violent than felsic lava eruptions.

    a. 1700 Cascadia earthquake
    b. 1509 Istanbul earthquake
    c. 1703 Genroku earthquake
    d. Mafic

4. _____ is a measure of the resistance of a fluid which is being deformed by either shear stress or extensional stress. In everyday terms (and for fluids only), _____ is 'thickness'. Thus, water is 'thin', having a lower _____, while honey is 'thick' having a higher _____.
    a. Viscosity
    b. Shear stress
    c. Thixotropy
    d. Tensile stress

5. _____ include a variety of substances given off by active (or, at times, by dormant) volcanoes. These include gases trapped in cavities (vesicles) in volcanic rocks, dissolved or dissociated gases in magma and lava, or gases emanating directly from lava or indirectly through ground water heated by volcanic action.

The sources of _____ on Earth include:

- primordial and recycled constituents from the Earth's mantle,
- assimilated constituents from the Earth's crust,
- groundwater and the Earth's atmosphere.

Substances that may become gaseous or give off gases when heated are termed volatile substances.

Gases are released from magma through volatile constituents reaching such high concentrations in the base magma that they evaporate.

   a. Pit crater
   b. Cinder
   c. Volcanic ash
   d. Volcanic gases

Chapter 4. Volcanism and Volcanoes

6. The _____ is a chronologic schema (or idealized model) relating stratigraphy to time that is used by geologists, paleontologists and other earth scientists to describe the timing and relationships between events that have occurred during the history of the Earth. The table of geologic time spans presented here agrees with the dates and nomenclature proposed by the International Commission on Stratigraphy, and uses the standard color codes of the United States Geological Survey.

Evidence from radiometric dating indicates that the Earth is about 4.570 billion years old.

    a. 1703 Genroku earthquake   b. Geologic time scale
    c. 1509 Istanbul earthquake   d. 1700 Cascadia earthquake

7. _____ is molten rock that is found beneath the surface of the Earth, and may also exist on other terrestrial planets. Besides molten rock, _____ may also contain suspended crystals and gas bubbles. _____ often collects in a _____ chamber inside a volcano. _____ is capable of intrusion into adjacent rocks, extrusion onto the surface as lava, and explosive ejection as tephra to form pyroclastic rock.

    a. Vesicular texture   b. Metavolcanic rock
    c. Magma   d. Rock cycle

8. A _____ is an opening in a planet's surface or crust, which allows hot, molten rock, ash, and gases to escape from below the surface. Volcanic activity involving the extrusion of rock tends to form mountains or features like mountains over a period of time.

    a. 1703 Genroku earthquake   b. 1700 Cascadia earthquake
    c. 1509 Istanbul earthquake   d. Volcano

9. _____ is molten rock expelled by a volcano during eruption. When first expelled from a volcanic vent, it is a liquid at temperatures from 700 >°C to 1,200 >°C (1,300 >°F to 2,200 >°F.) Although _____ is quite viscous, with about 100,000 times the viscosity of water, it can flow great distances before cooling and solidifying, because of both its thixotropic and shear thinning properties.

    a. Pumice   b. Pyroclastic flow
    c. Cinder   d. Lava

10. _____ are natural conduits through which lava travels beneath the surface of a lava flow, expelled by a volcano during an eruption. They can be actively draining lava from a source, or can be extinct, meaning the lava flow has ceased and the rock has cooled and left a long, cave-like channel.

_____ are formed when an active low-viscosity lava flow develops a continuous and hard crust,which thickens and forms a roof above the still-flowing lava stream.

    a. 1703 Genroku earthquake   b. 1700 Cascadia earthquake
    c. Lava tubes   d. 1509 Istanbul earthquake

11. _____ is a form of air pollution that results when sulfur dioxide and other gases emitted by an erupting volcano react with oxygen and moisture in the presence of sunlight. The term is in common use in the Hawaiian islands, where the KÄ«lauea volcano, on the island of Hawai>Ê»i, has been erupting continuously since 1983.

    a. 1509 Istanbul earthquake   b. Vog
    c. 1700 Cascadia earthquake   d. 1703 Genroku earthquake

Chapter 4. Volcanism and Volcanoes

12. The _____ is part of the larger Great Rift Valley. It is a continental rift zone that appears to be a developing divergent tectonic plate boundary. The rift is a narrow zone in which the African Plate is in the process of splitting into two new plates called the Nubian and Somalian subplates or protoplates.
    a. AASHTO Soil Classification System
    b. East African Rift
    c. AL 333
    d. AL 129-1

13. A _____ is a type of mudflow or landslide composed of pyroclastic material and water that flows down from a volcano, typically along a river valley. The term '_____' originated in the Javanese language of Indonesia. They can be best described as volcanic mudflows. They may not necessarily be caused by volcanic activity, but at the very least do originate from some type of volcanism.
    a. 1703 Genroku earthquake
    b. 1700 Cascadia earthquake
    c. 1509 Istanbul earthquake
    d. Lahar

14. In geology, a _____ is a place where the Earth's crust and lithosphere are being pulled apart and is an example of extensional tectonics.

    Typical _____ features are a central linear downdropped fault segment, called a graben, with parallel normal faulting and _____-flank uplifts on either side forming a _____ valley, where the _____ remains above sea level. The axis of the _____ area commonly contains volcanic rocks and active volcanism is a part of many, but not all active _____ systems.

    a. 1703 Genroku earthquake
    b. Rift
    c. 1700 Cascadia earthquake
    d. 1509 Istanbul earthquake

15. A _____ or mudslide is the most rapid (up to 80 km/h, or 50 mph) and fluid type of downhill mass wasting. It is a rapid movement of a large mass of mud formed from loose earth and water. Similar terms are mudslide (not very liquid), mud stream, debris flow (e.g. in high mountains), j>ökulhlaup, and lahar
    a. 1703 Genroku earthquake
    b. 1700 Cascadia earthquake
    c. Mudflow
    d. 1509 Istanbul earthquake

16. In geology a _____ is the smallest division of a geologic formation or stratigraphic rock series marked by well-defined divisional planes (bedding planes) separating it from layers above and below. A _____ is the smallest lithostratigraphic unit, usually ranging in thickness from a centimeter to several meters and distinguishable from _____s above and below it. _____s can be differentiated in various ways, including rock or mineral type and particle size.
    a. Bed
    b. Sequence stratigraphy
    c. Biozones
    d. Cyclostratigraphy

17. In geology the term _____ refers to a fracture in rock where there has been no lateral movement in the plane of the fracture (up, down or sideways) of one side relative to the other. This makes it different from a fault which is defined as a fracture in rock where one side slides laterally past to the other. _____s normally have a regular spacing related to either the mechanical properties of the individual rock or the thickness of the layer involved.
    a. 1703 Genroku earthquake
    b. 1700 Cascadia earthquake
    c. 1509 Istanbul earthquake
    d. Joint

Chapter 4. Volcanism and Volcanoes

18. _____ is the removal of solids (sediment, soil, rock and other particles) in the natural environment. It usually occurs due to transport by wind, water, or ice; by down-slope creep of soil and other material under the force of gravity; or by living organisms, such as burrowing animals, in the case of bioerosion.

_____ is distinguished from weathering, which is the process of chemical or physical breakdown of the minerals in the rocks, although the two processes may occur concurrently.

   a. Erosion
   b. AL 129-1
   c. AASHTO Soil Classification System
   d. AL 333

19. _____ is the part of Earth's lithosphere that surfaces in the ocean basins. _____ is primarily composed of mafic rocks, or sima. It is thinner than continental crust, or sial, generally less than 10 kilometers thick, however it is denser, having a mean density of about 3.3 grams per cubic centimeter.
   a. AL 333
   b. AL 129-1
   c. Oceanic crust
   d. AASHTO Soil Classification System

20. _____ are pillow-shaped structures sometimes seen in lavas and are attributed to the congealment of lava under water, or subaqeous extrusion. A pillow structure in certain extrusive igneous rock is characterized by discontinuous pillow-shaped masses, commonly up to 1 metre in diameter. _____ commonly occur at Constructive plate boundaries, forming part of a mid-ocean ridge.
   a. Pillow lava
   b. Corrasion
   c. Metamorphic reaction
   d. Compression

21. _____ is a size classification term for tephra, which is material that falls out of the air during a volcanic eruption. They are in some senses similar to ooids or pisoids in calcareous sediments.

By definition _____ range in size from 2 mm to 64 mm in diameter. A pyroclastic particle greater than 64 mm in diameter is correctly known as a volcanic bomb when molten, or a volcanic block when solid.

   a. Supervolcano
   b. Pumice
   c. Volcanic gases
   d. Lapilli

22. _____ is a caldera lake located in the U.S. state of Oregon. It is the main feature of _____ National Park and famous for its deep blue color and water clarity. The lake partly fills a nearly 1,958 foot (597 m) deep caldera that was formed around 7,700 (>± 150) BC by the collapse of the volcano Mount Mazama.
   a. 1700 Cascadia earthquake
   b. 1509 Istanbul earthquake
   c. 1703 Genroku earthquake
   d. Crater Lake

23. A _____ is a mountain rising from the ocean seafloor that does not reach to the water's surface (sea level), and thus is not an island. These are typically formed from extinct volcanoes, that rise abruptly and are usually found rising from a seafloor of 1,000-4,000 meters depth. They are defined by oceanographers as independent features that rise to at least 1,000 meters above the seafloor.
   a. 1700 Cascadia earthquake
   b. 1509 Istanbul earthquake
   c. 1703 Genroku earthquake
   d. Seamount

Chapter 4. Volcanism and Volcanoes

24. _____ is the largest volcano on earth in terms of area covered and one of five volcanoes that form the Island of Hawaii in the U.S. state of Hawai>Ê»i in the Pacific Ocean. It is an active shield volcano, with a volume estimated at approximately 18,000 cubic miles (75,000 kmÂ³), although its peak is about 120 feet (37 m) lower than that of its neighbor, Mauna Kea. The Hawaiian name '_____' means 'Long Mountain'.
   a. Mauna Loa
   b. 1703 Genroku earthquake
   c. 1700 Cascadia earthquake
   d. 1509 Istanbul earthquake

25. A _____ is generally a large area of exposed Precambrian crystalline igneous and high-grade metamorphic rocks that form tectonically stable areas. In all cases, the age of these rocks is greater than 570 million years and sometimes dates back 2 to 3.5 billion years. They have been little affected by tectonic events following the end of the Precambrian Era, and are relatively flat regions where mountain building, faulting, and other tectonic processes are greatly diminished compared with the activity that occurs at the margins of the _____s and the boundaries between tectonic plates.
   a. 1509 Istanbul earthquake
   b. 1703 Genroku earthquake
   c. Shield
   d. 1700 Cascadia earthquake

26. A _____ is a large volcano with shallow-sloping sides.

They are formed by lava flows of low viscosity - lava that flows easily. Consequently, a volcanic mountain having a broad profile is built up over time by flow after flow of relatively fluid basaltic lava issuing from vents or fissures on the surface of the volcano

   a. 1703 Genroku earthquake
   b. 1700 Cascadia earthquake
   c. 1509 Istanbul earthquake
   d. Shield volcano

27. The _____ is the volcanic caldera in Yellowstone National Park in the United States. The caldera is located in the northwest corner of Wyoming, in which the vast majority of the park is contained. The major features of the caldera measure about 55 kilometers (34 mi) by 72 kilometers (45 mi) as determined by geological field work conducted by Bob Christiansen of the United States Geological Survey in the 1960s and 1970s.
   a. 1700 Cascadia earthquake
   b. 1703 Genroku earthquake
   c. 1509 Istanbul earthquake
   d. Yellowstone caldera

28. A _____ is a pyroclastic material. They are extrusive igneous rocks, and are similar to pumice, which has so many cavities and is such low-density that it can float on water.
   a. Wadati-Benioff zone
   b. Lapilli
   c. Pumice
   d. Cinder

29. A _____ or scoria cone is a steep conical hill of volcanic fragments that accumulate around and downwind from a volcanic vent. The rock fragments, often called cinders or scoria, are glassy and contain numerous gas bubbles 'frozen' into place as magma exploded into the air and then cooled quickly. _____s range in size from tens to hundreds of meters tall.
   a. Cinder cone
   b. 1703 Genroku earthquake
   c. 1509 Istanbul earthquake
   d. 1700 Cascadia earthquake

Chapter 4. Volcanism and Volcanoes

30. A _____ is an upwelling of abnormally hot rock within the Earth's mantle. As the heads of _____s can partly melt when they reach shallow depths, they are thought to be the cause of volcanic centers known as hotspots and probably also to have caused flood basalts. It is a secondary way that Earth loses heat, much less important in this regard than is heat loss at plate margins.
    a. Mazuku
    b. Strainmeter
    c. Mantle plume
    d. Seismic refraction

31. A _____ or super volcanic eruption is a volcanic eruption which is substantially larger than any volcano in historic times (generally accepted to be greater than 1,000 cubic kilometres). They occur when magma in the Earth rises into the crust from a hotspot but is unable to break through the crust. Pressure builds in a large and growing magma pool until the crust is unable to contain the pressure.
    a. Lava
    b. Volcanic gases
    c. Supervolcano
    d. Volcanic ash

32. _____ is a type of rock consisting of consolidated volcanic ash ejected from vents during a volcanic eruption. _____ is sometimes called tufa, particularly when used as construction material, although tufa also refers to a quite different rock.

The products of a volcanic eruption are volcanic gases, lava, steam, and tephra. Magma is blown apart when it interacts violently with volcanic gases and steam. Solid material produced and thrown into the air by such volcanic eruptions is called tephra, regardless of composition or fragment size. If the resulting pieces of ejecta are small enough, the material is called volcanic ash, defined as such particles less than 2 mm in diameter, sand-sized or smaller.

    a. Tuff
    b. Country rock
    c. Scoria
    d. Charnockite

33. _____ is an igneous, volcanic rock, of intermediate composition, with aphanitic to porphyritic texture. The mineral assemblage is typically dominated by plagioclase plus pyroxene and/or hornblende. Magnetite, zircon, apatite, ilmenite, biotite, and garnet are common accessory minerals.
    a. AL 129-1
    b. AL 333
    c. AASHTO Soil Classification System
    d. Andesite

34. A _____, sometimes called a composite volcano, is a tall, conical volcano with many layers (strata) of hardened lava, tephra, and volcanic ash. They are characterized by a steep profile and periodic, explosive eruptions. The lava that flows from a _____ tends to be viscous; it cools and hardens before spreading far.
    a. Mount Overlord
    b. Broken Top
    c. Nevado Sajama
    d. Stratovolcano

35. In volcanology, a _____ is a roughly circular mound-shaped protrusion resulting from the slow extrusion of viscous lava from a volcano. The geochemistry of _____s can vary from basalt to rhyolite although most preserved domes tend to have high silica content.

The characteristic dome shape is attributed to high viscosity that prevents the lava from flowing very far. This high viscosity can be obtained in two ways: by high levels of silica in the magma, or by degassing of fluid magma.

Chapter 4. Volcanism and Volcanoes

a. 1703 Genroku earthquake
b. 1509 Istanbul earthquake
c. Lava dome
d. 1700 Cascadia earthquake

36. _____ is the youngest group of lava domes in Lassen Volcanic National Park, California, having been formed as five dacite domes 1,100-1,000 years ago. The cluster of domes are located north of Lassen Peak.

From the base of the crags and extending toward the northwest corner of the park is Chaos Jumbles, a cold rock avalanche which undermined _____' northwest slope 300 years ago.

a. 1509 Istanbul earthquake
b. Chaos Jumbles
c. Chaos Crags
d. 1700 Cascadia earthquake

37. From the base of the crags and extending toward the northwest corner of the park is _____, a cold rock avalanche which undermined Chaos Crags' northwest slope 300 years ago. Riding on a cushion of compressed air , the rock debris traveled at about 100 miles per hour (160 km/h), flattened the forest before it, and dammed Manzanita Creek, forming Manzanita Lake.

In 1974 the United States Park Service took the advice of the USGS and closed the visitor center and accommodations at Manzanita Lake.

a. Chaos Jumbles
b. 1509 Istanbul earthquake
c. 1700 Cascadia earthquake
d. Chaos Crags

38. _____ is a common extrusive volcanic rock. It is usually grey to black and fine-grained due to rapid cooling of lava at the surface of a planet. It may be porphyritic containing larger crystals in a fine matrix, or vesicular, or frothy scoria.

a. 1700 Cascadia earthquake
b. Basalt
c. 1703 Genroku earthquake
d. 1509 Istanbul earthquake

39. In the earth sciences and geology sub-fields, a _____ or physical feature comprises a geomorphological unit, and is largely defined by its surface form and location in the landscape, as part of the terrain, and as such, is typically an element of topography. _____ elements also include seascape and oceanic waterbody interface features such as bays, peninsulas, seas and so forth, including sub-surface terrain features such as submersed mountain ranges, volcanoes, and the great ocean basins under the thin skin of water, for the whole earth is the province and domain of geology. This panorama in Great Smoky Mountains National Park has the readily identifiable physical features of a rolling plain, actually part of a broad valley, distant foothills, and a backdrop of the old much weathered Appalachian mountain range.

_____s are categorised by characteristic physical attributes such as elevation, slope, orientation, stratification, rock exposure, and soil type.

a. 1703 Genroku earthquake
b. 1700 Cascadia earthquake
c. 1509 Istanbul earthquake
d. Landform

40. _____ is a pyroclastic rock, of any origin, that was sufficiently hot at the time of deposition to weld together. Strictly speaking, if the rock contains scattered pea-sized fragments or fiamme in it, it is called a welded lapilli-tuff. They (and welded lapilli-tuffs) can be of fallout origin, or deposited from pyroclastic density currents, as in the case of ignimbrites.

Chapter 4. Volcanism and Volcanoes

a. Litchfieldite
b. Welded tuff
c. Charnockite
d. Country rock

41. A _____ is a geological phenomenon which includes a wide range of ground movement, such as rock falls, deep failure of slopes and shallow debris flows, which can occur in offshore, coastal and onshore environments. Although the action of gravity is the primary driving force for a _____ to occur, there are other contributing factors affecting the original slope stability. Typically, pre-conditional factors build up specific sub-surface conditions that make the area/slope prone to failure, whereas the actual _____ often requires a trigger before being released.
   a. 1700 Cascadia earthquake
   b. Landslide
   c. Soil liquefaction
   d. 1509 Istanbul earthquake

42. _____ is a depression in eastern California that is adjacent to Mammoth Mountain. The valley is one of the largest calderas on earth, measuring about 32 kilometres (20 mi) long (east-west) and 17 kilometres (11 mi) wide (north-south.) The elevation of the floor of the caldera is 6,500 feet (2,000 m) in the east and 8,500 feet (2,600 m) in the west.
   a. 1700 Cascadia earthquake
   b. 1509 Istanbul earthquake
   c. 1703 Genroku earthquake
   d. Long Valley caldera

43. _____ is the geomorphic process by which soil, regolith, and rock move downslope under the force of gravity. Types of _____ include creep, slides, flows, topples, and falls, each with its own characteristic features, and taking place over timescales from seconds to years. _____ occurs on both terrestrial and submarine slopes, and has been observed on Earth, Mars, and Venus.
   a. Soil liquefaction
   b. Mass wasting
   c. 1700 Cascadia earthquake
   d. 1509 Istanbul earthquake

44. _____, meaning 'new eruption', is a volcano located on the Alaska Peninsula in Katmai National Park and Preserve, about 290 miles (470 km) southwest of Anchorage. Formed in 1912 during one of the largest volcanic eruptions of the 20th century, _____ released 30 times the volume of magma as the 1980 eruption of Mount St. Helens. Map showing volcanoes of Alaska.

One of the largest eruptions of the 20th century occurred in 1912, from June 6 to June 8, to form _____.

   a. 1700 Cascadia earthquake
   b. 1703 Genroku earthquake
   c. 1509 Istanbul earthquake
   d. Novarupta

45. The _____, also known as the local magnitude (M_L) scale, assigns a single number to quantify the amount of seismic energy released by an earthquake. It is a base-10 logarithmic scale obtained by calculating the logarithm of the combined horizontal amplitude of the largest displacement from zero on a Wood-Anderson torsion seismometer output. So, for example, an earthquake that measures 5.0 on the Richter scale has a shaking amplitude 10 times larger than one that measures 4.0.
   a. Seismic scale
   b. Mercalli intensity scale
   c. Moment magnitude scale
   d. Richter Magnitude Scale

46. An _____ is the result of a sudden release of energy in the Earth's crust that creates seismic waves. They are recorded with a seismometer or the related and mostly obsolete Richter magnitude, with a magnitude 3 or lower _____ being mostly imperceptible and magnitude 7 causing serious damage over large areas.

a. AASHTO Soil Classification System
b. AL 333
c. Earthquake
d. AL 129-1

47. _____ describes a long-duration release of seismic energy with distinct spectral (harmonic) lines that and often precedes or accompanies volcanic eruptions. More generally, volcanic tremor, is a sustained signal that may or may not possess these harmonic spectral features.

_____ is a sustained release of seismic and/or infrasonic energy typically associated with the underground movement or venting of magma and/or volcanic gases.

a. Seismic shadowing
b. Teleseism
c. Volcanic tremor
d. Harmonic tremor

48. A _____ is an instrument designed to measure very small changes from the horizontal level, either on the ground or in structures. A similar term, in less common usage, is the inclinometer. They are used extensively for monitoring volcanos, the response of dams to filling, the small movements of potential landslides, the orientation and volume of hydraulic fractures, and the response of structures to various influences such as loading and foundation settlement.

a. 1703 Genroku earthquake
b. 1700 Cascadia earthquake
c. 1509 Istanbul earthquake
d. Tiltmeter

49. Harmonic tremor describes a long-duration release of seismic energy with distinct spectral (harmonic) lines that and often precedes or accompanies volcanic eruptions. More generally, _____, is a sustained signal that may or may not possess these harmonic spectral features.

Harmonic tremor is a sustained release of seismic and/or infrasonic energy typically associated with the underground movement or venting of magma and/or volcanic gases.

a. Maximum magnitude
b. Receiver function
c. Harmonic tremor
d. Volcanic tremor

50. The lithosphere is broken up into what are called _____. In the case of Earth, there are eight major and many minor plates The lithospheric plates ride on the asthenosphere. These plates move in relation to one another at one of three types of plate boundaries: convergent, or collisional boundaries; divergent boundaries, also called spreading centers; and transform boundaries.

a. Juan de Fuca Ridge
b. Lithosphere
c. Subduction
d. Tectonic plates

51. _____ describes the large scale motions of Earth's lithosphere. The theory encompasses the older concepts of continental drift, developed during the first decades of the 20th century by Alfred Wegener, and seafloor spreading, understood during the 1960s.

The outermost part of the Earth's interior is made up of two layers: the lithosphere and the asthenosphere.

a. Lithosphere
b. Supercontinent cycle
c. Copperbelt Province
d. Plate tectonics

Chapter 4. Volcanism and Volcanoes

52. The term _____ can be used to describe both the conduct of a survey for geological purposes and an institution holding geological information.

A _____ is the systematic investigation of the subsurface of a given piece of ground for the purpose of creating a geological map or model. A _____ employs techniques from the traditional walk-over survey, studying outcrops and landforms, to intrusive methods, such as hand augering and machine driven boreholes, to the use of geophysical techniques and remote sensing methods, such as aerial photography and satellite imagery.

   a. Leaverite
   c. Reading Prong
   b. Paralithic
   d. Geological Survey

53. A _____ is an underwater mountain range, typically having a valley known as a rift running along its spine, formed by plate tectonics. This type of oceanic ridge is characteristic of what is known as an oceanic spreading center, which is responsible for seafloor spreading. The uplifted sea floor results from convection currents which rise in the mantle as magma at a linear weakness in the oceanic crust, and emerge as lava, creating new crust upon cooling.

   a. Mid-ocean ridge
   c. Deposition
   b. Wave pounding
   d. Hydrothermal circulation

54. The _____ is a tectonic plate which includes the continent of Africa, as well as oceanic crust which lies between the continent and various surrounding ocean ridges.

The westerly side is a divergent boundary with the North American Plate to the north and the South American Plate to the south forming the central and southern part of the Mid-Atlantic Ridge. The _____ is bounded on the northeast by the Arabian Plate, the southeast by the Indo-Australian Plate, the north by the Eurasian Plate and the Anatolian Plate, and on the south by the Antarctic Plate.

   a. Arabian Plate
   c. Eurasian Plate
   b. Easter Plate
   d. African plate

55. A _____ or dyke in geology is a type of sheet intrusion referring to any geologic body that cuts discordantly across

   - planar wall rock structures, such as bedding or foliation
   - massive rock formations, like igneous/magmatic intrusions and salt diapirs.

They can therefore be either intrusive or sedimentary in origin.

An intrusive _____ is an igneous body with a very high aspect ratio, which means that its thickness is usually much smaller than the other two dimensions. Thickness can vary from sub-centimeter scale to many meters and the lateral dimensions can extend over many kilometers. A _____ is an intrusion into an opening cross-cutting fissure, shouldering aside other pre-existing layers or bodies of rock; this implies that a _____ is always younger than the rocks that contain it.

   a. Dike
   c. Fabric
   b. Schmidt hammer
   d. Haloclasty

Chapter 4. Volcanism and Volcanoes

56. The _____ is a mid-oceanic ridge, a divergent tectonic plate boundary located along the floor of the Pacific Ocean. It separates the Pacific Plate to the west from (north to south) the North American Plate, the Rivera Plate, the Cocos Plate, the Nazca Plate, and the Antarctic Plate. It runs from an undefined point near Antarctica in the south northward to its termination at the northern end of the Gulf of California in the Salton Sea basin in southern California.
   a. Azores-Gibraltar Transform Fault
   b. East Pacific Rise
   c. Elastic rebound theory
   d. Obduction

57. _____ refers to a large group of dark, coarse-grained, intrusive igneous rocks chemically equivalent to basalt. The rocks are plutonic, formed when molten magma is trapped beneath the Earth's surface and cools into a crystalline mass.

The vast majority of the Earth's surface is underlain by _____ within the oceanic crust, produced by basalt magmatism at mid-ocean ridges.

   a. Gabbro
   b. 1703 Genroku earthquake
   c. 1509 Istanbul earthquake
   d. 1700 Cascadia earthquake

58. The _____ is a mid-ocean ridge, a divergent tectonic plate boundary located along the floor of the Atlantic Ocean, and the longest mountain range in the world. It separates the Eurasian Plate and North American Plate in the North Atlantic, and the African Plate from the South American Plate in the South Atlantic. The MAR extends from a junction with the Gakkel Ridge (Mid-Arctic Ridge) northeast of Greenland southward to the Bouvet Triple Junction in the South Atlantic.
   a. 1703 Genroku earthquake
   b. 1700 Cascadia earthquake
   c. 1509 Istanbul earthquake
   d. Mid-Atlantic Ridge

59. A _____ in geology is an intrusive igneous rock body that crystallized from a magma slowly cooling below the surface of the Earth. _____s include batholiths, dikes, sills, laccoliths, lopoliths, and other igneous bodies. In practice, '_____' usually refers to a distinctive mass of igneous rock, typically kilometers in dimension, without a tabular shape like those of dikes and sills.
   a. Pluton
   b. Metavolcanic rock
   c. Metamorphic rock
   d. Petrology

60. The _____ is an area where large numbers of earthquakes and volcanic eruptions occur in the basin of the Pacific Ocean. In a 40,000 km horseshoe shape, it is associated with a nearly continuous series of oceanic trenches, volcanic arcs, and volcanic belts and/or plate movements. The _____ has 452 volcanoes and is home to over 75% of the world's active and dormant volcanoes.
   a. 1703 Genroku earthquake
   b. 1509 Istanbul earthquake
   c. 1700 Cascadia earthquake
   d. Pacific Ring of Fire

61. The _____ is a tectonic plate covering the continent of South America and extending eastward to the Mid-Atlantic Ridge.

The easterly side is a divergent boundary with the African Plate forming the southern part of the Mid-Atlantic Ridge. The southerly side is a complex boundary with the Antarctic Plate and the Scotia Plate.

a. Kermadec Plate
b. South American plate
c. Somali Plate
d. Sunda Plate

62. In geology, _____ is the process that takes place at convergent boundaries by which one tectonic plate moves under another tectonic plate, sinking into the Earth's mantle, as the plates converge. A _____ zone is an area on Earth where two tectonic plates move towards one another and _____ occurs. Rates of _____ are typically measured in centimeters per year, with the average rate of convergence being approximately 2 to 8 centimeters per year (about the rate a fingernail grows.)

a. Forearc
b. Panthalassa
c. Thrust fault
d. Subduction

63. A _____ is a large emplacement of igneous intrusive rock that forms from cooled magma deep in the Earth's crust. they are almost always made mostly of felsic or intermediate rock-types, such as granite, quartz monzonite, or diorite

Although they may appear uniform, _____s are in fact structures with complex histories and compositions.

a. Batholith
b. Tuff
c. Scoria
d. Great Dyke

64. The _____ is the zone of the ocean floor that separates the thin oceanic crust from thick continental crust. _____s constitute about 28% of the oceanic area.

The transition from continental to oceanic crust commonly occurs within the outer part of the margin, called continental rise.

a. Cuspate forelands
b. Longshore drift
c. Continental margin
d. 1509 Istanbul earthquake

Chapter 5. Weathering, Erosion, and Soil

1. _____ is the geological process by which material is added to a landform or land mass. Fluids such as wind and water, as well as sediment gravity flows, transport previously eroded sediment, which, at the loss of enough kinetic energy in the fluid, is deposited, building up layers of sediment.

   _____ occurs when the forces responsible for sediment transportation are no longer sufficient to overcome the forces of particle weight and friction, which resist motion.

   a. Hydraulic action
   c. Stoping
   b. Hydrothermal circulation
   d. Deposition

2. _____ is the removal of solids (sediment, soil, rock and other particles) in the natural environment. It usually occurs due to transport by wind, water, or ice; by down-slope creep of soil and other material under the force of gravity; or by living organisms, such as burrowing animals, in the case of bioerosion.

   _____ is distinguished from weathering, which is the process of chemical or physical breakdown of the minerals in the rocks, although the two processes may occur concurrently.

   a. AL 333
   c. AASHTO Soil Classification System
   b. Erosion
   d. AL 129-1

3. Two important classifications of weathering processes exist -- _____ and chemical weathering. Mechanical or _____ involves the breakdown of rocks and soils through direct contact with atmospheric conditions, such as heat, water, ice and pressure. The second classification, chemical weathering, involves the direct effect of atmospheric chemicals or biologically produced chemicals (also known as biological weathering) in the breakdown of rocks, soils and minerals.

   a. Weathering
   c. 1509 Istanbul earthquake
   b. Physical weathering
   d. Frost disintegration

4. The _____ is a fundamental concept in geology that describes the dynamic transitions through geologic time among the three main rock types: sedimentary, metamorphic, and igneous. Each type of rock is altered or destroyed when it is forced out of its equilibrium conditions. An igneous rock such as basalt may break down and dissolve when exposed to the atmosphere, or melt as it is subducted under a continent.

   a. Magma
   c. Metamorphic zone
   b. Petrology
   d. Rock cycle

5. _____ is one of the three main rock types (the others being igneous and metamorphic rock.) _____ is formed by deposition and consolidation of mineral and organic material and from precipitation of minerals from solution. The processes that form _____ occur at the surface of the Earth and within bodies of water.

   a. Groundmass
   c. Migmatite
   b. Sedimentary rock
   d. Pluton

6. _____ is the naturally occurring, unconsolidated or loose covering on the Earth's surface. _____ is composed of particles of broken rock that have been altered by chemical, biological and environmental processes including weathering and erosion. _____ is different from its parent rock(s) source(s), altered by interactions between the lithosphere, hydrosphere, atmosphere, and the biosphere.

   a. Topsoil
   c. 1509 Istanbul earthquake
   b. Slump
   d. Soil

Chapter 5. Weathering, Erosion, and Soil

7. _____ is the decomposition of Earth rocks, soils and their minerals through direct contact with the planet's atmosphere. _____ occurs in situ, or 'with no movement', and thus should not be confused with erosion, which involves the movement of rocks and minerals by agents such as water, ice, wind and gravity.

Two important classifications of _____ processes exist -- physical and chemical _____.

  a. Physical weathering
  b. Frost disintegration
  c. 1509 Istanbul earthquake
  d. Weathering

8. _____ is the process of determining a specific date for an archaeological or palaeontological site or artifact. Some archaeologists prefer the terms chronometric or calendar dating, as use of the word 'absolute' implies a certainty and precision that is rarely possible in archaeology. _____ is usually based on the physical or chemical properties of the materials of artifacts, buildings, or other items that have been modified by humans.

  a. Uranium-lead dating
  b. AASHTO Soil Classification System
  c. Absolute dating
  d. Erathem

9. Two important classifications of weathering processes exist -- physical and _____. Mechanical or physical weathering involves the breakdown of rocks and soils through direct contact with atmospheric conditions, such as heat, water, ice and pressure. The second classification, _____, involves the direct effect of atmospheric chemicals or biologically produced chemicals (also known as biological weathering) in the breakdown of rocks, soils and minerals.

  a. Frost disintegration
  b. Chemical weathering
  c. 1509 Istanbul earthquake
  d. Physical weathering

10. A _____ is a large, slow-moving mass of ice, formed from compacted layers of snow, that slowly deforms and flows in response to gravity and high pressure.

_____ ice is the largest reservoir of fresh water on Earth, and second only to oceans as the largest reservoir of total water.

  a. Greenhouse gases
  b. Pacific Decadal Oscillation
  c. Little Ice Age
  d. Glacier

11. _____ is a silvery white and ductile member of the boron group of chemical elements. It has the symbol Al; its atomic number is 13. It is not soluble in water under normal circumstances. _____ is the most abundant metal in the Earth's crust, and the third most abundant element therein, after oxygen and silicon. It makes up about 8% by weight of the Earth'e;s solid surface.

  a. AASHTO Soil Classification System
  b. AL 129-1
  c. AL 333
  d. Aluminum

12. _____ is the difference in degree of discoloration, disintegration, etc., of rocks of different kinds exposed to the same environment. Quartz deposits in basaltic flows will weather slower than the surrounding rock, while being exposed to the same forces of weathering.

_____ occurs when some parts of a rock weathers at different rates than others.

a. Toreva block
b. Fault scarp
c. Gravitational erosion
d. Differential weathering

13. _____, is a type of salt weathering common on coastal and semi-arid granites, sandstones and limestones. _____ is not limited to natural settings and can be seen to develop on buildings where a rate of development can be established. This rate can be as fast as several centimeters in 100 years
   a. Honeycomb weathering
   b. Leaverite
   c. Geotechnics
   d. Stream Load

14. An _____ is a type of rock that contains minerals such as gemstones and metals that can be extracted through mining and refined for use. Samples of _____ in the form of exceptionally beautiful crystals, exotic layering visible when sectioned or polished or metallic presentations such as large nuggets or crystalline formations of metals such as gold or copper may command a value far beyond their value as mere _____ or raw metal for subsequent reduction to utilitarian purposes.

   The grade or concentration of an _____ mineral, or metal, as well as its form of occurrence, will directly affect the costs associated with mining the _____.

   a. Ore genesis
   b. Iron ores
   c. AASHTO Soil Classification System
   d. Ore

15. _____ in the French school of pedology are two regressive evolution processes associated with the loss of equilibrium of a stable soil. Retrogression is primarily due to erosion and corresponds to a phenomenon where succession reverts back to pioneer conditions (such as bare ground.) Degradation is an evolution, different of natural evolution, related to the locale climate and vegetation.
   a. Soils retrogression and degradation
   b. 1703 Genroku earthquake
   c. 1509 Istanbul earthquake
   d. 1700 Cascadia earthquake

16. _____ can also be called frost shattering or frost-wedging. This type of weathering is common in mountain areas where the temperature is around freezing point. Frost induced weathering, although often attributed to the expansion of freezing water captured in cracks, is generally independent of the water-to-ice expansion. It has long been known that moist soils expand or frost heave upon freezing as a result of water migrating along from unfrozen areas via thin films to collect at growing ice lenses. This same phenomena occurs within pore spaces of rocks.
   a. Physical weathering
   b. Weathering
   c. 1509 Istanbul earthquake
   d. Frost disintegration

17. _____ is a common and widely occurring type of intrusive, felsic, igneous rock. _____ has a medium to coarse texture, occasionally with some individual crystals larger than the groundmass forming a rock known as porphyry. _____s can be pink to dark gray or even black, depending on their chemistry and mineralogy.
   a. 1703 Genroku earthquake
   b. 1700 Cascadia earthquake
   c. 1509 Istanbul earthquake
   d. Granite

18. _____ is a term given to an accumulation of broken rock fragments at the base of crags, mountain cliffs, or valley shoulders. Landforms associated with these materials are sometimes called _____ slopes or talus piles. These deposits typically have a concave upwards form, while the maximum inclination of such deposits corresponds to the angle of repose of the mean debris size.

Chapter 5. Weathering, Erosion, and Soil

a. 1509 Istanbul earthquake
b. 1703 Genroku earthquake
c. 1700 Cascadia earthquake
d. Scree

19. In geology the term _____ refers to a fracture in rock where there has been no lateral movement in the plane of the fracture (up, down or sideways) of one side relative to the other. This makes it different from a fault which is defined as a fracture in rock where one side slides laterally past to the other. _____s normally have a regular spacing related to either the mechanical properties of the individual rock or the thickness of the layer involved.
 a. 1509 Istanbul earthquake
 b. 1703 Genroku earthquake
 c. Joint
 d. 1700 Cascadia earthquake

20. A _____ is a large emplacement of igneous intrusive rock that forms from cooled magma deep in the Earth's crust. they are almost always made mostly of felsic or intermediate rock-types, such as granite, quartz monzonite, or diorite

Although they may appear uniform, _____s are in fact structures with complex histories and compositions.

 a. Tuff
 b. Scoria
 c. Great Dyke
 d. Batholith

21. _____ is the process by which the freezing of water-saturated soil causes the deformation and upward thrust of the ground surface. This process can damage plant roots through breaking or desiccation, cause cracks in pavement, and damage the foundations of buildings, even below the frost line. Moist, fine-grained soil at certain temperatures is most susceptible to _____.
 a. Frost heaving
 b. 1700 Cascadia earthquake
 c. 1509 Istanbul earthquake
 d. 1703 Genroku earthquake

22. A _____ in geology is an intrusive igneous rock body that crystallized from a magma slowly cooling below the surface of the Earth. _____s include batholiths, dikes, sills, laccoliths, lopoliths, and other igneous bodies. In practice, '_____' usually refers to a distinctive mass of igneous rock, typically kilometers in dimension, without a tabular shape like those of dikes and sills.
 a. Metamorphic rock
 b. Metavolcanic rock
 c. Pluton
 d. Petrology

23. _____ or sheet joints are surface-parallel fracture systems in rock often leading to erosion of concentric slabs.
 a. AL 129-1
 b. AL 333
 c. AASHTO Soil Classification System
 d. Exfoliation joints

24. A _____ column (or _____) is a column of rising air in the lower altitudes of the Earth's atmosphere. They are created by the uneven heating of the Earth's surface from solar radiation, and an example of convection. The Sun warms the ground, which in turn warms the air directly above it.
 a. 1700 Cascadia earthquake
 b. 1509 Istanbul earthquake
 c. Thermal
 d. 1703 Genroku earthquake

25. _____ are a distinctive type of rock often found in primordial sedimentary rocks. The structures consist of repeated thin layers of iron oxides, either magnetite or hematite, alternating with bands of iron-poor shale and chert. Some of the oldest known rock formations, formed around three thousand million years before present, include banded iron layers, and the banded layers are a common feature in sediments for much of the Earth's early history.

a. Sandstone
b. Banded Iron Formations
c. Diatomaceous earth
d. Coquina

26. _____ is a naturally occurring material composed primarily of fine-grained minerals, which show plasticity through a variable range of water content, and which can be hardened when dried and/or fired. _____ deposits are mostly composed of _____ minerals (phyllosilicate minerals), minerals which impart plasticity and harden when fired and/or dried, and variable amounts of water trapped in the mineral structure by polar attraction. Organic materials which do not impart plasticity may also be a part of _____ deposits.
   a. 1509 Istanbul earthquake
   b. 1703 Genroku earthquake
   c. 1700 Cascadia earthquake
   d. Clay

27. _____ are hydrous aluminium phyllosilicates, sometimes with variable amounts of iron, magnesium, alkali metals, alkaline earths and other cations. Clays have structures similar to the micas and therefore form flat hexagonal sheets.
   _____ are common weathering products (including weathering of feldspar) and low temperature hydrothermal alteration products.
   a. 1509 Istanbul earthquake
   b. Clay minerals
   c. Glauconite
   d. Kaolinite

28. _____ is a chemical element. It has the symbol K, atomic number 19, and atomic mass 39.0983. _____ was first isolated from potash.
   a. Potassium
   b. 1509 Istanbul earthquake
   c. 1703 Genroku earthquake
   d. 1700 Cascadia earthquake

29. _____ are a group of rock-forming tectosilicate minerals which make up as much as 60% of the Earth's crust.

   _____ crystallize from magma in both intrusive and extrusive igneous rocks, as veins, and are also present in many types of metamorphic rock. Rock formed entirely of plagioclase feldspar is known as anorthosite.

   a. 1703 Genroku earthquake
   b. 1509 Istanbul earthquake
   c. Feldspars
   d. 1700 Cascadia earthquake

30. _____ is a carbonate mineral and the most stable polymorph of calcium carbonate ($CaCO_3$.) The other polymorphs are the minerals aragonite and vaterite. Aragonite will change to _____ at 470>°C, and vaterite is even less stable.

   _____ is a common constituent of sedimentary rocks, limestone in particular, much of which is formed from the shells of dead marine organisms. Approximately 10% of sedimentary rock is limestone.

   a. 1703 Genroku earthquake
   b. 1700 Cascadia earthquake
   c. 1509 Istanbul earthquake
   d. Calcite

31. _____ is water located beneath the ground surface in soil pore spaces and in the fractures of lithologic formations. A unit of rock or an unconsolidated deposit is called an aquifer when it can yield a usable quantity of water. The depth at which soil pore spaces or fractures and voids in rock become completely saturated with water is called the water table.

Chapter 5. Weathering, Erosion, and Soil

a. 1700 Cascadia earthquake
b. 1509 Istanbul earthquake
c. Depression focused recharge
d. Groundwater

32. An _____ is a confined aquifer containing groundwater that will flow upward through a well without the need for pumping. Water may even reach the ground surface if the natural pressure is high enough, in which case the well is called a flowing artesian well. An aquifer provides the water for an artesian well.
    a. Artesian aquifer
    b. AL 333
    c. AASHTO Soil Classification System
    d. AL 129-1

33. _____ is the name of a sedimentary carbonate rock and a mineral, both composed of calcium magnesium carbonate $CaMg_2$ found in crystals.

    _____ rock (also dolostone) is composed predominantly of the mineral _____. Limestone that is partially replaced by _____ is referred to as dolomitic limestone, or in old U.S. geologic literature as magnesian limestone.

    a. Diatomaceous earth
    b. Dolomite
    c. Sandstone
    d. Keystone

34. _____ are the materials left over after the process of separating the valuable fraction from the worthless fraction of an ore.

    _____ represent external costs of mining. As mining techniques and the price of minerals improve, it is not unusual for _____ to be reprocessed using new methods, or more thoroughly with old methods, to recover additional minerals.

    a. 1703 Genroku earthquake
    b. Tailings
    c. 1509 Istanbul earthquake
    d. 1700 Cascadia earthquake

35. A _____ is a compound containing an anion in which one or more central silicon atoms are surrounded by electronegative ligands. This definition is broad enough to include species such as hexafluorosilicate ('fluorosilicate'), $[SiF_6]^{2-}$, but the _____ species that are encountered most often consist of silicon with oxygen as the ligand. _____ anions, with a negative net electrical charge, must have that charge balanced by other cations to make an electrically neutral compound.
    a. 1509 Istanbul earthquake
    b. 1700 Cascadia earthquake
    c. Silicate
    d. 1703 Genroku earthquake

36. The _____ is a wooded mountain range in Baden-W>ürttemberg, southwestern Germany. It is bordered by the Rhine valley to the west and south. The highest peak is the Feldberg with an elevation of 1,493 meters (4,898 ft.).

Geologically, the _____ consists of a cover of sandstone on top of a core of gneiss. During the last glacial period of the W>ürm glaciation, the _____ was covered by glaciers; several tarn lakes such as the Mummelsee are remains of this period.

Chapter 5. Weathering, Erosion, and Soil

a. 1700 Cascadia earthquake
b. 1703 Genroku earthquake
c. 1509 Istanbul earthquake
d. Black Forest

37. _____ is a chemical reaction during which one or more water molecules are split into hydrogen and hydroxide ions which may go on to participate in further reactions. It is the type of reaction that is used to break down certain polymers, especially those made by step-growth polymerization. Such polymer degradation is usually catalysed by either acid e.g. concentrated sulphuric acid [H_2SO_4] or alkali e.g. sodium hydroxide [NaOH] attack, often increasing with their strength or pH.

a. 1509 Istanbul earthquake
b. 1700 Cascadia earthquake
c. 1703 Genroku earthquake
d. Hydrolysis

38. _____ is molten rock expelled by a volcano during eruption. When first expelled from a volcanic vent, it is a liquid at temperatures from 700 >°C to 1,200 >°C (1,300 >°F to 2,200 >°F.) Although _____ is quite viscous, with about 100,000 times the viscosity of water, it can flow great distances before cooling and solidifying, because of both its thixotropic and shear thinning properties.

a. Cinder
b. Pyroclastic flow
c. Pumice
d. Lava

39. _____ is a sedimentary rock composed largely of the mineral calcite (calcium carbonate: $CaCO_3$.) The deposition of _____ strata is often a by-product and indicator of biological activity in the geologic record. Calcium (along with nitrogen, phosphorus, and potassium) is a key mineral to plant nutrition: soils overlying _____ bedrock tend to be pre-fertilized with calcium.

a. 1703 Genroku earthquake
b. 1509 Istanbul earthquake
c. Limestone
d. 1700 Cascadia earthquake

40. _____ is a sedimentary rock composed mainly of sand-size mineral or rock grains. Most _____ is composed of quartz and/or feldspar because these are the most common minerals in the Earth's crust. Like sand, _____ may be any color, but the most common colors are tan, brown, yellow, red, gray and white.

a. Dolomite
b. Porcellanite
c. Dolostone
d. Sandstone

41. A _____ is an opening in a planet's surface or crust, which allows hot, molten rock, ash, and gases to escape from below the surface. Volcanic activity involving the extrusion of rock tends to form mountains or features like mountains over a period of time.

a. 1700 Cascadia earthquake
b. 1703 Genroku earthquake
c. 1509 Istanbul earthquake
d. Volcano

42. _____ is a gas consisting primarily of methane. It is found associated with fossil fuels, in coal beds, as methane clathrates, and is created by methanogenic organisms in marshes, bogs, and landfills. It is an important fuel source, a major feedstock for fertilizers, and a potent greenhouse gas.

a. Natural gas
b. 1703 Genroku earthquake
c. 1509 Istanbul earthquake
d. 1700 Cascadia earthquake

43. The chemical compound silicon dioxide, also known as _____ , is an oxide of silicon with a chemical formula of SiO_2 and has been known for its hardness since antiquity. _____ is most commonly found in nature as sand or quartz, as well as in the cell walls of diatoms. It is a principal component of most types of glass and substances such as concrete.

Chapter 5. Weathering, Erosion, and Soil

a. 1700 Cascadia earthquake
b. Silica
c. 1509 Istanbul earthquake
d. 1703 Genroku earthquake

44. In geology, a _____ or _____ line is a planar fracture in rock in which the rock on one side of the fracture has moved with respect to the rock on the other side. Large _____s within the Earth's crust are the result of differential or shear motion and active _____ zones are the causal locations of most earthquakes. Earthquakes are caused by energy release during rapid slippage along a _____.
   a. Combe
   b. Cohesion
   c. Geothermal
   d. Fault

45. _____ refers to the diameter of individual grains of sediment, or the lithified particles in clastic rocks. The term may also be applied to other granular materials. This is different from the crystallite size, which is the size of a single crystal inside the particles or grains.
   a. 1509 Istanbul earthquake
   b. 1703 Genroku earthquake
   c. 1700 Cascadia earthquake
   d. Particle size

46. _____ is a type of chemical weathering that creates rounded boulders and helps to create domed monoliths. This should not be confused with stream abrasion, a physical process which also creates rounded rocks on a much smaller scale. A good example of _____ can be found in the Alabama Hills area of eastern California.
   a. Saltation
   b. Wave pounding
   c. Transgression
   d. Spheroidal weathering

47. '_____' is degraded organic material in soil, which causes some soil layers to be dark brown or black.

In soil science, _____ refers to any organic matter that has reached a point of stability, where it will break down no further and might, if conditions do not change, remain essentially as it is for centuries, if not millennia.

   a. 1700 Cascadia earthquake
   b. 1509 Istanbul earthquake
   c. 1703 Genroku earthquake
   d. Humus

48. _____ is a homogeneous, typically nonstratified, porous, friable, slightly coherent, often calcareous, fine-grained, silty, pale yellow or buff, windblown (aeolian) sediment. It generally occurs as a widespread blanket deposit that covers areas of hundreds of square kilometers and tens of meters thick. _____ often stands in either steep or vertical faces.
   a. 1509 Istanbul earthquake
   b. 1700 Cascadia earthquake
   c. 1703 Genroku earthquake
   d. Loess

49. _____ is the second most abundant mineral in the Earth's continental crust. It is made up of a framework of silicon-oxygen tetrahedra SiO_4, with each silicon shared between two oxygens to give the overall formula SiO_2. _____ has a hardness of 7 on the Mohs scale and a density of 2.65 g/cm³.
   a. 1509 Istanbul earthquake
   b. Shocked quartz
   c. 1700 Cascadia earthquake
   d. Quartz

50. _____ is a layer of loose, heterogeneous material covering solid rock. It includes dust, soil, broken rock, and other related materials and is present on Earth, the Moon, some asteroids, and other planets. The term was first defined by George P. Merrill in 1897 who stated, 'In places this covering is made up of material originating through rock-weathering or plant growth in situ. In other instances it is of fragmental and more or less decomposed matter drifted by wind, water or ice from other sources. This entire mantle of unconsolidated material, whatever its nature or origin, it is proposed to call the _____.'
   a. 1703 Genroku earthquake
   b. 1509 Istanbul earthquake
   c. 1700 Cascadia earthquake
   d. Regolith

51. A _____ is a specific layer in the soil which measures parallel to the soil surface and possesses physical characteristics which differ from the layers above and beneath. Horizon formation is a function of a range of geological, chemical, and biological processes and occurs over long time periods. Soils vary in the degree to which horizons are expressed.
   a. Soil horizon
   b. Mollisols
   c. Podsol
   d. Laterite

52. _____ is a sedimentary rock, a hardened deposit of calcium carbonate. This calcium carbonate cements together other materials, including gravel, sand, clay, and silt. It is found in aridisol and mollisol soil orders.
   a. 1509 Istanbul earthquake
   b. 1700 Cascadia earthquake
   c. Caliche
   d. 1703 Genroku earthquake

53. _____ is a surface formation in hot and wet tropical areas which is enriched in iron and aluminium and develops by intensive and long lasting weathering of the underlying parent rock. Nearly all kinds of rocks can be deeply decomposed by the action of high rainfall and elevated temperatures. The percolating rain water causes dissolution of primary rock minerals and decrease of easily soluble elements as sodium, potassium, calcium, magnesium and silicon.
   a. Soil structure
   b. Vertisol
   c. Podsol
   d. Laterite

54. The _____ is the epoch from 1.8 million to 11550 years BP covering the world's recent period of repeated glaciations. The _____ epoch follows the Pliocene epoch and is followed by the Holocene epoch. The _____ is the third epoch of the Neogene period or 6th epoch of the Cenozoic Era. The end of the _____ corresponds with the retreat of the last continental glacier. It also corresponds with the end of the Paleolithic age used in archaeology.
   a. Late Pleistocene
   b. Tyrrhenian
   c. Sicilian Stage
   d. Pleistocene

55. _____ is the layer of soil under the topsoil on the surface of the ground. The _____ may include substances such as clay and has only been partially broken down by air, sunlight, water etc., to produce true soil. Below the _____ is the substratum, which can be residual bedrock, sediments, or aeolian deposits, largely unaffected by soil-forming factors active in the _____.
   a. 1509 Istanbul earthquake
   b. 1700 Cascadia earthquake
   c. 1703 Genroku earthquake
   d. Subsoil

56. _____ is the upper, outermost layer of soil, usually the top 2 inches (5.1 cm) to 8 inches (20 cm.) It has the highest concentration of organic matter and microorganisms and is where most of the Earth's biological soil activity occurs. Plants generally concentrate their roots in and obtain most of their nutrients from this layer.

Chapter 5. Weathering, Erosion, and Soil

a. Soil
b. Slump
c. 1509 Istanbul earthquake
d. Topsoil

57. _____ consists of cutting and burning of forests or woodlands to create fields for agriculture or pasture for livestock, or for a variety of other purposes. It is sometimes part of shifting cultivation agriculture, and of transhumance livestock herding.

Historically, the practice of _____ has been widely practiced throughout most of the world, in grasslands as well as woodlands, and known by many names.

a. 1509 Istanbul earthquake
b. 1703 Genroku earthquake
c. 1700 Cascadia earthquake
d. Slash and burn

58. _____ is a common extrusive volcanic rock. It is usually grey to black and fine-grained due to rapid cooling of lava at the surface of a planet. It may be porphyritic containing larger crystals in a fine matrix, or vesicular, or frothy scoria.

a. 1703 Genroku earthquake
b. 1509 Istanbul earthquake
c. Basalt
d. 1700 Cascadia earthquake

59. _____ is a hard metamorphic rock which was originally sandstone. Sandstone is converted into _____ through heating and pressure usually related to tectonic compression within orogenic belts. Pure _____ is usually white to grey, though _____s often occur in various shades of pink and red due to varying amounts of iron oxide .

a. Facies
b. Quartzite
c. Shock metamorphism
d. Schist

60. In stratigraphy, _____ is the native consolidated rock underlying the surface of a terrestrial planet, usually the Earth. Above the _____ is usually an area of broken and weathered unconsolidated rock in the basal subsoil. The top of the _____ is known as rockhead and identifying this, via excavations, drilling or geophysical methods, is an important task in most civil engineering projects.

a. Sequence stratigraphy
b. Polystrate
c. Biozones
d. Bedrock

61. The _____ is a chronologic schema (or idealized model) relating stratigraphy to time that is used by geologists, paleontologists and other earth scientists to describe the timing and relationships between events that have occurred during the history of the Earth. The table of geologic time spans presented here agrees with the dates and nomenclature proposed by the International Commission on Stratigraphy, and uses the standard color codes of the United States Geological Survey.

Evidence from radiometric dating indicates that the Earth is about 4.570 billion years old.

a. 1703 Genroku earthquake
b. 1700 Cascadia earthquake
c. 1509 Istanbul earthquake
d. Geologic time scale

62. _____ is the solid-state recrystallization of pre-existing rocks due to changes in physical and chemical conditions, primarily heat, pressure, and the introduction of chemically active fluids. Both mineralogical, chemical and crystallographic changes can occur during this process.

Three types of _____ exist: dynamic, contact and regional.

a. Gradualism
b. Cross-bedding
c. Metamorphism
d. Dike

63. The _____ or the Dirty Thirties was a period of severe dust storms causing major ecological and agricultural damage to American and Canadian prairie lands from 1930 to 1936 (in some areas until 1940.) The phenomenon was caused by severe drought coupled with decades of extensive farming without crop rotation or other techniques to prevent erosion. Deep plowing of the virgin topsoil of the Great Plains had killed the natural grasses that normally kept the soil in place and trapped moisture even during periods of drought and high winds.
a. 1509 Istanbul earthquake
b. 1700 Cascadia earthquake
c. 1703 Genroku earthquake
d. Dust Bowl

64. A _____ is a narrow and shallow incision into soil resulting from erosion by overland flow that has been focused into a thin thread by soil surface roughness. Rilling, the process of _____ formation, is common on agricultural land and unvegetated ground.
a. Transition zone
b. Cross-cutting relationships
c. Rill
d. Fort Union Formation

65. _____ or contour farming is the farming practice of plowing across a slope following its elevation contour lines. The rows formed have the effect of slowing water run-off during rainstorms so that the soil is not washed away and allows the water to percolate into the soil. In _____, the ruts made by the plough run perpendicular rather than parallel to slopes, generally resulting in furrows that curve around the land and are level.
a. 1509 Istanbul earthquake
b. 1700 Cascadia earthquake
c. 1703 Genroku earthquake
d. Contour plowing

66. _____ or Crop sequencing is the practice of growing a series of dissimilar types of crops in the same area in sequential seasons for various benefits such as to avoid the build up of pathogens and pests that often occurs when one species is continuously cropped. _____ also seeks to balance the fertility demands of various crops to avoid excessive depletion of soil nutrients. A traditional component of _____ is the replenishment of nitrogen through the use of green manure in sequence with cereals and other crops.
a. 1700 Cascadia earthquake
b. 1509 Istanbul earthquake
c. Crop rotation
d. 1703 Genroku earthquake

67. _____ is the most important aluminium ore. It consists largely of the minerals gibbsite Al(OH)$_3$, boehmite >γ-AlO(OH), and diaspore >α-AlO(OH), together with the iron oxides goethite and hematite, the clay mineral kaolinite and small amounts of anatase TiO$_2$. It was named after the village Les Baux in southern France, where it was first discovered in 1821 by the geologist Pierre Berthier.
a. 1700 Cascadia earthquake
b. 1509 Istanbul earthquake
c. Bauxite
d. 1703 Genroku earthquake

68. _____ are rocks and minerals from which metallic iron can be economically extracted. The ores are usually rich in iron oxides and vary in color from dark grey, bright yellow, deep purple, to rusty red. The iron itself is usually found in the form of magnetite (Fe$_3$O$_4$), haematite (Fe$_2$O$_3$), goethite, limonite or siderite.
a. AASHTO Soil Classification System
b. Iron ores
c. Ore
d. Ore genesis

Chapter 6. Sediment and Sedimentary Rocks

1. In geology a _____ is the smallest division of a geologic formation or stratigraphic rock series marked by well-defined divisional planes (bedding planes) separating it from layers above and below. A _____ is the smallest lithostratigraphic unit, usually ranging in thickness from a centimeter to several meters and distinguishable from _____s above and below it. _____s can be differentiated in various ways, including rock or mineral type and particle size.
   - a. Biozones
   - b. Bed
   - c. Cyclostratigraphy
   - d. Sequence stratigraphy

2. The _____ is the layer of igneous, sedimentary, and metamorphic rocks which form the continents and the areas of shallow seabed close to their shores, known as continental shelves. This layer is sometimes called sial due to more felsic, or granitic, bulk composition, which lies in contrast to the oceanic crust, called sima due to its mafic, or basaltic rock. (Based on the change in velocity of seismic waves, it is believed that at a certain depth sial becomes close in its physical properties to sima.
   - a. Divergent boundary
   - b. Mirovia
   - c. Continental crust
   - d. Plate tectonics

3. _____ is the geological process by which material is added to a landform or land mass. Fluids such as wind and water, as well as sediment gravity flows, transport previously eroded sediment, which, at the loss of enough kinetic energy in the fluid, is deposited, building up layers of sediment.

   _____ occurs when the forces responsible for sediment transportation are no longer sufficient to overcome the forces of particle weight and friction, which resist motion.
   - a. Hydraulic action
   - b. Deposition
   - c. Stoping
   - d. Hydrothermal circulation

4. _____ are the preserved remains or traces of animals, plants, and other organisms from the remote past. The totality of _____, both discovered and undiscovered, and their placement in fossiliferous rock formations and sedimentary layers (strata) is known as the fossil record. The study of _____ across geological time, how they were formed, and the evolutionary relationships between taxa (phylogeny) are some of the most important functions of the science of paleontology.
   - a. 1509 Istanbul earthquake
   - b. 1700 Cascadia earthquake
   - c. Fossils
   - d. 1703 Genroku earthquake

5. _____ is rock that is of a specific particle size range. Specifically, it is any loose rock that is larger than two millimeters (2mm) in its largest dimension (about 1/12 of an inch) and no more than 64 millimeters (about 2.5 inches.) The next smaller size class in geology is sand, which is >0.0625 mm to 2 mm in size.
   - a. 1700 Cascadia earthquake
   - b. 1703 Genroku earthquake
   - c. 1509 Istanbul earthquake
   - d. Gravel

6. _____ is the part of Earth's lithosphere that surfaces in the ocean basins. _____ is primarily composed of mafic rocks, or sima. It is thinner than continental crust, or sial, generally less than 10 kilometers thick, however it is denser, having a mean density of about 3.3 grams per cubic centimeter.
   - a. AASHTO Soil Classification System
   - b. AL 333
   - c. AL 129-1
   - d. Oceanic crust

Chapter 6. Sediment and Sedimentary Rocks

7. The _____ is the epoch from 1.8 million to 11550 years BP covering the world's recent period of repeated glaciations. The _____ epoch follows the Pliocene epoch and is followed by the Holocene epoch. The _____ is the third epoch of the Neogene period or 6th epoch of the Cenozoic Era. The end of the _____ corresponds with the retreat of the last continental glacier. It also corresponds with the end of the Paleolithic age used in archaeology.

   a. Late Pleistocene   b. Tyrrhenian
   c. Sicilian Stage   d. Pleistocene

8. The _____ is a fundamental concept in geology that describes the dynamic transitions through geologic time among the three main rock types: sedimentary, metamorphic, and igneous. Each type of rock is altered or destroyed when it is forced out of its equilibrium conditions. An igneous rock such as basalt may break down and dissolve when exposed to the atmosphere, or melt as it is subducted under a continent.

   a. Metamorphic zone   b. Magma
   c. Petrology   d. Rock cycle

9. _____ is any particulate matter that can be transported by fluid flow, and which eventually is deposited.

They are most often transported by water (fluvial processes) transported by wind (aeolian processes) and glaciers. Beach sands and river channel deposits are examples of fluvial transport and deposition, though _____ also often settles out of slow-moving or standing water in lakes and oceans.

   a. Salt glacier   b. Bovey Beds
   c. Sediment   d. Quick clay

10. _____ is one of the three main rock types (the others being igneous and metamorphic rock.) _____ is formed by deposition and consolidation of mineral and organic material and from precipitation of minerals from solution. The processes that form _____ occur at the surface of the Earth and within bodies of water.

   a. Pluton   b. Sedimentary rock
   c. Migmatite   d. Groundmass

11. _____ is the process of determining a specific date for an archaeological or palaeontological site or artifact. Some archaeologists prefer the terms chronometric or calendar dating, as use of the word 'absolute' implies a certainty and precision that is rarely possible in archaeology. _____ is usually based on the physical or chemical properties of the materials of artifacts, buildings, or other items that have been modified by humans.

   a. Uranium-lead dating   b. Erathem
   c. AASHTO Soil Classification System   d. Absolute dating

12. A _____ is a large emplacement of igneous intrusive rock that forms from cooled magma deep in the Earth's crust. they are almost always made mostly of felsic or intermediate rock-types, such as granite, quartz monzonite, or diorite

Although they may appear uniform, _____s are in fact structures with complex histories and compositions.

   a. Tuff   b. Scoria
   c. Batholith   d. Great Dyke

Chapter 6. Sediment and Sedimentary Rocks

13. _____ is the movement of the Earth's continents relative to each other. The hypothesis that continents 'drift' was first put forward by Abraham Ortelius in 1596 and was fully developed by Alfred Wegener in 1912. However, it was not until the development of the theory of plate tectonics in the 1960s, that a sufficient geological explanation of that movement was found.
   a. Subduction
   b. Continental drift
   c. Nappe
   d. Mirovia

14. In geology, _____ is transported rock debris overlying the solid bedrock. The term is also sometimes refers to organic debris so-transported. In the largest sense, it refers to the material left behind by retreating continental glaciers.
   a. Contact metamorphism
   b. Geostrophic current
   c. Detritus
   d. Drift

15. _____ is the removal of solids (sediment, soil, rock and other particles) in the natural environment. It usually occurs due to transport by wind, water, or ice; by down-slope creep of soil and other material under the force of gravity; or by living organisms, such as burrowing animals, in the case of bioerosion.

   _____ is distinguished from weathering, which is the process of chemical or physical breakdown of the minerals in the rocks, although the two processes may occur concurrently.

   a. AL 129-1
   b. AL 333
   c. AASHTO Soil Classification System
   d. Erosion

16. _____ is a gas consisting primarily of methane. It is found associated with fossil fuels, in coal beds, as methane clathrates, and is created by methanogenic organisms in marshes, bogs, and landfills. It is an important fuel source, a major feedstock for fertilizers, and a potent greenhouse gas.
   a. 1703 Genroku earthquake
   b. Natural gas
   c. 1509 Istanbul earthquake
   d. 1700 Cascadia earthquake

17. The lithosphere is broken up into what are called _____. In the case of Earth, there are eight major and many minor plates The lithospheric plates ride on the asthenosphere. These plates move in relation to one another at one of three types of plate boundaries: convergent, or collisional boundaries; divergent boundaries, also called spreading centers; and transform boundaries.
   a. Tectonic plates
   b. Juan de Fuca Ridge
   c. Subduction
   d. Lithosphere

18. The _____ is the extended perimeter of each continent and associated coastal plain, and was part of the continent during the glacial periods, but is undersea during interglacial periods such as the current epoch by relatively shallow seas (known as shelf seas) and gulfs.

   The continental rise is below the slope, but landward of the abyssal plains. Its gradient is intermediate between the slope and the shelf, on the order of 0.5-1°.

   a. Continental shelf
   b. Continental slope
   c. Surface runoff
   d. Mud

64 Chapter 6. Sediment and Sedimentary Rocks

19. _____ is mechanical scraping of a rock surface by friction between rocks and moving particles during their transport in wind, glacier, waves, gravity or running water, after friction, the moving particles dislodge loose and weak debris from the side of the rock, these particles can be dissolved in the water source.

The intensity of _____ depends on the hardness, concentration, velocity and mass of moving particles.

A virtually smooth marine platform cut by the ocean waves at a coastline.

   a. AASHTO Soil Classification System
   b. AL 333
   c. AL 129-1
   d. Abrasion

20. _____ is a naturally occurring material composed primarily of fine-grained minerals, which show plasticity through a variable range of water content, and which can be hardened when dried and/or fired. _____ deposits are mostly composed of _____ minerals (phyllosilicate minerals), minerals which impart plasticity and harden when fired and/or dried, and variable amounts of water trapped in the mineral structure by polar attraction. Organic materials which do not impart plasticity may also be a part of _____ deposits.
   a. 1700 Cascadia earthquake
   b. 1703 Genroku earthquake
   c. 1509 Istanbul earthquake
   d. Clay

21. _____ is a geological term used to describe particles of rock derived from pre-existing rock through processes of weathering and erosion. Thesel particles can consist of lithic fragments (particles of recognisable rock), or of monomineralic fragments (mineral grains.) These particles are often transported through sedimentary processes into depositional systems such as riverbeds, lakes or the ocean forming sedimentary successions.
   a. Perched coastline
   b. Dispersion
   c. Metamorphism
   d. Detritus

22. _____ is a sedimentary rock composed largely of the mineral calcite (calcium carbonate: $CaCO_3$.) The deposition of _____ strata is often a by-product and indicator of biological activity in the geologic record. Calcium (along with nitrogen, phosphorus, and potassium) is a key mineral to plant nutrition: soils overlying _____ bedrock tend to be pre-fertilized with calcium.
   a. 1509 Istanbul earthquake
   b. 1700 Cascadia earthquake
   c. 1703 Genroku earthquake
   d. Limestone

23. _____ is a liquid or semi-liquid mixture of water and some combination of soil, silt, and clay. Ancient _____ deposits harden over geological time to form sedimentary rock such as siltstone or solid, mudrock lutites. When geological deposits of _____ are formed in estuaries the resultant layers are termed bay _____s.
   a. Continental slope
   b. Surface runoff
   c. Mud
   d. Continental shelf

24. _____ is a naturally occurring granular material composed of finely divided rock and mineral particles.

As the term is used by geologists, _____ particles range in diameter from 0.0625 (or $>^1\!\!>\!\!/_{16}$ mm, or 62.5 micrometers) to 2 millimeters. An individual particle in this range size is termed a _____ grain.

Chapter 6. Sediment and Sedimentary Rocks

a. 1703 Genroku earthquake
b. Sand
c. 1700 Cascadia earthquake
d. 1509 Istanbul earthquake

25. _____ is soil or rock derived granular material of a grain size between sand and clay. _____ may occur as a soil or as suspended sediment in a surface water body. It may also exist as soil deposited at the bottom of a water body.
   a. 1703 Genroku earthquake
   b. 1700 Cascadia earthquake
   c. Silt
   d. 1509 Istanbul earthquake

26. _____ is the decomposition of Earth rocks, soils and their minerals through direct contact with the planet's atmosphere. _____ occurs in situ, or 'with no movement', and thus should not be confused with erosion, which involves the movement of rocks and minerals by agents such as water, ice, wind and gravity.

Two important classifications of _____ processes exist -- physical and chemical _____.

   a. 1509 Istanbul earthquake
   b. Physical weathering
   c. Frost disintegration
   d. Weathering

27. A _____ is a large, slow-moving mass of ice, formed from compacted layers of snow, that slowly deforms and flows in response to gravity and high pressure.

_____ ice is the largest reservoir of fresh water on Earth, and second only to oceans as the largest reservoir of total water.

   a. Little Ice Age
   b. Greenhouse gases
   c. Pacific Decadal Oscillation
   d. Glacier

28. _____ refers to the process by which a sediment progressively loses its porosity due to the effects of loading. This forms part of the process of lithification. When a layer of sediment is originally deposited, it contains an open framework of particles with the pore space being usually filled with water.
   a. Submersion
   b. Cleavage
   c. Depression
   d. Compaction

29. In geology, sedimentary _____ describes the combination of physical, chemical and biological processes associated with the deposition of a particular type of sediment and, therefore, the rock types that will be formed after lithification, if the sediment is preserved in the rock record. In most cases the environments associated with particular rock types or associations of rock types can be matched to existing analogues. However, the further back in geological time sediments were deposited, the more likely that direct modern analogues are not available (e.g. banded iron formations.)
   a. 1509 Istanbul earthquake
   b. Depositional environment
   c. 1703 Genroku earthquake
   d. 1700 Cascadia earthquake

30. _____ is the process in which sediments compact under pressure, expel connate fluids, and gradually become solid rock. Essentially, _____ is a process of porosity destruction through compaction and cementation. _____ includes all the processes which convert unconsolidated sediments into sedimentary rocks.
   a. Lithification
   b. Dolomite
   c. Sedimentary deposits
   d. Metasediment

Chapter 6. Sediment and Sedimentary Rocks

31. _____ is the chemical element with the symbol Ca and atomic number 20. It has an atomic mass of 40.078 amu. _____ is a soft grey alkaline earth metal, and is the fifth most abundant element by mass in the Earth's crust.
    a. 1509 Istanbul earthquake
    b. 1703 Genroku earthquake
    c. 1700 Cascadia earthquake
    d. Calcium

32. _____ is a chemical compound with the chemical formula $CaCO_3$. It is a common substance found in rock in all parts of the world, and is the main component of shells of marine organisms, snails, pearls, and eggshells. _____ is the active ingredient in agricultural lime, and is usually the principal cause of hard water.
    a. Calcium carbonate
    b. 1700 Cascadia earthquake
    c. 1509 Istanbul earthquake
    d. 1703 Genroku earthquake

33. _____ is water located beneath the ground surface in soil pore spaces and in the fractures of lithologic formations. A unit of rock or an unconsolidated deposit is called an aquifer when it can yield a usable quantity of water. The depth at which soil pore spaces or fractures and voids in rock become completely saturated with water is called the water table.
    a. Depression focused recharge
    b. 1509 Istanbul earthquake
    c. Groundwater
    d. 1700 Cascadia earthquake

34. The chemical compound silicon dioxide, also known as _____ , is an oxide of silicon with a chemical formula of SiO_2 and has been known for its hardness since antiquity. _____ is most commonly found in nature as sand or quartz, as well as in the cell walls of diatoms. It is a principal component of most types of glass and substances such as concrete.
    a. 1509 Istanbul earthquake
    b. Silica
    c. 1700 Cascadia earthquake
    d. 1703 Genroku earthquake

35. In chemistry, a _____ is a salt or ester of carbonic acid.

To test for the presence of the _____ anion in a salt, the addition of dilute mineral acid (e.g. hydrochloric acid) will yield carbon dioxide gas.

_____-containing salts are industrially and mineralogically ubiquitous.

    a. 1700 Cascadia earthquake
    b. 1703 Genroku earthquake
    c. Carbonate
    d. 1509 Istanbul earthquake

36. A _____ is a compound containing an anion in which one or more central silicon atoms are surrounded by electronegative ligands. This definition is broad enough to include species such as hexafluorosilicate ('fluorosilicate'), $[SiF_6]^{2-}$, but the _____ species that are encountered most often consist of silicon with oxygen as the ligand. _____ anions, with a negative net electrical charge, must have that charge balanced by other cations to make an electrically neutral compound.
    a. 1700 Cascadia earthquake
    b. 1703 Genroku earthquake
    c. 1509 Istanbul earthquake
    d. Silicate

37. _____ rocks are composed of fragments of pre-existing rock. The term is most commonly, but not uniquely, applied to sedimentary rocks.

Chapter 6. Sediment and Sedimentary Rocks 67

_____ metamorphic rocks include breccias formed in faults, as well as some protomylonite and pseudotachylite.

a. 1700 Cascadia earthquake
b. 1509 Istanbul earthquake
c. 1703 Genroku earthquake
d. Clastic

38. A _____ is a rock consisting of individual stones that have become cemented together. They are sedimentary rocks consisting of rounded fragments and are thus differentiated from breccias, which consist of angular clasts. Both _____s and breccias are characterized by clasts larger than sand (>2 mm).
   a. Superficial deposits
   b. Keystone
   c. Concretion
   d. Conglomerate

39. _____ is broken stone, of irregular size, shape and texture. This word is closely connected in derivation with 'rubbish', which was formerly also applied to what we now call '_____'. _____ naturally found in the soil is known also as 'brash' (compare cornbrash).
   a. 1509 Istanbul earthquake
   b. 1703 Genroku earthquake
   c. 1700 Cascadia earthquake
   d. Rubble

40. _____ is a rock composed of angular fragments of minerals or rocks in a matrix (cementing material), that may be similar or different in composition to the fragments. A _____ may have a variety of different origins, as indicated by the named types including sedimentary _____, tectonic _____, igneous _____, impact _____ and hydrothermal _____.

Sedimentary _____s are a type of clastic sedimentary rock which are composed of angular to subangular, randomly oriented clasts of other sedimentary rocks.

a. 1509 Istanbul earthquake
b. Coprolite
c. Ventifacts
d. Breccia

41. In materials science, _____ is the distribution of crystallographic orientations of a polycrystalline sample. A sample in which these orientations are fully random is said to have no _____. If the crystallographic orientations are not random, but have some preferred orientation, then the sample has a weak, strong, or moderate _____.
   a. Melange
   b. Deformation
   c. Texture
   d. Streak

42. _____ is a detrital sedimentary rock, specifically a type of sandstone containing at least 25% feldspar., Arkosic sand is sand that is similarly rich in feldspar, and thus the potential precursor of _____. The other mineral components may vary, but quartz is commonly dominant, and some mica is often present. Apart from the mineral content, rock fragments may also be a significant component.
   a. AASHTO Soil Classification System
   b. AL 129-1
   c. AL 333
   d. Arkose

Chapter 6. Sediment and Sedimentary Rocks

43. _____ is a fine-grained silica-rich microcrystalline, cryptocrystalline or microfibrous sedimentary rock that may contain small fossils. It varies greatly in color (from white to black), but most often manifests as gray, brown, grayish brown and light green to rusty red; its color is an expression of trace elements present in the rock, and both red and green are most often related to traces of iron (in its oxidized and reduced forms respectively.)

_____ occurs as oval to irregular nodules in greensand, limestone, chalk, and dolostone formations as a replacement mineral, where it is formed as a result of some type of diagenesis.

   a. 1703 Genroku earthquake
   c. 1700 Cascadia earthquake
   b. Chert
   d. 1509 Istanbul earthquake

44. _____, in structural geology and related disciplines, describes the tendency of a rock to break along preferred planes of weakness.

Rocks deformed under very low to low metamorphic grade often develop planes along which the rock can easily be split. Slates are an example of a rock with a penetrative _____ caused partly by the realignment of phyllosilicate minerals with increasing flattening strain.

   a. Depression
   c. Cleavage
   b. Combe
   d. Fault

45. _____ are a group of rock-forming tectosilicate minerals which make up as much as 60% of the Earth's crust.

_____ crystallize from magma in both intrusive and extrusive igneous rocks, as veins, and are also present in many types of metamorphic rock. Rock formed entirely of plagioclase feldspar is known as anorthosite.

   a. 1700 Cascadia earthquake
   c. 1703 Genroku earthquake
   b. 1509 Istanbul earthquake
   d. Feldspars

46. _____ is the second most abundant mineral in the Earth's continental crust. It is made up of a framework of silicon-oxygen tetrahedra SiO_4, with each silicon shared between two oxygens to give the overall formula SiO_2. _____ has a hardness of 7 on the Mohs scale and a density of 2.65 g/cm³.

   a. 1700 Cascadia earthquake
   c. Quartz
   b. 1509 Istanbul earthquake
   d. Shocked quartz

47. _____ is a sedimentary rock composed mainly of sand-size mineral or rock grains. Most _____ is composed of quartz and/or feldspar because these are the most common minerals in the Earth's crust. Like sand, _____ may be any color, but the most common colors are tan, brown, yellow, red, gray and white.

   a. Sandstone
   c. Dolostone
   b. Porcellanite
   d. Dolomite

48. _____ are hydrous aluminium phyllosilicates, sometimes with variable amounts of iron, magnesium, alkali metals, alkaline earths and other cations. Clays have structures similar to the micas and therefore form flat hexagonal sheets.

_____ are common weathering products (including weathering of feldspar) and low temperature hydrothermal alteration products.

a. Glauconite
b. 1509 Istanbul earthquake
c. Kaolinite
d. Clay minerals

49. _____ is a geological term used to describe a sedimentary rock that is composed primarily of clay-sized particles . It does not refer to those rocks that are laminated or easily split into thin layers (clay shales.) _____s are distinct from mudstones, which are partly hardened muds that slake when wetted; _____ is fully-hardened material.
   a. Siltstone
   b. Claystone
   c. Pelagic sediments
   d. Keystone

50. _____ is a fine grained sedimentary rock whose original constituents were clays or muds. Grain size is up to 0.0625 mm with individual grains too small to be distinguished without a microscope. With increased pressure over time the platey clay minerals may become aligned, with the appearance of fissility or parallel layering.
   a. Mudstone
   b. Pelagic sediments
   c. Sandstone
   d. Porcellanite

51. _____ is a fine-grained sedimentary rock whose original constituents were clay minerals or muds. It is characterized by thin laminae breaking with an irregular curving fracture, often splintery and usually parallel to the often-indistinguishable bedding plane. This property is called fissility.
   a. Sandstone
   b. Siltstone
   c. Shale
   d. Diatomaceous earth

52. _____ is a sedimentary rock which has a composition intermediate in grain size between the coarser sandstones and the finer mudstones and shales.

As its name implies, it is primarily composed (greater than 2/3) of silt sized particles, defined as grains between 3.9 and 62.5 micrometres or 4 to 8 on the Krumbein phi (>φ) scale. _____s differ significantly from sandstones due to their smaller pores and higher propensity for containing a significant clay fraction.

   a. Sandstone
   b. Carbonate rocks
   c. Shale
   d. Siltstone

53. Two important classifications of weathering processes exist -- physical and _____. Mechanical or physical weathering involves the breakdown of rocks and soils through direct contact with atmospheric conditions, such as heat, water, ice and pressure. The second classification, _____, involves the direct effect of atmospheric chemicals or biologically produced chemicals (also known as biological weathering) in the breakdown of rocks, soils and minerals.
   a. 1509 Istanbul earthquake
   b. Chemical weathering
   c. Physical weathering
   d. Frost disintegration

54. _____ is a carbonate mineral and the most stable polymorph of calcium carbonate ($CaCO_3$.) The other polymorphs are the minerals aragonite and vaterite. Aragonite will change to _____ at 470>°C, and vaterite is even less stable.

_____ is a common constituent of sedimentary rocks, limestone in particular, much of which is formed from the shells of dead marine organisms. Approximately 10% of sedimentary rock is limestone.

Chapter 6. Sediment and Sedimentary Rocks

a. 1509 Istanbul earthquake
b. Calcite
c. 1703 Genroku earthquake
d. 1700 Cascadia earthquake

55. _____ are a class of sedimentary rocks composed primarily of carbonate minerals. The two major types are limestone and dolomite, composed of calcite ($CaCO_3$) and the mineral dolomite ($CaMg(CO_3)_2$) respectively. Chalk and tufa are also minor sedimentary carbonates.

a. Carbonate rocks
b. Concretion
c. Porcellanite
d. Shale

56. _____ is a soft, white, porous sedimentary rock, a form of limestone composed of the mineral calcite. It forms under relatively deep marine conditions from the gradual accumulation of minute calcite plates shed from micro-organisms called coccolithophores. It is common to find flint and chert nodules embedded in _____.

a. 1509 Istanbul earthquake
b. 1703 Genroku earthquake
c. Chalk
d. 1700 Cascadia earthquake

57. _____ is an incompletely consolidated sedimentary rock. _____ was formed in association with marine reefs and is a variety of 'coral rag', technically a subset of limestone.

_____ is mainly composed of mineral calcite, often including some phosphate, in the form of seashells or coral.

a. Superficial deposits
b. Lithification
c. Coquina
d. Diatomaceous earth

58. _____ or dolomite rock is a sedimentary carbonate rock that contains a high percentage of the mineral dolomite. In old U.S.G.S. publications it was referred to as magnesian limestone. Most _____ formed as a magnesium replacement of limestone or lime mud prior to lithification.

a. Sandstone
b. Pelagic sediments
c. Metasediment
d. Dolostone

59. _____ are water-soluble mineral sediments that result from the evaporation of bodies of surficial water. _____ are considered sedimentary rocks.

Although all water bodies on the surface and in aquifers contain dissolved salts, the water must evaporate into the atmosphere for the minerals to precipitate.

a. AL 333
b. AL 129-1
c. AASHTO Soil Classification System
d. Evaporites

60. _____ is a sedimentary rock. It is a natural chemical precipitate of carbonate minerals; typically aragonite, but often recrystallized to, or primarily, calcite.

_____ forms as calcium carbonate is deposited from the water of mineral springs or rivulets that are saturated with dissolved calcium bicarbonate. The spring water from which the calcium carbonate precipitates can be hot, warm or cold. The rate of deposition increases with the temperature of the water, or alternatively, when biotic material accelerates the process of precipitation.

Chapter 6. Sediment and Sedimentary Rocks

a. 1703 Genroku earthquake
b. 1509 Istanbul earthquake
c. Travertine
d. 1700 Cascadia earthquake

61. _____ are a distinctive type of rock often found in primordial sedimentary rocks. The structures consist of repeated thin layers of iron oxides, either magnetite or hematite, alternating with bands of iron-poor shale and chert. Some of the oldest known rock formations, formed around three thousand million years before present, include banded iron layers, and the banded layers are a common feature in sediments for much of the Earth's early history.

a. Diatomaceous earth
b. Coquina
c. Sandstone
d. Banded Iron Formations

62. A _____ in petrology or mineralogy is a secondary structure, generally spherical or irregularly rounded in shape. They are typically solid replacement bodies of chert or iron oxides formed during diagenesis of a sedimentary rock. They may be hollow as geodes or vugs or filled with crystals and intricate geometric shrinkage patterns as in septarian _____s.

a. Heavy metal
b. Stratification
c. Nodule
d. Tarn

63. _____ is an accumulation of partially decayed vegetation matter. _____ forms in wetlands or peatlands, variously called bogs, moors, muskegs, pocosins, mires, and _____ swamp forests. By volume there are about 4 trillion mÂÂ³ of _____ in the world covering a total of around 2% of global land mass (about 3 million km^2), containing about 8 billion terajoules of energy.

a. Peat
b. 1703 Genroku earthquake
c. 1509 Istanbul earthquake
d. 1700 Cascadia earthquake

64. _____ is a hard, compact variety of mineral coal that has a high lustre. It has the highest carbon count and contains the fewest impurities of all coals, despite its lower calorific content.

_____ is the highest of the metamorphic rank, in which the carbon content is between 92% and 98%. .

a. AASHTO Soil Classification System
b. AL 129-1
c. AL 333
d. Anthracite

65. _____ is a relatively soft coal containing a tarlike substance called bitumen. It is of higher quality than lignite coal but of poorer quality than anthracite coal.

_____ is a sedimorphic rock formed by diagenetic and submetamorphic compression of peat bog material.

a. 1700 Cascadia earthquake
b. 1703 Genroku earthquake
c. 1509 Istanbul earthquake
d. Bituminous coal

66. _____ is a geological process occurring when areas of submerged seafloor are exposed above the sea level. The opposite event, marine transgression, occurs when flooding from the sea covers previously exposed land.

Evidence of _____ and transgression occurs throughout the fossil record, and these fluctuations are thought to have caused (or contributed to) several mass extinctions, among them the Permian-Triassic extinction event (250 million years ago) and Cretaceous-Tertiary extinction event (65 Ma.)

Chapter 6. Sediment and Sedimentary Rocks

a. 1703 Genroku earthquake
b. 1509 Istanbul earthquake
c. Marine regression
d. 1700 Cascadia earthquake

67. In geology, _____ are a body of rock with specified characteristics. Ideally, a _____ is a distinctive rock unit that forms under certain conditions of sedimentation, reflecting a particular process or environment.

The term _____ was introduced by the Swiss geologist Amanz Gressly in 1838 and was part of his significant contribution to the foundations of modern stratigraphy, [Cross and Homewood (1997)] which replaced the earlier notions of Neptunism.

a. Jadeitite
b. Slate
c. Porphyroblast
d. Facies

68. A marine _____ is a geologic event during which sea level rises relative to the land and the shoreline moves toward higher ground, resulting in flooding. They can be caused either by the land sinking or the ocean basins filling with water (or decreasing in capacity.) Transgresssions and regressions may be caused by tectonic events such as orogenies, severe climate change such as ice ages or isostatic adjustments following removal of ice or sediment load.

a. Diagenesis
b. Hydrothermal circulation
c. Hydraulic action
d. Transgression

69. The general term '_____' or, more precisely, 'glacial age' denotes a geological period of long-term reduction in the temperature of the Earth's surface and atmosphere, resulting in an expansion of continental ice sheets, polar ice sheets and alpine glaciers. Within a long-term _____, individual pulses of extra cold climate are termed 'glaciations'. Glaciologically, _____ implies the presence of extensive ice sheets in the northern and southern hemispheres; by this definition we are still in an _____

a. AL 129-1
b. AL 333
c. AASHTO Soil Classification System
d. Ice Age

70. The _____, usually referred to as the Moho, is the boundary between the Earth's crust and the mantle. The Moho serves to separate both oceanic crust and continental crust from underlying mantle. The Moho mostly lies entirely within the lithosphere; only beneath mid-ocean ridges does it define the lithosphere-asthenosphere boundary.

a. Gorda Ridge
b. Copperbelt Province
c. Panthalassa
d. Mohorovičić discontinuity

71. _____ refers to natural mountain building, and may be studied as a tectonic structural event, (b) as a geographical event, and (c) a chronological event. Orogenic events (a) cause distinctive structural phenomena and related tectonic activity, (b) affect certain regions of rocks and crust, and (c) happen within a specific period of time.

a. Antler orogeny
b. Orogenesis
c. Alice Springs Orogeny
d. Orogeny

72. _____ occurs at mid-ocean ridges, where new oceanic crust is formed through volcanic activity and then gradually moves away from the ridge. _____ helps explain continental drift in the theory of plate tectonics.

Chapter 6. Sediment and Sedimentary Rocks 73

Earlier theories (e.g., by Alfred Wegener) of continental drift were that continents 'plowed' through the sea. The idea that the seafloor itself moves (and carries the continents with it) as it expands from a central axis was proposed by Harry Hess from Princeton University in the 1960s. The theory is well-accepted now, and the phenomenon is known to be caused by convection currents in the plastic, very weak upper mantle, or asthenosphere.

- a. Seafloor spreading
- b. Headward erosion
- c. Deposition
- d. Downcutting

73. In geology, engineering, and surveying, _____ is the motion of a surface (usually, the Earth's surface) as it shifts downward relative to a datum such as sea-level. The opposite of _____ is uplift, which results in an increase in elevation. There are several types of _____.
    - a. Pothole
    - b. Subsidence
    - c. 1700 Cascadia earthquake
    - d. 1509 Istanbul earthquake

74. In chronostratigraphy, a _____ is a succession of rock strata laid down in an single age on the geologic timescale, which usually represents millions of years of deposition. A given _____ of rock and the corresponding age of time will by convention have the same name, and the same boundaries.
    - a. Global Boundary Stratotype Section and Point
    - b. Lichenometry
    - c. Relative dating
    - d. Stage

75. In geology, _____ refers to inclined sedimentary structures in a horizontal unit of rock. These tilted structures are deposits from bedforms such as ripples and dunes, and they indicate that the depositional environment contained a flowing fluid (typically, water or wind.) This is a case in geology when original depositional layering is tilted, and that the tilting is not a result of post-depositional deformation.
    - a. Paralithic
    - b. Perched coastline
    - c. Geopetal
    - d. Cross-bedding

76. In geology, a _____ is one characterized by a systematic change in grain or clast size from the base of the bed to the top. Most commonly this takes the form of normal grading, with coarser sediments at the base, which grade upward into progressively finer ones. Normally _____s generally represent depositional environments which decrease in transport energy as time passes, but also form during rapid depositional events.
    - a. 1700 Cascadia earthquake
    - b. 1509 Istanbul earthquake
    - c. Graded bed
    - d. 1703 Genroku earthquake

77. In geology, _____ are sedimentary structures that indicate agitation by water (current or waves) or wind. _____ formed by water consist of two basic types:

    1. Current _____ are asymmetrical in profile, with a gentle up-current slope and a steeper down-current slope. The down-current slope depends on the shape of the sediment, with 33>° being typical.
    2. Wave-formed _____ have a symmetrical, almost sinusoidal profile; they indicate an environment with weak currents where water motion is dominated by wave oscillations.

Ripples will not form in sediment larger than course sand.

Chapter 6. Sediment and Sedimentary Rocks

a. 1703 Genroku earthquake
b. Ripple marks
c. 1509 Istanbul earthquake
d. 1700 Cascadia earthquake

78. _____ are those structures formed during sediment deposition.

_____ such as cross bedding, graded bedding and ripple marks are utilized in stratigraphic studies to indicate original position of strata in geologically complex terranes.

There are two kinds of flow regimes, which at varying speeds and velocities produce different structures.

a. 1700 Cascadia earthquake
b. 1703 Genroku earthquake
c. Sedimentary structures
d. 1509 Istanbul earthquake

79. _____ is a type of fossil: it consists of fossil wood where all the organic materials have been replaced with minerals, while retaining the original structure of the wood. The petrifaction process occurs underground, when wood becomes buried under sediment and is initially preserved due to a lack of oxygen. Mineral-rich water flowing through the sediment deposits minerals in the plant's cells and as the plant's lignin and cellulose decay away, a stone mould forms in its place.

a. 1509 Istanbul earthquake
b. Pteridospermatophyta
c. Glossopteris
d. Petrified wood

80. _____ are geological records of biological activity. _____ may be impressions made on the substrate by an organism: for example, burrows, borings, footprints and feeding marks, and root cavities. The term in its broadest sense also includes the remains of other organic material produced by an organism - for example coprolites or chemical markers - or sedimentological structures produced by biological means - for example, stromatolites.

a. 1703 Genroku earthquake
b. 1509 Istanbul earthquake
c. 1700 Cascadia earthquake
d. Trace fossils

81. _____ are an extinct group of marine animals of the subclass Ammonoidea in the class Cephalopoda, phylum Mollusca. They are excellent index fossils, and it is often possible to link the rock layer in which they are found to specific geological time periods.

_____ ' closest living relative is probably not the modern Nautilus (which they outwardly resemble), but rather the subclass Coleoidea (octopus, squid, and cuttlefish.)

a. AASHTO Soil Classification System
b. AL 333
c. AL 129-1
d. Ammonites

82. A _____ is fossilized animal dung. They are classified as trace fossils as opposed to body fossils, as they give evidence for the animal's behavior (in this case, diet) rather than morphology. They were first described by William Buckland in 1829.

a. Fault breccia
b. 1509 Istanbul earthquake
c. Ventifacts
d. Coprolite

Chapter 6. Sediment and Sedimentary Rocks

83. _____ is the term for the conversion of an a organic substance into carbon or a carbon-containing residue through pyrolysis or destructive distillation. It is often used in organic chemistry with reference to the generation of coal gas and coal tar from raw coal. Fossil fuels in general are the products of the _____ of vegetable matter.
   a. 1509 Istanbul earthquake
   b. Carbonization
   c. Recrystallization
   d. 1700 Cascadia earthquake

84. The _____ is an Eocene geologic formation that records the sedimentation in a series of intermountain lakes. The sedimentary layers were formed in a large area of interconnecting lakes a tributary of the Colorado River. The area of the formation exists as three separate basins around the Uinta Mountains of northeastern Utah: an area in northwestern Colorado east of the Uintas, a larger area in the southwest corner of Wyoming just north of the Uintas known as Lake Gosiute, and the largest area, which lies in northeastern Utah and western Colorado south of the Uintas, known as Lake Uinta.
   a. Green River Formation
   b. 1700 Cascadia earthquake
   c. 1703 Genroku earthquake
   d. 1509 Istanbul earthquake

85. _____ is the principle that the same scientific laws and processes are constant throughout space and time. It applies specifically to sciences that require a long timescale such as geology, astronomy, and paleontology. It was first defined by Charles Lyell (1797 - 1875), who incorporated James Hutton's gradualism into the idea of _____.
   a. AASHTO Soil Classification System
   b. Uniformitarianism
   c. AL 333
   d. AL 129-1

86. _____ is a geologic formation in the Glen Canyon Group that is spread across the U.S. states of northern Arizona, northwest Colorado, Nevada, and Utah (the unit is not part of a group in Nevada.) It is located in the Colorado Plateau province of the United States. This rock formation is particularly prominent in southern Utah, where it forms the main attractions of a number of national parks and monuments including Zion National Park, Capitol Reef National Park, Glen Canyon National Recreation Area, Grand Staircase-Escalante National Monument, and Canyonlands National Park.

_____ frequently occurs as spectacular cliffs, cuestas, domes, and bluffs rising from the desert floor. It can be distinguished from adjacent Jurassic sandstones by its white to light pink color, meter-scale cross-bedding, and distinctive rounded weathering.

   a. 1703 Genroku earthquake
   b. 1509 Istanbul earthquake
   c. 1700 Cascadia earthquake
   d. Navajo Sandstone

87. _____ are rocks and minerals from which metallic iron can be economically extracted. The ores are usually rich in iron oxides and vary in color from dark grey, bright yellow, deep purple, to rusty red. The iron itself is usually found in the form of magnetite (Fe_3O_4), haematite (Fe_2O_3), goethite, limonite or siderite.
   a. Ore
   b. AASHTO Soil Classification System
   c. Ore genesis
   d. Iron ores

88. A _____ is an elevated area of land with a flat top and sides that are usually steep cliffs. It takes its name from its characteristic table-top shape. It is a characteristic landform of arid environments, particularly the southwestern United States.

_____s form usually in areas where horizontally layered rocks are uplifted by tectonic activity, but may form also in its absence.

Chapter 6. Sediment and Sedimentary Rocks

_____s are formed by weathering and erosion. Variations in the ability of different types of rock to resist weathering and erosion cause the weaker types of rocks to be eroded away, leaving the more resistant types of rocks topographically higher relative to their surroundings. This process is called differential erosion.

   a. Mesa   b. 1509 Istanbul earthquake
   c. Palustrine   d. Truncated spur

89. An _____ is a type of rock that contains minerals such as gemstones and metals that can be extracted through mining and refined for use. Samples of _____ in the form of exceptionally beautiful crystals, exotic layering visible when sectioned or polished or metallic presentations such as large nuggets or crystalline formations of metals such as gold or copper may command a value far beyond their value as mere _____ or raw metal for subsequent reduction to utilitarian purposes.

The grade or concentration of an _____ mineral, or metal, as well as its form of occurrence, will directly affect the costs associated with mining the _____.

   a. Iron ores   b. Ore
   c. AASHTO Soil Classification System   d. Ore genesis

90. In organic chemistry, a _____ is an organic compound consisting entirely of hydrogen and carbon. With relation to chemical terminology, aromatic _____s or arenes, alkanes, alkenes and alkyne-based compounds composed entirely of carbon or hydrogen are referred to as 'pure' _____s, whereas other _____s with bonded compounds or impurities of sulfur or nitrogen, are referred to as 'impure', and remain somewhat erroneously referred to as _____s.

_____s are referred to as consisting of a 'backbone' or 'skeleton' composed entirely of carbon and hydrogen and other bonded compounds, and have a functional group that generally facilitates combustion.

   a. 1700 Cascadia earthquake   b. 1509 Istanbul earthquake
   c. Hydrocarbon   d. 1703 Genroku earthquake

91. _____ in the earth sciences (commonly symbolized as κ a rock or k) is a measure of the ability of a material (typically unconsolidated material) to transmit fluids. It is of great importance in determining the flow characteristics of hydrocarbons in oil and gas reservoirs, and of groundwater in aquifers. It is typically measured in the lab by application of Darcy's law under steady state conditions or, more generally, by application of various solutions to the diffusion equation for unsteady flow conditions.

   a. Saltwater intrusion   b. Porosity
   c. Permeability   d. Phreatic zone

92. _____ or phosphorite is a general description applied to several kinds of rock which contain significant concentrations of phosphate minerals, which are minerals that contain the phosphate ion in their chemical structure.

Many kinds of rock contain mineral components containing phosphate or other phosphorus compounds in small amounts. However, rocks which contain phosphate in quantity and concentration which are economic to mine as ore for their phosphate content are not particularly common.

Chapter 6. Sediment and Sedimentary Rocks

a. Skarn
b. Slyne-Erris Trough
c. Diapir
d. Phosphate rock

93. In geology, a _____ deposit or _____ is an accumulation of valuable minerals formed by deposition of dense mineral phases in a trap site. Types of _____ deposits include alluvium, eluvium, beach _____s, and paleoplacers.

Typical locations for alluvial _____ deposits are on the inside bends of rivers and creeks, in natural hollows, at the break of slope on a stream, the base of an escarpment, waterfall or other barrier, within sand dunes, beach profiles or in gravel beds.

a. 1703 Genroku earthquake
b. 1509 Istanbul earthquake
c. Placer
d. 1700 Cascadia earthquake

94. A _____ is a type of structural dome formed when a thick bed of evaporite minerals found at depth intrudes vertically into surrounding rock strata, forming a diapir.

The salt that forms these domes was deposited within restricted marine basins. Due to restricted flow of water into a basin, evaporation occurs resulting in the precipitation of salts from solution, depositing evaporites.

a. 1703 Genroku earthquake
b. Salt dome
c. 1509 Istanbul earthquake
d. 1700 Cascadia earthquake

95. In petroleum geology _____ refers to rocks from which hydrocarbons have been generated or are capable of being generated. They form one of the necessary elements of a working hydrocarbon system. They are organic rich sediments that may have been deposited in a variety of environments including deepwater marine, lacustrine and deltaic.
a. 1700 Cascadia earthquake
b. 1509 Istanbul earthquake
c. 1703 Genroku earthquake
d. Source rock

96. A _____ or sandstorm is a meteorological phenomenon common in arid and semi-arid regions and arises when a gust front passes or when the wind force exceeds the threshold value where loose sand and dust are removed from the dry surface. Particles are transported by saltation and suspension, causing soil erosion from one place and deposition in another. The Sahara and drylands around the Arabian peninsula are the main source of airborne dust, with some contributions from Iran, Pakistan and India into the Arabian Sea, and China's storms deposit dust in the Pacific.
a. 1700 Cascadia earthquake
b. 1509 Istanbul earthquake
c. 1703 Genroku earthquake
d. Dust storm

97. _____ is a potassium uranium vanadate mineral with chemical formula: $K_2(UO_2)_2(VO_4)_2·3H_2O$. The water content can vary and small amounts of calcium, barium, magnesium, iron, and sodium are often present.

_____ is a bright to greenish yellow mineral that occurs typically as crusts and flakes in sandstones.

a. 1509 Istanbul earthquake
b. 1703 Genroku earthquake
c. 1700 Cascadia earthquake
d. Carnotite

Chapter 6. Sediment and Sedimentary Rocks

98. _____ is a mixture of organic chemical compounds that make up a portion of the organic matter in sedimentary rocks. It is insoluble in normal organic solvents because of the huge molecular weight (upwards of 1,000 Daltons) of its component compounds. The soluble portion is known as bitumen.
   a. 1509 Istanbul earthquake
   b. 1703 Genroku earthquake
   c. Kerogen
   d. 1700 Cascadia earthquake

99. _____ is a type of coal whose properties range from those of lignite to those of bituminous coal and are used primarily as fuel for steam-electric power generation.

_____s may be dull, dark brown to black, soft and crumbly at the lower end of the range, to bright jet-black, hard, and relatively strong at the upper end. They contain 15-30% inherent moisture by weight and are non-coking (undergo little swelling upon heating.)

   a. Sub-bituminous coal
   b. 1700 Cascadia earthquake
   c. 1509 Istanbul earthquake
   d. 1703 Genroku earthquake

100. _____ or extra heavy oil, is a type of bitumen deposit. The sands are naturally occurring mixtures of sand or clay, water and an extremely dense and viscous form of petroleum called bitumen. They are found in large amounts in many countries throughout the world, but are found in extremely large quantities in Canada and Venezuela.
   a. AL 129-1
   b. Oil sands
   c. AL 333
   d. AASHTO Soil Classification System

Chapter 7. Metamorphism and Metamorphic Rocks

1. _____ usually refers to the thick foundation of ancient, and oldest metamorphic and igneous rock that forms the crust of continents, often in the form of granite. _____ is contrasted to overlying sedimentary rocks which are laid down on top of the _____s after the continent was formed, such as sandstone and limestone. The sedimentary rocks which may be deposited on top of the basement usually form a relatively thin veneer, but can be more than 3 miles thick.
   a. Polystrate
   b. Bed
   c. Key bed
   d. Basement rock

2. The _____ -- also called the Laurentian Plateau, or Bouclier Canadien -- is a massive geological shield covered by a thin layer of soil that forms the nucleus of the North American or Laurentia craton. It has a deep, common, joined bedrock region in eastern and central Canada and stretches North from the Great Lakes to the Arctic Ocean, covering over half of Canada; it also extends south into the northern reaches of the United States. Population is scarce, and industrial development is minimal, although the region has a large hydroelectric power potential.
   a. Yilgarn Craton
   b. Gawler craton
   c. Sahara pump theory
   d. Canadian Shield

3. The _____ is the layer of igneous, sedimentary, and metamorphic rocks which form the continents and the areas of shallow seabed close to their shores, known as continental shelves. This layer is sometimes called sial due to more felsic, or granitic, bulk composition, which lies in contrast to the oceanic crust, called sima due to its mafic, or basaltic rock. (Based on the change in velocity of seismic waves, it is believed that at a certain depth sial becomes close in its physical properties to sima.
   a. Divergent boundary
   b. Mirovia
   c. Plate tectonics
   d. Continental crust

4. _____, whose name derives from the Greek word kyanos, meaning blue, is a typically blue silicate mineral, commonly found in aluminium-rich metamorphic pegmatites and/or sedimentary rock. _____ in metamorphic rocks generally indicates pressures higher than 4 kilobars. Although potentially stable at lower pressure and low temperature, the activity of water is usually high enough under such conditions that it is replaced by hydrous aluminosilicates such as muscovite, pyrophyllite, or kaolinite.
   a. 1700 Cascadia earthquake
   b. 1703 Genroku earthquake
   c. Kyanite
   d. 1509 Istanbul earthquake

5. _____ is the result of the transformation of an existing rock type, the protolith, in a process called metamorphism, which means 'change in form'. The protolith is subjected to heat and pressure (temperatures greater than 150 to 200 >°C and pressures of 1500 bars) causing profound physical and/or chemical change. The protolith may be sedimentary rock, igneous rock or another older _____.
   a. Volcanic rock
   b. Sedimentary rock
   c. Phenocryst
   d. Metamorphic rock

6. _____ is the part of Earth's lithosphere that surfaces in the ocean basins. _____ is primarily composed of mafic rocks, or sima. It is thinner than continental crust, or sial, generally less than 10 kilometers thick, however it is denser, having a mean density of about 3.3 grams per cubic centimeter.
   a. Oceanic crust
   b. AL 333
   c. AASHTO Soil Classification System
   d. AL 129-1

Chapter 7. Metamorphism and Metamorphic Rocks

7. A _____ is generally a large area of exposed Precambrian crystalline igneous and high-grade metamorphic rocks that form tectonically stable areas. In all cases, the age of these rocks is greater than 570 million years and sometimes dates back 2 to 3.5 billion years. They have been little affected by tectonic events following the end of the Precambrian Era, and are relatively flat regions where mountain building, faulting, and other tectonic processes are greatly diminished compared with the activity that occurs at the margins of the _____s and the boundaries between tectonic plates.

a. 1700 Cascadia earthquake
b. 1509 Istanbul earthquake
c. Shield
d. 1703 Genroku earthquake

8. _____ is a fine-grained, foliated, homogeneous metamorphic rock derived from an original shale-type sedimentary rock composed of clay or volcanic ash through low grade regional metamorphism. The result is a foliated rock in which the foliation may not correspond to the original sedimentary layering. _____ is frequently grey in colour especially when seen en masse covering roofs.

a. Talc carbonate
b. Granulites
c. Shock metamorphism
d. Slate

9. _____ is a mineral composed of hydrated magnesium silicate with the chemical formula H_2Mg_{34} or $Mg_3Si_4O_{10}(OH)_2$. In loose form, it is the widely used substance known as talcum powder. It occurs as foliated to fibrous masses, its monoclinic crystals being so rare as to be almost unknown.

_____ is a metamorphic mineral resulting from the metamorphism of magnesian minerals such as pyroxene, amphibole, olivine and other similar minerals in the presence of carbon dioxide and water. This is known as _____ carbonation or steatization and produces a suite of rocks known as _____ carbonates.

a. 1509 Istanbul earthquake
b. 1700 Cascadia earthquake
c. 1703 Genroku earthquake
d. Talc

10. A _____ is a large emplacement of igneous intrusive rock that forms from cooled magma deep in the Earth's crust. they are almost always made mostly of felsic or intermediate rock-types, such as granite, quartz monzonite, or diorite

Although they may appear uniform, _____s are in fact structures with complex histories and compositions.

a. Tuff
b. Scoria
c. Great Dyke
d. Batholith

11. _____ defines an important group of generally dark-colored rock-forming inosilicate minerals, composed of double chain SiO_4 tetrahedra, linked at the vertices and generally containing ions of iron and/or magnesium in their structures. They crystallize into two crystal systems, monoclinic and orthorhombic. In chemical composition and general characteristics they are similar to the pyroxenes. They are minerals of either igneous or metamorphic origin; in the former case occurring as constituents (hornblende) of igneous rocks, such as granite, diorite, andesite and others. Those of metamorphic origin include examples such as those developed in limestones by contact metamorphism (tremolite) and those formed by the alteration of other ferromagnesian minerals (hornblende).

a. AL 129-1
b. AL 333
c. Amphibole
d. AASHTO Soil Classification System

Chapter 7. Metamorphism and Metamorphic Rocks

12. _____ or white asbestos is the most commonly encountered form of asbestos, accounting for approximately 95% of the asbestos in place in the United States and a similar proportion in other countries. It is a soft, fibrous silicate mineral in the serpentine group of phyllosilicates: as such, it is distinct from other asbestiform minerals in the amphibole group. Its idealized chemical formula is $Mg_3(Si_2O_5)(OH)_4$, in which some of the magnesium ions may be substituted by iron or other cations.

   a. 1509 Istanbul earthquake
   b. Clay minerals
   c. Kaolinite
   d. Chrysotile

13. Some forms of riebeckite are asbestiform, notably _____, also known as blue asbestos.

The riebeckite granite known as ailsite, found on the island of Ailsa Craig in western Scotland, is prized for its use in the manufacture of curling stones.

Canton viaduct

Riebeckite granite was used for the facing stones of the Canton Viaduct from Moyles Quarry (a.k.a. Canton Viaduct Quarry) now part of Borderland State Park in Massachusetts.

   a. 1700 Cascadia earthquake
   b. 1703 Genroku earthquake
   c. 1509 Istanbul earthquake
   d. Crocidolite

14. _____ is a geological term meaning the rock native to an area. It is similar and in many cases interchangeable with the terms basement and wall rocks.

The term is used to denote the usual strata of a region in relation to the rock which is being discussed or observed.

   a. Pyroclastic rocks
   b. Coldwell Complex
   c. Great Dyke
   d. Country rock

15. In geology, _____ refers to heat sources within the planet. _____ is technically an adjective (e.g., _____ energy) but in U.S. English the word has attained frequent use as a noun.

The planet's internal heat was originally generated during its accretion, due to gravitational binding energy, and since then additional heat has continued to be generated by decay heat from the radioactive decay of elements.

   a. Combe
   b. Cleavage
   c. Geothermal
   d. Stratification

16. The _____ is the rate of increase in temperature per unit depth in the Earth. It varies with location and is typically measured by determining the bottom open-hole temperature after borehole drilling. To achieve accuracy the drilling fluid needs time to reach the ambient temperature.

   a. Geothermal power
   b. Hot Dry Rock Geothermal Energy
   c. Geothermal heat pump
   d. Geothermal gradient

82 Chapter 7. Metamorphism and Metamorphic Rocks

17. Overburden pressure, _____, and vertical stress are terms that denote the pressure or stress imposed on a layer of soil or rock by the weight of overlying material.

The overburden pressure at a depth z is given by

$$>$$

where $>\rho(z)$ is the density of the overlying rock at depth z and g is the acceleration due to gravity. p_0 is the datum pressure, like the pressure at the surface.

    a. Wave-cut platform   b. Siliceous ooze
    c. Lithostatic pressure   d. Palynomorph

18. _____ is the solid-state recrystallization of pre-existing rocks due to changes in physical and chemical conditions, primarily heat, pressure, and the introduction of chemically active fluids. Both mineralogical, chemical and crystallographic changes can occur during this process.

Three types of _____ exist: dynamic, contact and regional.

    a. Gradualism   b. Metamorphism
    c. Dike   d. Cross-bedding

19. A _____ in geology is an intrusive igneous rock body that crystallized from a magma slowly cooling below the surface of the Earth. _____s include batholiths, dikes, sills, laccoliths, lopoliths, and other igneous bodies. In practice, '_____' usually refers to a distinctive mass of igneous rock, typically kilometers in dimension, without a tabular shape like those of dikes and sills.

    a. Metamorphic rock   b. Metavolcanic rock
    c. Pluton   d. Petrology

20. In geology, solid-state _____ is a metamorphic process that occurs under situations of intense temperature and pressure where grains, atoms or molecules of a rock or mineral are packed closer together, creating a new crystal structure. The basic composition remains the same. This process can be illustrated by observing how snow recrystallizes to ice without melting.

    a. 1509 Istanbul earthquake   b. Vitrification
    c. Recrystallization   d. 1700 Cascadia earthquake

21. A _____ is a compound containing an anion in which one or more central silicon atoms are surrounded by electronegative ligands. This definition is broad enough to include species such as hexafluorosilicate ('fluorosilicate'), $[SiF_6]^{2-}$, but the _____ species that are encountered most often consist of silicon with oxygen as the ligand. _____ anions, with a negative net electrical charge, must have that charge balanced by other cations to make an electrically neutral compound.

    a. 1703 Genroku earthquake   b. 1700 Cascadia earthquake
    c. Silicate   d. 1509 Istanbul earthquake

Chapter 7. Metamorphism and Metamorphic Rocks

22. In geology, _____ is the process that takes place at convergent boundaries by which one tectonic plate moves under another tectonic plate, sinking into the Earth's mantle, as the plates converge. A _____ zone is an area on Earth where two tectonic plates move towards one another and _____ occurs. Rates of _____ are typically measured in centimeters per year, with the average rate of convergence being approximately 2 to 8 centimeters per year (about the rate a fingernail grows.)
   a. Thrust fault
   b. Panthalassa
   c. Forearc
   d. Subduction

23. The _____ is the zone of the ocean floor that separates the thin oceanic crust from thick continental crust. _____s constitute about 28% of the oceanic area.

The transition from continental to oceanic crust commonly occurs within the outer part of the margin, called continental rise.

   a. Longshore drift
   b. 1509 Istanbul earthquake
   c. Cuspate forelands
   d. Continental margin

24. The lithosphere is broken up into what are called _____. In the case of Earth, there are eight major and many minor plates The lithospheric plates ride on the asthenosphere. These plates move in relation to one another at one of three types of plate boundaries: convergent, or collisional boundaries; divergent boundaries, also called spreading centers; and transform boundaries.
   a. Subduction
   b. Juan de Fuca Ridge
   c. Lithosphere
   d. Tectonic plates

25. _____ occurs typically around intrusive igneous rocks as a result of the temperature increase caused by the intrusion of magma into cooler country rock. The area surrounding the intrusion (called aureoles) where the _____ effects are present is called the metamorphic aureole. Contact metamorphic rocks are usually known as hornfels.
   a. Seismic to simulation
   b. Slope Mass Rating
   c. Contact metamorphism
   d. Cross-bedding

26. A _____ or dyke in geology is a type of sheet intrusion referring to any geologic body that cuts discordantly across

- planar wall rock structures, such as bedding or foliation
- massive rock formations, like igneous/magmatic intrusions and salt diapirs.

They can therefore be either intrusive or sedimentary in origin.

An intrusive _____ is an igneous body with a very high aspect ratio, which means that its thickness is usually much smaller than the other two dimensions. Thickness can vary from sub-centimeter scale to many meters and the lateral dimensions can extend over many kilometers. A _____ is an intrusion into an opening cross-cutting fissure, shouldering aside other pre-existing layers or bodies of rock; this implies that a _____ is always younger than the rocks that contain it.

   a. Fabric
   b. Dike
   c. Haloclasty
   d. Schmidt hammer

84 *Chapter 7. Metamorphism and Metamorphic Rocks*

27. _____ is a term used in geology to refer to silicate minerals, magma, and rocks which are enriched in the lighter elements such as silicon, oxygen, aluminium, sodium, and potassium. _____ minerals are usually light in color and have specific gravities less than 3. Common _____ minerals include quartz, muscovite, orthoclase, and the sodium-rich plagioclase feldspars.
   a. Laccolith
   b. Phenocryst
   c. Sedimentary rock
   d. Felsic

28. The _____ is a chronologic schema (or idealized model) relating stratigraphy to time that is used by geologists, paleontologists and other earth scientists to describe the timing and relationships between events that have occurred during the history of the Earth. The table of geologic time spans presented here agrees with the dates and nomenclature proposed by the International Commission on Stratigraphy, and uses the standard color codes of the United States Geological Survey.

Evidence from radiometric dating indicates that the Earth is about 4.570 billion years old.

   a. 1703 Genroku earthquake
   b. 1700 Cascadia earthquake
   c. 1509 Istanbul earthquake
   d. Geologic time scale

29. _____ is an adjective describing a silicate mineral or rock that is rich in magnesium and iron; the term was derived by contracting 'magnesium' and 'ferric'. Most _____ minerals are dark in color and the specific gravity is greater than 3. Common rock-forming _____ minerals include olivine, pyroxene, amphibole, and biotite.

_____ lava, before cooling, has a low viscosity, in comparison to felsic lava, due to the lower silica content in _____ magma. Water and other volatiles can more easily and gradually escape from _____ lava, so eruptions of volcanoes made of _____ lavas are less explosively violent than felsic lava eruptions.

   a. 1509 Istanbul earthquake
   b. 1700 Cascadia earthquake
   c. 1703 Genroku earthquake
   d. Mafic

30. _____ refers to natural mountain building, and may be studied as a tectonic structural event, (b) as a geographical event, and (c) a chronological event. Orogenic events (a) cause distinctive structural phenomena and related tectonic activity, (b) affect certain regions of rocks and crust, and (c) happen within a specific period of time.
   a. Orogenesis
   b. Antler orogeny
   c. Alice Springs Orogeny
   d. Orogeny

31. _____ is molten rock that is found beneath the surface of the Earth, and may also exist on other terrestrial planets. Besides molten rock, _____ may also contain suspended crystals and gas bubbles. _____ often collects in a _____ chamber inside a volcano. _____ is capable of intrusion into adjacent rocks, extrusion onto the surface as lava, and explosive ejection as tephra to form pyroclastic rock.
   a. Vesicular texture
   b. Magma
   c. Metavolcanic rock
   d. Rock cycle

32. _____ is a naturally occurring material composed primarily of fine-grained minerals, which show plasticity through a variable range of water content, and which can be hardened when dried and/or fired. _____ deposits are mostly composed of _____ minerals (phyllosilicate minerals), minerals which impart plasticity and harden when fired and/or dried, and variable amounts of water trapped in the mineral structure by polar attraction. Organic materials which do not impart plasticity may also be a part of _____ deposits.

a. 1703 Genroku earthquake
b. Clay
c. 1700 Cascadia earthquake
d. 1509 Istanbul earthquake

33. _____ are hydrous aluminium phyllosilicates, sometimes with variable amounts of iron, magnesium, alkali metals, alkaline earths and other cations. Clays have structures similar to the micas and therefore form flat hexagonal sheets. _____ are common weathering products (including weathering of feldspar) and low temperature hydrothermal alteration products.
   a. Glauconite
   b. Kaolinite
   c. 1509 Istanbul earthquake
   d. Clay minerals

34. _____ or dolomite rock is a sedimentary carbonate rock that contains a high percentage of the mineral dolomite. In old U.S.G.S. publications it was referred to as magnesian limestone. Most _____ formed as a magnesium replacement of limestone or lime mud prior to lithification.
   a. Pelagic sediments
   b. Sandstone
   c. Metasediment
   d. Dolostone

35. In geology, a _____ or _____ line is a planar fracture in rock in which the rock on one side of the fracture has moved with respect to the rock on the other side. Large _____s within the Earth's crust are the result of differential or shear motion and active _____ zones are the causal locations of most earthquakes. Earthquakes are caused by energy release during rapid slippage along a _____.
   a. Geothermal
   b. Fault
   c. Cohesion
   d. Combe

36. _____ circulation in its most general sense is the circulation of hot water; 'hydros' in the Greek meaning water and 'thermos' meaning heat. _____ circulation occurs most often in the vicinity of sources of heat within the Earth's crust. This generally occurs near volcanic activity, but can occur in the deep crust related to the intrusion of granite, or as the result of orogeny or metamorphism.
   a. Transgression
   b. Wave pounding
   c. Headward erosion
   d. Hydrothermal

37. _____ is a sedimentary rock composed largely of the mineral calcite (calcium carbonate: $CaCO_3$.) The deposition of _____ strata is often a by-product and indicator of biological activity in the geologic record. Calcium (along with nitrogen, phosphorus, and potassium) is a key mineral to plant nutrition: soils overlying _____ bedrock tend to be pre-fertilized with calcium.
   a. 1703 Genroku earthquake
   b. 1509 Istanbul earthquake
   c. Limestone
   d. 1700 Cascadia earthquake

38. A _____ is in geology an area where, as a result of metamorphism, the same combination of minerals occur in the bed rocks. These zones occur because most metamorphic minerals are only stable in certain intervals of temperature and pressure.

The temperature and pressure at which the mineralogical composition of a rock equilibrated can vary laterally through a metamorphic terrane.

a. Metamorphic rock
b. Rock cycle
c. Metamorphic zone
d. Serpentinite

39. _____ is a fine grained sedimentary rock whose original constituents were clays or muds. Grain size is up to 0.0625 mm with individual grains too small to be distinguished without a microscope. With increased pressure over time the platey clay minerals may become aligned, with the appearance of fissility or parallel layering.
   a. Porcellanite
   b. Sandstone
   c. Pelagic sediments
   d. Mudstone

40. _____ is a fine-grained, compact rock produced by dynamic crystallization of the constituent minerals resulting in a reduction of the grain size of the rock. It is classified as a metamorphic rock. _____ can have many different mineralogical compositions; it is a classification based on the textural appearance of the rock.
   a. Greenschist
   b. Shock metamorphism
   c. Greenstone belts
   d. Mylonite

41. The _____ is a continental transform fault that runs a length of roughly 800 miles (1,300 km) through California in the United States. The fault's motion is right-lateral strike-slip (horizontal motion.) It forms the tectonic boundary between the Pacific Plate and the North American Plate.
   a. 1700 Cascadia earthquake
   b. San Andreas fault
   c. 1703 Genroku earthquake
   d. 1509 Istanbul earthquake

42. _____ is a sedimentary rock composed mainly of sand-size mineral or rock grains. Most _____ is composed of quartz and/or feldspar because these are the most common minerals in the Earth's crust. Like sand, _____ may be any color, but the most common colors are tan, brown, yellow, red, gray and white.
   a. Dolostone
   b. Porcellanite
   c. Dolomite
   d. Sandstone

43. _____ is a fine-grained sedimentary rock whose original constituents were clay minerals or muds. It is characterized by thin laminae breaking with an irregular curving fracture, often splintery and usually parallel to the often-indistinguishable bedding plane. This property is called fissility.
   a. Diatomaceous earth
   b. Sandstone
   c. Siltstone
   d. Shale

44. Two important classifications of weathering processes exist -- physical and _____. Mechanical or physical weathering involves the breakdown of rocks and soils through direct contact with atmospheric conditions, such as heat, water, ice and pressure. The second classification, _____, involves the direct effect of atmospheric chemicals or biologically produced chemicals (also known as biological weathering) in the breakdown of rocks, soils and minerals.
   a. Chemical weathering
   b. 1509 Istanbul earthquake
   c. Physical weathering
   d. Frost disintegration

45. In materials science, _____ is the distribution of crystallographic orientations of a polycrystalline sample. A sample in which these orientations are fully random is said to have no _____. If the crystallographic orientations are not random, but have some preferred orientation, then the sample has a weak, strong, or moderate _____.
   a. Melange
   b. Streak
   c. Deformation
   d. Texture

Chapter 7. Metamorphism and Metamorphic Rocks

46. _____ is the decomposition of Earth rocks, soils and their minerals through direct contact with the planet's atmosphere. _____ occurs in situ, or 'with no movement', and thus should not be confused with erosion, which involves the movement of rocks and minerals by agents such as water, ice, wind and gravity.

Two important classifications of _____ processes exist -- physical and chemical _____.

a. Physical weathering
b. 1509 Istanbul earthquake
c. Frost disintegration
d. Weathering

47. _____, in structural geology and related disciplines, describes the tendency of a rock to break along preferred planes of weakness.

Rocks deformed under very low to low metamorphic grade often develop planes along which the rock can easily be split. Slates are an example of a rock with a penetrative _____ caused partly by the realignment of phyllosilicate minerals with increasing flattening strain.

a. Fault
b. Cleavage
c. Depression
d. Combe

48. An _____ is used in geology to determine the degree of metamorphism a rock has experienced. Depending on the original composition of and the pressure and temperature experienced by the protolith (parent rock), chemical reactions between minerals in the solid state produce new minerals. When an _____ is found in a metamorphosed rock, it indicates the minimum pressure and temperature the protolith must have achieved in order for that mineral to form.

a. AL 129-1
b. AL 333
c. AASHTO Soil Classification System
d. Index mineral

49. _____ is a feature of rocks containing platy minerals. Platy minerals include clay minerals and micas, with a long thin shape. When these align, they form a series of planes along which the rock tends to split.

a. Wave-cut platform
b. Teilzone
c. Sclavia craton
d. Slaty cleavage

50. _____ is a type of foliated metamorphic rock primarily composed of quartz, sericite mica, and chlorite; the rock represents a gradation in the degree of metamorphism between slate and mica schist. Minute crystals of graphite, sericite, or chlorite impart a silky, sometimes golden sheen to the surfaces of cleavage (or schistosity.) _____ is formed from the continued metamorphism of slate.

a. 1509 Istanbul earthquake
b. Phyllite
c. 1700 Cascadia earthquake
d. 1703 Genroku earthquake

51. _____ is the name given to a rock consisting mainly of hornblende amphibole, the use of the term being restricted, however, to metamorphic rocks. The modern terminology for a holocrystalline plutonic igneous rocks composed primarily of hornblende amphibole is a hornblendite, which are usually crystal cumulates. Rocks with >90% amphibole which have a feldspar groundmass may be a lamprophyre.

a. AASHTO Soil Classification System
b. Amphibolite
c. AL 333
d. AL 129-1

Chapter 7. Metamorphism and Metamorphic Rocks

52. _____ is a common and widely distributed type of rock formed by high-grade regional metamorphic processes from pre-existing formations that were originally either igneous or sedimentary rocks. Gneissic rocks are usually medium to coarse foliated and largely recrystallized but do not carry large quantities of micas, chlorite or other platy minerals. _____es that are metamorphosed igneous rocks or their equivalent are termed granite _____es, diorite _____es, etc.
   a. 1700 Cascadia earthquake
   b. 1509 Istanbul earthquake
   c. 1703 Genroku earthquake
   d. Gneiss

53. _____ forms a group of medium-grade metamorphic rocks, chiefly notable for the preponderance of lamellar minerals such as micas, chlorite, talc, hornblende, graphite, and others. Quartz often occurs in drawn-out grains to such an extent that a particular form called quartz _____ is produced. By definition, _____ contains more than 50% platy and elongated minerals, often finely interleaved with quartz and feldspar.
   a. Geothermobarometry
   b. Cataclasite
   c. Foliation
   d. Schist

54. _____ is any penetrative planar fabric present in rocks. _____ is common to rocks affected by regional metamorphic compression typical of orogenic belts. Rocks exhibiting _____ include the typical metamorphic rock sequence of slate, phyllite, schist and gneiss.
   a. Porphyroblast
   b. Metasomatism
   c. Hornfels
   d. Foliation

55. _____ - also known as greenstone - is a general field petrologic term applied to metamorphic and/or altered mafic volcanic rock. The green is due to abundant green chlorite, actinolite and epidote minerals that dominate the rock. However, basalts may remain quite black if primary pyroxene does not revert to chlorite or actinolite.
   a. Slate
   b. Greenschist
   c. Hornfels
   d. Metamorphic facies

56. _____ is the group designation for a series of contact metamorphic rocks that have been baked and indurated by the heat of intrusive igneous masses and have been rendered massive, hard, splintery, and in some cases exceedingly tough and durable. Most _____ are fine-grained, and while the original rocks may have been more or less fissile owing to the presence of bedding or cleavage planes, this structure is effaced or rendered inoperative in the _____. Though they may show banding, due to bedding, etc., they break across this as readily as along it; in fact, they tend to separate into cubical fragments rather than into thin plates.
   a. Slate
   b. Jadeitite
   c. Cataclasite
   d. Hornfels

57. _____ is a rock at the frontier between igneous and metamorphic rocks. They can also be known as diatexite.

_____ forms under extreme temperature conditions during prograde metamorphism, where partial melting occurs in pre-existing rocks.
   a. Petrology
   b. Serpentinite
   c. Migmatite
   d. Laccolith

Chapter 7. Metamorphism and Metamorphic Rocks

58. _____ is the second most abundant mineral in the Earth's continental crust. It is made up of a framework of silicon-oxygen tetrahedra SiO_4, with each silicon shared between two oxygens to give the overall formula SiO_2. _____ has a hardness of 7 on the Mohs scale and a density of 2.65 g/cmÂ³.
   a. 1700 Cascadia earthquake
   b. Quartz
   c. Shocked quartz
   d. 1509 Istanbul earthquake

59. _____ is a hard metamorphic rock which was originally sandstone. Sandstone is converted into _____ through heating and pressure usually related to tectonic compression within orogenic belts. Pure _____ is usually white to grey, though _____s often occur in various shades of pink and red due to varying amounts of iron oxide.
   a. Shock metamorphism
   b. Quartzite
   c. Schist
   d. Facies

60. _____ is a hard, compact variety of mineral coal that has a high lustre. It has the highest carbon count and contains the fewest impurities of all coals, despite its lower calorific content.

    _____ is the highest of the metamorphic rank, in which the carbon content is between 92% and 98%.

   a. AASHTO Soil Classification System
   b. AL 129-1
   c. AL 333
   d. Anthracite

61. _____ is a geological term that describes a series of metamorphic rocks, typically developed in the high ground which lies southeast of the Great Glen of Scotland. This was the old Celtic region of D>ál Riata (Dalriada), and in 1891 Sir A. Geikie proposed the name _____ as a convenient provisional designation for the complicated set of rocks to which it is difficult to assign a definite position in the stratigraphical sequence.

    In Sir A. Geikie's words, 'they consist in large proportion of altered sedimentary strata, now found in the form of mica-schist, graphite-schist, andalusite-schist, phyllite, schistose grit, greywacke and conglomerate, quartzite, limestone and other rocks, together with epidiorites, chlorite-schists, hornblende schists and other allied varieties, which probably mark sills, lava-sheets or beds of tuff, intercalated among the sediments.

   a. Metaconglomerate
   b. Geothermobarometry
   c. Metasomatism
   d. Dalradian

62. _____ are fine to medium-grained metamorphic rocks that have experienced high temperatures of metamorphism, composed mainly of feldspars sometimes associated with quartz and anhydrous ferromagnesian minerals, with granoblastic texture and gneissose to massive structure. They are of particular interest to geologists because many _____ represent samples of the deep continental crust. Some _____ experienced decompression from deep in the Earth to shallower crustal levels at high temperature; others cooled while remaining at depth in the Earth.
   a. Greenschist facies
   b. Granulites
   c. Jadeitite
   d. Hornfels

63. _____ is determined by the particular T-P conditions required to metamorphose basalt to form the typical _____ minerals chlorite, actinolite, and albite. _____ results from low temperature, moderate pressure metamorphism. Metamorphic conditions which create typical _____ assemblages are called the Barrovian Facies Sequence, and the lower-pressure Abukuma Facies Series.

a. Greenschist facies
c. Mylonite
b. Hornfels
d. Foliation

64. In geology, an _____ is a plane of constant metamorphic grade in the field; it separates metamorphic zones of different metamorphic index minerals. On geologic maps focusing on metamorphic terranes (or landscapes underlain by metamorphic rocks), the boundaries between rocks of different metamorphic grade are commonly demarcated by _____ lines. The garnet _____, for example, would mark the first occurrence of garnet in the rocks.

a. Espresso crema effect
c. Ostwald ripening
b. Exner equation
d. Isograd

65. The _____ are groups of mineral compositions in metamorphic rocks, that are typical for a certain field in pressure-temperature space. Rocks which contain certain minerals can therefore be linked to certain tectonic settings.

The name facies was first used for specific sedimentary environments in sedimentary rocks by Swiss geologist Amanz Gressly in 1838.

a. Shock metamorphism
c. Cataclasite
b. Metasomatism
d. Metamorphic facies

66. In geology, _____ are a body of rock with specified characteristics. Ideally, a _____ is a distinctive rock unit that forms under certain conditions of sedimentation, reflecting a particular process or environment.

The term _____ was introduced by the Swiss geologist Amanz Gressly in 1838 and was part of his significant contribution to the foundations of modern stratigraphy, [Cross and Homewood (1997)] which replaced the earlier notions of Neptunism.

a. Facies
c. Porphyroblast
b. Jadeitite
d. Slate

67. _____ is a rock that forms by the metamorphism of basalt and rocks with similar composition at high pressures and low temperatures, approximately corresponding to a depth of 15 to 30 kilometers and 200 to ~500 degrees Celsius. The blue color of the rock comes from the presence of the mineral glaucophane.

They are typically found within orogenic belts as terranes of lithology in faulted contact with greenschist or rarely eclogite facies rocks.

a. Quartzite
c. Shock metamorphism
b. Porphyroclast
d. Blueschist

68. _____ describes the large scale motions of Earth's lithosphere. The theory encompasses the older concepts of continental drift, developed during the first decades of the 20th century by Alfred Wegener, and seafloor spreading, understood during the 1960s.

The outermost part of the Earth's interior is made up of two layers: the lithosphere and the asthenosphere.

a. Supercontinent cycle
b. Copperbelt Province
c. Plate tectonics
d. Lithosphere

69. _____ are rocks and minerals from which metallic iron can be economically extracted. The ores are usually rich in iron oxides and vary in color from dark grey, bright yellow, deep purple, to rusty red. The iron itself is usually found in the form of magnetite (Fe_3O_4), haematite (Fe_2O_3), goethite, limonite or siderite.
   a. Ore genesis
   b. Ore
   c. AASHTO Soil Classification System
   d. Iron ores

70. An _____ is a type of rock that contains minerals such as gemstones and metals that can be extracted through mining and refined for use. Samples of _____ in the form of exceptionally beautiful crystals, exotic layering visible when sectioned or polished or metallic presentations such as large nuggets or crystalline formations of metals such as gold or copper may command a value far beyond their value as mere _____ or raw metal for subsequent reduction to utilitarian purposes.

The grade or concentration of an _____ mineral, or metal, as well as its form of occurrence, will directly affect the costs associated with mining the _____.

   a. Ore genesis
   b. Iron ores
   c. AASHTO Soil Classification System
   d. Ore

Chapter 8. Geologic Time: Concepts and Principles

1. _____ is the process of determining a specific date for an archaeological or palaeontological site or artifact. Some archaeologists prefer the terms chronometric or calendar dating, as use of the word 'absolute' implies a certainty and precision that is rarely possible in archaeology. _____ is usually based on the physical or chemical properties of the materials of artifacts, buildings, or other items that have been modified by humans.
   a. AASHTO Soil Classification System
   b. Absolute dating
   c. Erathem
   d. Uranium-lead dating

2. _____ is a technique used to date materials, usually based on a comparison between the observed abundance of a naturally occurring radioactive isotope and its decay products, using known decay rates. It is the principal source of information about the absolute age of rocks and other geological features, including the age of the Earth itself, and can be used to date a wide range of natural and man-made materials. Together with stratigraphic principles, _____ methods are used in geochronology to establish the geological time scale.
   a. Paleomagnetism
   b. Milankovitch Theory
   c. Chronostratigraphy
   d. Radiometric dating

3. Before the advent of absolute dating in the 20th century, archaeologists and geologists were largely limited to the use of the _____ techniques. It estimates the order of prehistoric and geological events determined by using basic stratigraphic rules, and by observing where fossil organisms lay in the geological record, often in horizontal, stratified bands of rocks present throughout the world.

   Though _____ can determine the sequential order in which a series of events occurred, not when they occur, it is in no way inferior to radiometric dating; in fact, _____ by biostratigraphy is the preferred method in paleontology, and is in some respects more accurate (Stanley, 167-9.)

   a. Chronozone
   b. Cenomanian
   c. Paleomagnetism
   d. Relative dating

4. The _____ is a chronologic schema (or idealized model) relating stratigraphy to time that is used by geologists, paleontologists and other earth scientists to describe the timing and relationships between events that have occurred during the history of the Earth. The table of geologic time spans presented here agrees with the dates and nomenclature proposed by the International Commission on Stratigraphy, and uses the standard color codes of the United States Geological Survey.

   Evidence from radiometric dating indicates that the Earth is about 4.570 billion years old.

   a. 1703 Genroku earthquake
   b. 1509 Istanbul earthquake
   c. 1700 Cascadia earthquake
   d. Geologic time scale

5. A _____ is a type of speleothem that rises from the floor of a limestone cave due to the dripping of mineralized solutions and the deposition of calcium carbonate.

   The corresponding formation on the ceiling of a cave is known as a stalactite. If these formations grow together, the result is known as a column.

   a. 1700 Cascadia earthquake
   b. 1509 Istanbul earthquake
   c. 1703 Genroku earthquake
   d. Stalagmite

Chapter 8. Geologic Time: Concepts and Principles

6. Uluru, also referred to as _____, is a large sandstone rock formation in the southern part of the Northern Territory, central Australia. It lies 335 km (208 mi) south west of the nearest large town, Alice Springs; 450 km (280 mi) by road. Kata Tjuta and Uluru are the two major features of the Uluru - Kata Tjuta National Park.

_____ is an inselberg, literally 'island mountain', an isolated remnant left after the slow erosion of an original mountain range. Uluru is also often referred to as a monolith, although this is a somewhat ambiguous term because of its multiple meanings, and thus a word generally avoided by geologists.

   a. AL 333
   c. AL 129-1
   b. AASHTO Soil Classification System
   d. Ayers Rock

7. _____ is the principle that the same scientific laws and processes are constant throughout space and time. It applies specifically to sciences that require a long timescale such as geology, astronomy, and paleontology. It was first defined by Charles Lyell (1797 - 1875), who incorporated James Hutton's gradualism into the idea of _____.
   a. AL 333
   c. Uniformitarianism
   b. AASHTO Soil Classification System
   d. AL 129-1

8. A _____ is a rock consisting of individual stones that have become cemented together. They are sedimentary rocks consisting of rounded fragments and are thus differentiated from breccias, which consist of angular clasts. Both _____s and breccias are characterized by clasts larger than sand (>2 mm).
   a. Conglomerate
   c. Concretion
   b. Superficial deposits
   d. Keystone

9. The _____ states that layers of sediment initially extend laterally in all directions; in other words, they are laterally continuous. As a result, rocks that are otherwise similar, but are now separated by a valley or other erosional feature, can be assumed to be originally continuous.

Layers of sediment do not extend indefinitely; rather, the limits can be recognized and are controlled by the amount and type of sediment available and the size and shape of the sedimentary basin.

   a. 1703 Genroku earthquake
   c. Principle of lateral continuity
   b. 1509 Istanbul earthquake
   d. 1700 Cascadia earthquake

10. The _____ was proposed by the Danish geological pioneer Nicholas Steno (1638-1686.) This principle states that layers of sediment are originally deposited horizontally. The principle is important to the analysis of folded and tilted strata.
    a. Cyclostratigraphy
    c. Principle of original horizontality
    b. Key bed
    d. Bedrock

11. The _____ is a key axiom based on observations of natural history that is a foundational principle of sedimentary stratigraphy and so of other geology dependent natural sciences: 'Sedimentary layers are deposited in a time sequence, with the oldest on the bottom and the youngest on the top.'

The principle was first proposed in the 11th century by the Persian geologist, Avicenna , and the law was later formulated more clearly in the 17th century by the Danish scientist Nicolas Steno.

While discussing the origins of mountains in The Book of Healing in 1027, Avicenna first outlined the principle of the superposition of strata.

a. Milankovitch Theory
b. Cenomanian
c. Paleomagnetism
d. Law of superposition

12. A _____ is a large emplacement of igneous intrusive rock that forms from cooled magma deep in the Earth's crust. they are almost always made mostly of felsic or intermediate rock-types, such as granite, quartz monzonite, or diorite

Although they may appear uniform, _____s are in fact structures with complex histories and compositions.

a. Scoria
b. Batholith
c. Great Dyke
d. Tuff

13. The principle of _____ states that a rock or fault is younger than any rock (or fault) through which it cuts. This principle was developed by James Hutton.

In a series of horizontal sedimentary beds, there is an igneous dyke which cuts vertically through them. The dyke is younger than the sediment beds though which it crosses, as the beds would have had to be around before the dyke could have intruded.

a. Morton Gneiss
b. Lithostatic pressure
c. Cross-cutting relationships
d. Marine clay

14. _____ are the preserved remains or traces of animals, plants, and other organisms from the remote past. The totality of _____, both discovered and undiscovered, and their placement in fossiliferous rock formations and sedimentary layers (strata) is known as the fossil record. The study of _____ across geological time, how they were formed, and the evolutionary relationships between taxa (phylogeny) are some of the most important functions of the science of paleontology.

a. 1703 Genroku earthquake
b. 1509 Istanbul earthquake
c. 1700 Cascadia earthquake
d. Fossils

15. _____ is one of the three main rock types (the others being sedimentary and metamorphic rock.) _____ is formed by magma (molten rock) being cooled and becoming solid . They may form with or without crystallization, either below the surface as intrusive (plutonic) rocks or on the surface as extrusive (volcanic) rocks. They make up approximately 95% of the upper part of the Earth's crust, but their great abundance is hidden on the Earth's surface by a relatively thin but widespread layer of sedimentary and metamorphic rocks.

a. AL 333
b. AASHTO Soil Classification System
c. AL 129-1
d. Igneous rock

16. _____ are chemical substances that may or may not be present in a cell, depending on the cell type. _____ are stored nutrients, secretory products, and pigment granules. Examples of _____ are; glycogen granules in the liver and muscle cells; lipid droplets in fat cells; pigment granules in certain cells of skin and hair; water containing vacuoles; and crystals of various types.

a. Inclusions
b. AASHTO Soil Classification System
c. AL 333
d. AL 129-1

17. A _____ in geology is an intrusive igneous rock body that crystallized from a magma slowly cooling below the surface of the Earth. _____s include batholiths, dikes, sills, laccoliths, lopoliths, and other igneous bodies. In practice, '_____' usually refers to a distinctive mass of igneous rock, typically kilometers in dimension, without a tabular shape like those of dikes and sills.
   a. Petrology
   b. Metamorphic rock
   c. Metavolcanic rock
   d. Pluton

18. The _____ states that, with sedimentary rocks, if inclusions (or clasts) are found in a formation, then the inclusions must be older than the formation that contains them. For example, in sedimentary rocks, it is common for gravel from an older formation to be ripped up and included in a newer layer. A similar situation with igneous rocks occurs when xenoliths are found. These foreign bodies are picked up as magma or lava flows, and are incorporated, later to cool in the matrix. As a result, xenoliths are older than the rock which contains them.
   a. Suspended load
   b. Strike-slip faults
   c. Loihi Seamount
   d. Principle of inclusions and components

19. _____ is one of the three main rock types (the others being igneous and metamorphic rock.) _____ is formed by deposition and consolidation of mineral and organic material and from precipitation of minerals from solution. The processes that form _____ occur at the surface of the Earth and within bodies of water.
   a. Groundmass
   b. Migmatite
   c. Pluton
   d. Sedimentary rock

20. _____ is the movement of the Earth's continents relative to each other. The hypothesis that continents 'drift' was first put forward by Abraham Ortelius in 1596 and was fully developed by Alfred Wegener in 1912. However, it was not until the development of the theory of plate tectonics in the 1960s, that a sufficient geological explanation of that movement was found.
   a. Mirovia
   b. Subduction
   c. Nappe
   d. Continental drift

21. In geology, _____ is transported rock debris overlying the solid bedrock. The term is also sometimes refers to organic debris so-transported. In the largest sense, it refers to the material left behind by retreating continental glaciers.
   a. Geostrophic current
   b. Drift
   c. Contact metamorphism
   d. Detritus

22. In geology a _____ is the smallest division of a geologic formation or stratigraphic rock series marked by well-defined divisional planes (bedding planes) separating it from layers above and below. A _____ is the smallest lithostratigraphic unit, usually ranging in thickness from a centimeter to several meters and distinguishable from _____s above and below it. _____s can be differentiated in various ways, including rock or mineral type and particle size.
   a. Biozones
   b. Cyclostratigraphy
   c. Sequence stratigraphy
   d. Bed

Chapter 8. Geologic Time: Concepts and Principles

23. _____ is molten rock expelled by a volcano during eruption. When first expelled from a volcanic vent, it is a liquid at temperatures from 700 >°C to 1,200 >°C (1,300 >°F to 2,200 >°F.) Although _____ is quite viscous, with about 100,000 times the viscosity of water, it can flow great distances before cooling and solidifying, because of both its thixotropic and shear thinning properties.
   a. Pumice
   b. Lava
   c. Cinder
   d. Pyroclastic flow

24. A _____ is an opening in a planet's surface or crust, which allows hot, molten rock, ash, and gases to escape from below the surface. Volcanic activity involving the extrusion of rock tends to form mountains or features like mountains over a period of time.
   a. 1703 Genroku earthquake
   b. 1700 Cascadia earthquake
   c. Volcano
   d. 1509 Istanbul earthquake

25. An _____ is a buried erosion surface separating two rock masses or strata of different ages, indicating that sediment deposition was not continuous. In general, the older layer was exposed to erosion for an interval of time before deposition of the younger, but the term is used to describe any break in the sedimentary geologic record. The phenomenon of angular unconformities was discovered by James Hutton, who found examples at Jedburgh in 1787 and at Siccar Point in 1788.
   a. AL 333
   b. Unconformity
   c. AASHTO Soil Classification System
   d. AL 129-1

26. _____ is the removal of solids (sediment, soil, rock and other particles) in the natural environment. It usually occurs due to transport by wind, water, or ice; by down-slope creep of soil and other material under the force of gravity; or by living organisms, such as burrowing animals, in the case of bioerosion.

   _____ is distinguished from weathering, which is the process of chemical or physical breakdown of the minerals in the rocks, although the two processes may occur concurrently.

   a. Erosion
   b. AASHTO Soil Classification System
   c. AL 129-1
   d. AL 333

27. A _____ or dyke in geology is a type of sheet intrusion referring to any geologic body that cuts discordantly across

   - planar wall rock structures, such as bedding or foliation
   - massive rock formations, like igneous/magmatic intrusions and salt diapirs.

They can therefore be either intrusive or sedimentary in origin.

An intrusive _____ is an igneous body with a very high aspect ratio, which means that its thickness is usually much smaller than the other two dimensions. Thickness can vary from sub-centimeter scale to many meters and the lateral dimensions can extend over many kilometers. A _____ is an intrusion into an opening cross-cutting fissure, shouldering aside other pre-existing layers or bodies of rock; this implies that a _____ is always younger than the rocks that contain it.

Chapter 8. Geologic Time: Concepts and Principles

a. Schmidt hammer
b. Haloclasty
c. Fabric
d. Dike

28. _____ refers to natural mountain building, and may be studied as a tectonic structural event, (b) as a geographical event, and (c) a chronological event. Orogenic events (a) cause distinctive structural phenomena and related tectonic activity, (b) affect certain regions of rocks and crust, and (c) happen within a specific period of time.
   a. Alice Springs Orogeny
   b. Orogenesis
   c. Antler orogeny
   d. Orogeny

29. The _____ is a physiographic region of the Intermontane Plateaus, roughly centered on the Four Corners region of the southwestern United States. The province covers an area of 337,000 km^2 within western Colorado, northwestern New Mexico, southern and eastern Utah, and northern Arizona. About 90% of the area is drained by the Colorado River and its main tributaries; the Green, San Juan and Little Colorado.

Development of the province has in large part been influenced by structural features in its oldest rocks. Part of the Wasatch Line and its various faults form the western edge of the province. Faults that run parallel to the Wasatch Fault that lies along the Wasatch Range form the boundaries between the plateaus in the High Plateaus Section. The Uinta Basin, Uncompahgre Uplift, and the Paradox Basin were also created by movement along structural weaknesses in the region's oldest rock.

   a. 1703 Genroku earthquake
   b. 1700 Cascadia earthquake
   c. 1509 Istanbul earthquake
   d. Colorado Plateau

30. In geology, a _____ is a widespread sedimentary layer that formed at a single time, such that it is useful for geologic correlations and dating over a large area. Examples of these are massive ashfalls, such as those produced by nearby normal volcanic eruptions, and far away in supervolcanic eruptions, as well as tills deposited by continental glaciers, and the global iridium layer deposited at the K-T boundary.
   a. Principle of original horizontality
   b. Key bed
   c. Sequence stratigraphy
   d. Bedrock

31. _____ are fossils used to define and identify geologic periods They work on the premise that, although different sediments may look different depending on the conditions under which they were laid down, they may include the remains of the same species of fossil. If the species concerned were short-lived, then it is certain that the sediments in question were deposited within that narrow time period.
   a. Allotrioceras
   b. Index fossils
   c. Indian bead
   d. Invertebrate paleontology

32. _____ is Latin for 'little tongue'. It can stand for:

- _____ a brachiopod genus of the family Lingulidae, which is among the few brachiopods surviving today but also known from fossils over 500 million years old.
- In anatomy:
    - the _____ of left lung is one of the segments of the left lung with a tongue-shape
    - The Sphenoidal _____ is part of the sphenoid bone
    - The _____ of mandible, a ridge on the medial aspect of the body of the mandible, just anterior to the mandibular foramen
    - the _____ of cerebellum

a. Fault
b. Dali
c. Cleavage
d. Lingula

33. _____ is a gas consisting primarily of methane. It is found associated with fossil fuels, in coal beds, as methane clathrates, and is created by methanogenic organisms in marshes, bogs, and landfills. It is an important fuel source, a major feedstock for fertilizers, and a potent greenhouse gas.

a. 1703 Genroku earthquake
b. 1509 Istanbul earthquake
c. 1700 Cascadia earthquake
d. Natural gas

34. _____ refers to any material (typically called solids) removed from a borehole while drilling petroleum wells. Although sand and shale make up the majority of the cuttings encountered while drilling a well, depending on the location, any number of formations will actually be encountered. These include but are not limited to: anhydrite, calcite, chalk, chert, clay, dolomite, feldspar, glauconite, granite, gypsum, hematite, iron, kaolinite, lime, marlstone, mica, mudstone, pisolite, pyrite, quartz, sand, sandstone, shale, silica, silt and sulfur.

a. Skarn
b. Diapir
c. Slyne-Erris Trough
d. Drill cuttings

35. The _____ is the extended perimeter of each continent and associated coastal plain, and was part of the continent during the glacial periods, but is undersea during interglacial periods such as the current epoch by relatively shallow seas (known as shelf seas) and gulfs.

The continental rise is below the slope, but landward of the abyssal plains. Its gradient is intermediate between the slope and the shelf, on the order of 0.5-1°.

a. Continental shelf
b. Mud
c. Surface runoff
d. Continental slope

36. _____ was a physicist and chemist of Polish upbringing and, subsequently, French citizenship. She was a pioneer in the field of radioactivity, the first person honored with two Nobel Prizes, and the first female professor at the University of Paris.

She was born Maria SkÅ‚odowska in Warsaw and lived there until she was 24.

Chapter 8. Geologic Time: Concepts and Principles

a. Ambulocetus
b. Milutin Milankovié
c. Amblypoda
d. Marie SkÅ‚odowska Curie

37. A _____ or sandstorm is a meteorological phenomenon common in arid and semi-arid regions and arises when a gust front passes or when the wind force exceeds the threshold value where loose sand and dust are removed from the dry surface. Particles are transported by saltation and suspension, causing soil erosion from one place and deposition in another. The Sahara and drylands around the Arabian peninsula are the main source of airborne dust, with some contributions from Iran, Pakistan and India into the Arabian Sea, and China's storms deposit dust in the Pacific.
   a. 1509 Istanbul earthquake
   b. 1700 Cascadia earthquake
   c. Dust storm
   d. 1703 Genroku earthquake

38. The _____ is the total number of protons and neutrons in an atomic nucleus. Because protons and neutrons both are baryons, the _____ A is identical with the baryon number B as of the nucleus as of the whole atom or ion. The _____ is different for each different isotope of a chemical element.
   a. 1509 Istanbul earthquake
   b. 1703 Genroku earthquake
   c. 1700 Cascadia earthquake
   d. Mass number

39. In chemistry and physics, the _____ is the number of protons found in the nucleus of an atom and therefore identical to the charge number of the nucleus. It is conventionally represented by the symbol Z. The _____ uniquely identifies a chemical element. In an atom of neutral charge, _____ is equal to the number of electrons.
   a. Atomic number
   b. AASHTO Soil Classification System
   c. AL 333
   d. AL 129-1

40. A _____ is a free neutron that is Boltzmann distributed with kT = 0.024 eV (4.0×10^{-21} J) at room temperature. This gives characteristic (not average, or median) speed of 2.2 km/s. The name 'thermal' comes from their energy being that of the room temperature gas or material they are permeating.
   a. 1509 Istanbul earthquake
   b. 1703 Genroku earthquake
   c. 1700 Cascadia earthquake
   d. Thermal neutron

41. _____ is a type of radioactive decay in which an atomic nucleus emits an alpha particle (two protons and two neutrons bound together into a particle identical to a helium nucleus) and transforms (or 'decays') into an atom with a mass number 4 less and atomic number 2 less. For example:

$$^{238}_{92}U \rightarrow \, ^{234}_{90}Th + \, ^{4}_{2}He^{2+}$$

although this is typically written as:

$$^{238}U \rightarrow \, ^{234}Th + \alpha$$

(The second form is preferred because the first form appears electrically unbalanced. Fundamentally, the recoiling nucleus is very quickly stripped of the two extra electrons which give it an unbalanced charge.

a. AL 333
b. AASHTO Soil Classification System
c. AL 129-1
d. Alpha decay

Chapter 8. Geologic Time: Concepts and Principles

42. In nuclear physics, _____ is a type of radioactive decay in which a beta particle (an electron or a positron) is emitted. In the case of electron emission, it is referred to as beta minus (>>β^{-}), while in the case of a positron emission as beta plus (>>β^{+}.) Kinetic energy of beta particles has continuous spectrum ranging from 0 to maximal available energy (Q), which depends on parent and daughter nuclear states participating in the decay.
   a. Decay product
   b. 1509 Istanbul earthquake
   c. Mass deficiency
   d. Beta decay

43. _____ is a decay mode for isotopes that will occur when there are too many protons in the nucleus of an atom and insufficient energy to emit a positron; however, it continues to be a viable decay mode for radioactive isotopes that can decay by positron emission. If the energy difference between the parent atom and the daughter atom is less than 1.022 MeV, positron emission is forbidden and _____ is the sole decay mode. For example, Rubidium-83 will decay to Krypton-83 solely by _____ (the energy difference is about 0.9 MeV.)
   a. Electron capture
   b. AL 129-1
   c. AASHTO Soil Classification System
   d. AL 333

44. _____ is an analytical technique for the determination of the elemental composition of a sample or molecule. It is also used for elucidating the chemical structures of molecules, such as peptides and other chemical compounds. The _____ principle consists of ionizing chemical compounds to generate charged molecules or molecule fragments and measurement of their mass-to-charge ratios.
   a. 1703 Genroku earthquake
   b. 1509 Istanbul earthquake
   c. Mass spectrometry
   d. 1700 Cascadia earthquake

45. In nuclear physics, a _____ is a nuclide produced by radioactive decay. Radioactive decay often involves a sequence of steps For example, U-238 decays to Th-234 which decays to Pa-234 which decays, and so on, to Pb-206:

In this example:

- Th-234, Pa-234,…,Pb-206 are the _____s of U-238.
- Th-234 is the daughter of the parent U-238.
- Pa-234 is the granddaughter of U-238.

Note that Th-234, Pa-234,…,Pb-206 might also be referred to as the daughter products of U-238.

_____s are extremely important in understanding radioactive decay and the management of radioactive waste.

   a. Decay product
   b. 1509 Istanbul earthquake
   c. Mass deficiency
   d. Mass excess

46. _____ is a phyllosilicate (mica group) mineral.

It can also be referred to as an iron silicate. It crystallizes with monoclinic geometry.

Normally, _____ is considered diagnostic of continental shelf marine depositional environments with slow rates of accumulation. Typically, it appears in Jurassic/lower Cretaceous deposits of greensand, so-called after the coloration provided by the _____.

  a. Clay minerals
  b. Kaolinite
  c. 1509 Istanbul earthquake
  d. Glauconite

47. _____ is the solid-state recrystallization of pre-existing rocks due to changes in physical and chemical conditions, primarily heat, pressure, and the introduction of chemically active fluids. Both mineralogical, chemical and crystallographic changes can occur during this process.

Three types of _____ exist: dynamic, contact and regional.

  a. Gradualism
  b. Dike
  c. Cross-bedding
  d. Metamorphism

48. _____ is a radiometric dating technique based on analyses of the damage trails left by fission fragments in certain uranium bearing minerals and glasses. Fission-track dating is a relatively simple but robust method of radiometric dating that has made a significant impact on understanding the thermal history of continental crust, the timing of volcanic events, and the source and age of different archeological artifacts. The method involves using the number of fission events produced from the spontaneous decay of uranium-238 in common accessory minerals to date the time of rock cooling below closure temperature.
  a. 1509 Istanbul earthquake
  b. Potassium-argon dating
  c. Fission track dating
  d. Helium dating

49. _____, is a radiometric dating method that uses the naturally occurring radioisotope carbon-14 (^{14}C) to determine the age of carbonaceous materials up to about 60,000 years. Raw, i.e. uncalibrated, radiocarbon ages are usually reported in radiocarbon years 'Before Present' (BP), 'Present' being defined as AD 1950. Such raw ages can be calibrated to give calendar dates.
  a. Global Standard Stratigraphic Age
  b. Relative dating
  c. Radiometric dating
  d. Carbon dating

50. _____ or tree-ring dating is the method of scientific dating based on the analysis of tree-ring growth patterns. This technique was developed during the first half of the 20th century originally by the astronomer A. E. Douglass, the founder of the Laboratory of Tree-Ring Research at the University of Arizona. Douglass sought to better understand cycles of sunspot activity and reasoned that changes in solar activity would affect climate patterns on earth which would subsequently be recorded by tree-ring growth patterns (i.e., sunspots >→ climate >→ tree rings.)
  a. 1509 Istanbul earthquake
  b. 1700 Cascadia earthquake
  c. 1703 Genroku earthquake
  d. Dendrochronology

51. _____ is an igneous rock of volcanic origin.

They are usually fine-grained or aphanitic to glassy in texture. They often contain clasts of other rocks and phenocrysts.

a. Metamorphic rock
b. Serpentinite
c. Laccolith
d. Volcanic rock

Chapter 9. Earthquakes

1. An _____ is the result of a sudden release of energy in the Earth's crust that creates seismic waves. They are recorded with a seismometer or the related and mostly obsolete Richter magnitude, with a magnitude 3 or lower _____ being mostly imperceptible and magnitude 7 causing serious damage over large areas.
   - a. AL 333
   - b. Earthquake
   - c. AASHTO Soil Classification System
   - d. AL 129-1

2. An _____ is an earthquake that occurs after a previous earthquake (the main shock.) An _____ is in the same region of the main shock but is always of smaller magnitude strength. If an _____ is larger than the main shock, the _____ is redesignated as the main shock and the original main shock is redesignated as a foreshock.
   - a. AL 333
   - b. Aftershock
   - c. AASHTO Soil Classification System
   - d. AL 129-1

3. In geology, a _____ or _____ line is a planar fracture in rock in which the rock on one side of the fracture has moved with respect to the rock on the other side. Large _____ s within the Earth's crust are the result of differential or shear motion and active _____ zones are the causal locations of most earthquakes. Earthquakes are caused by energy release during rapid slippage along a _____.
   - a. Geothermal
   - b. Combe
   - c. Cohesion
   - d. Fault

4. The _____ is a continental transform fault that runs a length of roughly 800 miles (1,300 km) through California in the United States. The fault's motion is right-lateral strike-slip (horizontal motion.) It forms the tectonic boundary between the Pacific Plate and the North American Plate.
   - a. 1509 Istanbul earthquake
   - b. 1703 Genroku earthquake
   - c. 1700 Cascadia earthquake
   - d. San Andreas fault

5. The _____ is the zone of the ocean floor that separates the thin oceanic crust from thick continental crust. _____ s constitute about 28% of the oceanic area.

The transition from continental to oceanic crust commonly occurs within the outer part of the margin, called continental rise.

   - a. Cuspate forelands
   - b. Continental margin
   - c. 1509 Istanbul earthquake
   - d. Longshore drift

6. In materials science, _____ is a change in the shape or size of an object due to an applied force. This can be a result of tensile (pulling) forces, compressive (pushing) forces, shear, bending or torsion (twisting.) _____ is often described as strain.
   - a. Stack
   - b. Melange
   - c. Combe
   - d. Deformation

7. The lithosphere is broken up into what are called _____. In the case of Earth, there are eight major and many minor plates The lithospheric plates ride on the asthenosphere. These plates move in relation to one another at one of three types of plate boundaries: convergent, or collisional boundaries; divergent boundaries, also called spreading centers; and transform boundaries.
   - a. Subduction
   - b. Lithosphere
   - c. Juan de Fuca Ridge
   - d. Tectonic plates

Chapter 9. Earthquakes

8.   The _____ is an explanation for how energy is spread during earthquakes. As plates shift on opposite sides of a fault are subjected to force, they accumulate energy and slowly deform until their internal strength is exceeded. At that time, a sudden movement occurs along the fault, releasing the accumulated energy, and the rocks snap back to their original undeformed shape.

   a. Azores-Gibraltar Transform Fault
   b. Obduction
   c. East Pacific Rise
   d. Elastic rebound theory

9.   _____ is the solid-state recrystallization of pre-existing rocks due to changes in physical and chemical conditions, primarily heat, pressure, and the introduction of chemically active fluids. Both mineralogical, chemical and crystallographic changes can occur during this process.

Three types of _____ exist: dynamic, contact and regional.

   a. Dike
   b. Cross-bedding
   c. Gradualism
   d. Metamorphism

10.   The term _____ can be used to describe both the conduct of a survey for geological purposes and an institution holding geological information.

A _____ is the systematic investigation of the subsurface of a given piece of ground for the purpose of creating a geological map or model. A _____ employs techniques from the traditional walk-over survey, studying outcrops and landforms, to intrusive methods, such as hand augering and machine driven boreholes, to the use of geophysical techniques and remote sensing methods, such as aerial photography and satellite imagery.

   a. Reading Prong
   b. Paralithic
   c. Leaverite
   d. Geological Survey

11.   _____ describes the large scale motions of Earth's lithosphere. The theory encompasses the older concepts of continental drift, developed during the first decades of the 20th century by Alfred Wegener, and seafloor spreading, understood during the 1960s.

The outermost part of the Earth's interior is made up of two layers: the lithosphere and the asthenosphere.

   a. Copperbelt Province
   b. Supercontinent cycle
   c. Lithosphere
   d. Plate tectonics

12.   _____ is the scientific study of earthquakes and the propagation of elastic waves through the Earth. The field also includes studies of earthquake effects, such as tsunamis as well as diverse seismic sources such as volcanic, tectonic, oceanic, atmospheric, and artificial processes . A related field that uses geology to infer information regarding past earthquakes is paleoseismology.

   a. 1509 Istanbul earthquake
   b. 1703 Genroku earthquake
   c. 1700 Cascadia earthquake
   d. Seismology

Chapter 9. Earthquakes

13. A _____ or sandstorm is a meteorological phenomenon common in arid and semi-arid regions and arises when a gust front passes or when the wind force exceeds the threshold value where loose sand and dust are removed from the dry surface. Particles are transported by saltation and suspension, causing soil erosion from one place and deposition in another. The Sahara and drylands around the Arabian peninsula are the main source of airborne dust, with some contributions from Iran, Pakistan and India into the Arabian Sea, and China's storms deposit dust in the Pacific.

- a. Dust storm
- b. 1703 Genroku earthquake
- c. 1509 Istanbul earthquake
- d. 1700 Cascadia earthquake

14. The _____ is an oceanic tectonic plate beneath the Pacific Ocean.

To the north the easterly side is a divergent boundary with the Explorer Plate, the Juan de Fuca Plate and the Gorda Plate forming respectively the Explorer Ridge, the Juan de Fuca Ridge and the Gorda Ridge. In the middle the easterly side is a transform boundary with the North American Plate along the San Andreas Fault and a boundary with the Cocos Plate.

- a. Pacific plate
- b. Juan de Fuca Plate
- c. North American Plate
- d. South Bismarck Plate

15. A _____ is an opening in a planet's surface or crust, which allows hot, molten rock, ash, and gases to escape from below the surface. Volcanic activity involving the extrusion of rock tends to form mountains or features like mountains over a period of time.

- a. Volcano
- b. 1703 Genroku earthquake
- c. 1509 Istanbul earthquake
- d. 1700 Cascadia earthquake

16. The _____ or epicentre is the point on the Earth's surface that is directly above the hypocenter or focus, the point where an earthquake or underground explosion originates.

The _____ is usually the location of greatest damage. However, in some cases the _____ is above the start of a much larger event.

- a. AL 129-1
- b. AASHTO Soil Classification System
- c. Epicenter
- d. AL 333

17. The _____, refers to the site of an earthquake or to that of a nuclear explosion. In the former, it is a synonym of the focus; in the latter, of ground zero.

The location of an earthquake's _____ is the position where the energy stored in the strain in the rock is released, which occurs at the focal depth below the epicentre. The focal depth can be calculated from measurements based on seismic wave phenomena.

- a. Receiver function
- b. Hypocenter
- c. Seismic waves
- d. Meizoseismal area

Chapter 9. Earthquakes

18. _____ are waves that travel through the Earth or other elastic body, for example as the result of an earthquake, explosion, or some other process that imparts forces to the body. _____ are also continually excited on Earth by the incessant pounding of ocean waves (referred to as the microseism) and the wind. _____ are studied by seismologists, and measured by a seismograph, which records the output of a seismometer, or geophone.
    a. Paleoliquefaction
    b. Seismic gap
    c. Strong ground motion
    d. Seismic waves

19. A _____ is a deep active seismic area in a subduction zone. Differential motion along the zone produces deep-seated earthquakes, the foci of which may be as deep as about 700 kilometres (435 miles.) They develop beneath volcanic island arcs and continental margins above active subduction zones.
    a. Lava
    b. Wadati-Benioff zone
    c. Pit crater
    d. Pumice

20. The _____ are hemispheric-scale long but narrow topographic depressions of the sea floor. They are also the deepest parts of the ocean floor.

_____ define one of the most important natural boundaries on the Earth's solid surface, thatlie between two lithospheric plates. There are three types of lithospheric plate boundaries: divergent (where lithosphere and oceanic crust is created at mid-ocean ridges), convergent (where one lithospheric plate sinks beneath another and returns to the mantle), and transform (where two lithospheric plates slide past each other).

    a. AL 129-1
    b. AASHTO Soil Classification System
    c. AL 333
    d. Oceanic trenches

21. The _____ is located in the Pacific Ocean and is 10,882 meters (35,702 ft) deep at its deepest point, known as the Horizon Deep.

The trench lies at the northern end of the Kermadec-Tonga Subduction Zone, an active subduction zone where the Pacific Plate is being subducted below the Tonga Plate and the Indo-Australian Plate. The _____ extends north-northeast from the Kermadec Islands north of the North Island of New Zealand.

    a. 1700 Cascadia earthquake
    b. Tonga Trench
    c. 1509 Istanbul earthquake
    d. 1703 Genroku earthquake

22. An _____ is an earthquake that occurs in the interior of a tectonic plate, whereas an interplate earthquake is one that occurs at a plate boundary.

_____s are rare compared to earthquakes at plate boundaries. Nonetheless, very large _____s can inflict heavy damage.

    a. AL 333
    b. AL 129-1
    c. AASHTO Soil Classification System
    d. Intraplate earthquake

23. In seismology, _____ are surface seismic waves that cause horizontal shifting of the earth during an earthquake. A.E.H. Love predicted the existence of _____ mathematically in 1911. They form a distinct class, different from other types of seismic waves, such as P-waves and S-waves (both body waves), or Rayleigh waves (another type of surface wave). _____ travel with a slower velocity than P- or S- waves, but faster than Rayleigh waves.
   a. Love waves
   b. Strainmeter
   c. Mazuku
   d. Seismic refraction

24. _____ are type of elastic wave, also called seismic waves, that can travel through gases, elastic solids and liquids, including the Earth. _____ can be produced by earthquakes and recorded by seismometers.
   a. 1509 Istanbul earthquake
   b. 1700 Cascadia earthquake
   c. 1703 Genroku earthquake
   d. P-waves

25. _____ are a type of elastic surface wave that travel on solids. They are produced on the Earth by earthquakes, in which case they are also known as 'ground roll', or by other sources of seismic energy such as an explosion or even a sledgehammer impact. They are also produced in materials by acoustic transducers, and are used in non-destructive testing for detecting defects.
   a. Fault friction
   b. Teleseism
   c. Meizoseismal area
   d. Rayleigh waves

26. A type of seismic wave, the _____, secondary wave or shear wave (sometimes called an elastic _____) is one of the two main types of elastic body waves, so named because they move through the body of an object, unlike surface waves.

The _____ move as a shear or transverse wave, so motion is perpendicular to the direction of wave propagation: _____s, like waves in a rope, as opposed to waves moving through a slinky, the P-wave. The wave moves through elastic media, and the main restoring force comes from shear effects.

   a. 1703 Genroku earthquake
   b. S-wave
   c. 1509 Istanbul earthquake
   d. 1700 Cascadia earthquake

27. Study of geological _____ is related to the study of structural geology, rock microstructure or rock texture and fault mechanics.

_____ is the response of a rock to deformation usually by compressive stress and forms particular textures. _____ can be homogeneous or non-homogeneous, and may be pure _____ or simple _____.

   a. Shear
   b. Graben
   c. Syncline
   d. Petermann Orogeny

28. In physics, a _____ is a mechanical wave that propagates along the interface between differing media, usually two fluids with different densities. A _____ can also be an electromagnetic wave guided by a refractive index gradient. In radio transmission, a ground wave is a _____ that propagates close to the surface of the Earth.
   a. Surface wave
   b. 1700 Cascadia earthquake
   c. 1509 Istanbul earthquake
   d. 1703 Genroku earthquake

29. The _____ is a scale used for measuring the intensity of an earthquake. The scale quantifies the effects of an earthquake on the Earth's surface, humans, objects of nature, and man-made structures on a scale of I through XII, with I denoting not felt, and XII one that causes almost complete destruction. The values will differ based on the distance to the earthquake, with the highest intensities being around the epicentral area.
- a. Medvedev-Sponheuer-Karnik scale
- b. China Seismic Intensity Scale
- c. Rossi-Forel scale
- d. Mercalli Intensity Scale

30. The _____, also known as the local magnitude (M_L) scale, assigns a single number to quantify the amount of seismic energy released by an earthquake. It is a base-10 logarithmic scale obtained by calculating the logarithm of the combined horizontal amplitude of the largest displacement from zero on a Wood-Anderson torsion seismometer output. So, for example, an earthquake that measures 5.0 on the Richter scale has a shaking amplitude 10 times larger than one that measures 4.0.
- a. Moment magnitude scale
- b. Seismic scale
- c. Mercalli intensity scale
- d. Richter Magnitude Scale

31. In stratigraphy, _____ is the native consolidated rock underlying the surface of a terrestrial planet, usually the Earth. Above the _____ is usually an area of broken and weathered unconsolidated rock in the basal subsoil. The top of the _____ is known as rockhead and identifying this, via excavations, drilling or geophysical methods, is an important task in most civil engineering projects.
- a. Bedrock
- b. Polystrate
- c. Sequence stratigraphy
- d. Biozones

32. A _____ is a geological phenomenon which includes a wide range of ground movement, such as rock falls, deep failure of slopes and shallow debris flows, which can occur in offshore, coastal and onshore environments. Although the action of gravity is the primary driving force for a _____ to occur, there are other contributing factors affecting the original slope stability. Typically, pre-conditional factors build up specific sub-surface conditions that make the area/slope prone to failure, whereas the actual _____ often requires a trigger before being released.
- a. Soil liquefaction
- b. 1700 Cascadia earthquake
- c. 1509 Istanbul earthquake
- d. Landslide

33. _____ is the geomorphic process by which soil, regolith, and rock move downslope under the force of gravity. Types of _____ include creep, slides, flows, topples, and falls, each with its own characteristic features, and taking place over timescales from seconds to years. _____ occurs on both terrestrial and submarine slopes, and has been observed on Earth, Mars, and Venus.
- a. Soil liquefaction
- b. 1509 Istanbul earthquake
- c. 1700 Cascadia earthquake
- d. Mass wasting

34. _____ is the removal of solids (sediment, soil, rock and other particles) in the natural environment. It usually occurs due to transport by wind, water, or ice; by down-slope creep of soil and other material under the force of gravity; or by living organisms, such as burrowing animals, in the case of bioerosion.

_____ is distinguished from weathering, which is the process of chemical or physical breakdown of the minerals in the rocks, although the two processes may occur concurrently.

a. AASHTO Soil Classification System
b. AL 333
c. AL 129-1
d. Erosion

35. A _____ is the topographic expression of faulting attributed to the displacement of the land surface by movement along the fault. It can be caused by differential erosion along an old inactive geologic fault (a sort of old rupture) with hard and weak rock, or by a movement on an active fault. In many cases, bluffs form from the upthrown block and can be very steep.
   a. Stream gradient
   b. Shutter ridge
   c. Gravitational erosion
   d. Fault scarp

36. When building a house, regional _____ maps are used to find the best (or the worst) place to locate for earthquake shaking. Although greatly confused with its sister, seismic risk, _____ is the study of expected earthquake ground motions at any point on the earth. Surface motion map for a hypothetical earthquake on the northern portion of the Hayward Fault Zone and its presumed northern extension, the Rodgers Creek Fault Zone

The calculations for _____ can be quite complex.

   a. Seismic Hazard
   b. Seismic risk
   c. 1700 Cascadia earthquake
   d. 1509 Istanbul earthquake

37. A _____ is a segment of an active fault that has not slipped in an unusually long time when compared with other segments along the same structure. _____ hypothesis/theory states that, over long periods of time, the displacement on any segment must be equal to that experienced by all the other parts of the fault. Any large and longstanding gap is therefore considered to be the fault segment most likely to suffer future earthquakes.
   a. Harmonic tremor
   b. Teleseism
   c. Seismic shadowing
   d. Seismic gap

38. _____ uses the results of a seismic hazard analysis, and includes both consequence and probability. _____ has been defined, for most management purposes, as the potential economic, social and environmental consequences of hazardous events that may occur in a specified period of time. A building located in a region of high seismic hazard is at lower risk if it is built to sound seismic engineering principles.
   a. Seismic microzonation
   b. Seismic risk
   c. 1700 Cascadia earthquake
   d. 1509 Istanbul earthquake

39. A _____ material is one in which viscosity increases with the rate of shear. Such a shear thickening fluid, also known by the acronym STF, is an example of a non-Newtonian fluid.

The _____ effect occurs when closely packed particles are combined with enough liquid to fill the gaps between them.

   a. Dilatant
   b. Tensile stress
   c. Shear stress
   d. Viscosity

40. A _____ is an instrument designed to measure very small changes from the horizontal level, either on the ground or in structures. A similar term, in less common usage, is the inclinometer. They are used extensively for monitoring volcanos, the response of dams to filling, the small movements of potential landslides, the orientation and volume of hydraulic fractures, and the response of structures to various influences such as loading and foundation settlement.

a. 1509 Istanbul earthquake
b. Tiltmeter
c. 1703 Genroku earthquake
d. 1700 Cascadia earthquake

Chapter 10. Earth's Interior

1. The _____ is the layer of igneous, sedimentary, and metamorphic rocks which form the continents and the areas of shallow seabed close to their shores, known as continental shelves. This layer is sometimes called sial due to more felsic, or granitic, bulk composition, which lies in contrast to the oceanic crust, called sima due to its mafic, or basaltic rock. (Based on the change in velocity of seismic waves, it is believed that at a certain depth sial becomes close in its physical properties to sima.
   - a. Continental crust
   - b. Plate tectonics
   - c. Divergent boundary
   - d. Mirovia

2. The _____ is a chronologic schema (or idealized model) relating stratigraphy to time that is used by geologists, paleontologists and other earth scientists to describe the timing and relationships between events that have occurred during the history of the Earth. The table of geologic time spans presented here agrees with the dates and nomenclature proposed by the International Commission on Stratigraphy, and uses the standard color codes of the United States Geological Survey.

   Evidence from radiometric dating indicates that the Earth is about 4.570 billion years old.
   - a. Geologic time scale
   - b. 1700 Cascadia earthquake
   - c. 1703 Genroku earthquake
   - d. 1509 Istanbul earthquake

3. _____ is the part of Earth's lithosphere that surfaces in the ocean basins. _____ is primarily composed of mafic rocks, or sima. It is thinner than continental crust, or sial, generally less than 10 kilometers thick, however it is denser, having a mean density of about 3.3 grams per cubic centimeter.
   - a. AASHTO Soil Classification System
   - b. Oceanic crust
   - c. AL 333
   - d. AL 129-1

4. A _____ is a large emplacement of igneous intrusive rock that forms from cooled magma deep in the Earth's crust. they are almost always made mostly of felsic or intermediate rock-types, such as granite, quartz monzonite, or diorite

   Although they may appear uniform, _____ s are in fact structures with complex histories and compositions.
   - a. Great Dyke
   - b. Tuff
   - c. Scoria
   - d. Batholith

5. _____ are type of elastic wave, also called seismic waves, that can travel through gases, elastic solids and liquids, including the Earth. _____ can be produced by earthquakes and recorded by seismometers.
   - a. 1509 Istanbul earthquake
   - b. P-waves
   - c. 1703 Genroku earthquake
   - d. 1700 Cascadia earthquake

6. A type of seismic wave, the _____, secondary wave or shear wave (sometimes called an elastic _____) is one of the two main types of elastic body waves, so named because they move through the body of an object, unlike surface waves.

   The _____ move as a shear or transverse wave, so motion is perpendicular to the direction of wave propagation: _____ s, like waves in a rope, as opposed to waves moving through a slinky, the P-wave. The wave moves through elastic media, and the main restoring force comes from shear effects.

Chapter 10. Earth's Interior

    a. 1700 Cascadia earthquake
    b. 1509 Istanbul earthquake
    c. 1703 Genroku earthquake
    d. S-wave

7. _____s, sometimes called minor planets or planetoids, are small Solar System bodies in orbit around the Sun, especially in the inner Solar System; they are smaller than planets but larger than meteoroids. The term '_____' has historically been applied primarily to bodies in the inner Solar System since the outer Solar System was poorly known when it came into common usage. The distinction between _____s and comets is made on visual appearance: Comets show a perceptible coma while _____s do not.
    a. AL 129-1
    b. AL 333
    c. Asteroid
    d. AASHTO Soil Classification System

8. _____ is one of the three main rock types (the others being igneous and metamorphic rock.) _____ is formed by deposition and consolidation of mineral and organic material and from precipitation of minerals from solution. The processes that form _____ occur at the surface of the Earth and within bodies of water.
    a. Groundmass
    b. Sedimentary rock
    c. Migmatite
    d. Pluton

9. _____ is the process of determining a specific date for an archaeological or palaeontological site or artifact. Some archaeologists prefer the terms chronometric or calendar dating, as use of the word 'absolute' implies a certainty and precision that is rarely possible in archaeology. _____ is usually based on the physical or chemical properties of the materials of artifacts, buildings, or other items that have been modified by humans.
    a. Uranium-lead dating
    b. AASHTO Soil Classification System
    c. Erathem
    d. Absolute dating

10. The _____ is the extended perimeter of each continent and associated coastal plain, and was part of the continent during the glacial periods, but is undersea during interglacial periods such as the current epoch by relatively shallow seas (known as shelf seas) and gulfs.

The continental rise is below the slope, but landward of the abyssal plains. Its gradient is intermediate between the slope and the shelf, on the order of 0.5-1°.

    a. Mud
    b. Surface runoff
    c. Continental shelf
    d. Continental slope

11. _____ is a method of exploration geophysics that uses the principles of seismology to estimate the properties of the Earth's subsurface from reflected seismic waves. The method requires a controlled seismic source of energy, such as dynamite/Tovex, a specialized air gun or vibrators, commonly known by their trademark name Vibroseis. By noting the time it takes for a reflection to arrive at a receiver, it is possible to estimate the depth of the feature that generated the reflection.
    a. Coulomb stress transfer
    b. Geophone
    c. Plus minus methos
    d. Reflection seismology

12. _____ are waves that travel through the Earth or other elastic body, for example as the result of an earthquake, explosion, or some other process that imparts forces to the body. _____ are also continually excited on Earth by the incessant pounding of ocean waves (referred to as the microseism) and the wind. _____ are studied by seismologists, and measured by a seismograph, which records the output of a seismometer, or geophone.

Chapter 10. Earth's Interior

a. Strong ground motion
b. Seismic gap
c. Paleoliquefaction
d. Seismic waves

13. The _____ lies between the Earth's silicate mantle and its liquid iron-nickel outer core. This boundary is located at approximately 2900 km of depth beneath the Earth's surface. The boundary is observed via the discontinuity in seismic wave velocities at that depth. This discontinuity is due to the differences between the acoustic impedances of the solid mantle and the molten outer core. P-wave velocities are much slower in the outer core than in the deep mantle while S-waves do not exist at all in the liquid portion of the core.

a. 1509 Istanbul earthquake
b. Core-mantle boundary
c. Brittle-ductile transition zone
d. Seismogenic layer

14. A _____ is a sand- to boulder-sized particle of debris in the Solar System. The visible path of a _____ that enters Earth's (or another body's) atmosphere is called a meteor, or commonly a 'shooting star' or 'falling star.' If a _____ reaches the ground, it is then called a meteorite. Many meteors are part of a meteor shower.

a. 1509 Istanbul earthquake
b. 1700 Cascadia earthquake
c. 1703 Genroku earthquake
d. Meteoroid

15. _____ is the scientific study of earthquakes and the propagation of elastic waves through the Earth. The field also includes studies of earthquake effects, such as tsunamis as well as diverse seismic sources such as volcanic, tectonic, oceanic, atmospheric, and artificial processes . A related field that uses geology to infer information regarding past earthquakes is paleoseismology.

a. 1509 Istanbul earthquake
b. 1703 Genroku earthquake
c. Seismology
d. 1700 Cascadia earthquake

16. A _____ is an area in which an S-Wave (secondary seismic wave) is not detected due to it not being able to pass through the outer core of the earth due to it being liquid. When an earthquake occurs, seismographs near the epicenter, out to about 90° distance, are able to record both Primary and Secondary waves, but those at a greater distance no longer detect the S-wave. This is because shear waves cannot pass through liquids.

a. Tornillo event
b. Teleseism
c. Receiver function
d. Shadow zone

17. The _____ is the mechanically weak ductily-deforming region of the upper mantle of the Earth. It lies below the lithosphere, at depths between 100 and 200 km (~ 62 and 124 miles) below the surface, but perhaps extending as deep as 400 km (~ 249 miles.)

The _____ is a portion of the upper mantle just below the lithosphere that is involved in plate movements and isostatic adjustments. In spite of its heat, pressures keep it plastic, and it has a relatively low density. Seismic waves pass relatively slowly through the _____, compared to the overlying lithospheric mantle, thus it has been called the low-velocity zone. This was the observation that originally alerted seismologists to its presence and gave some information about its physical properties, as the speed of seismic waves decreases with decreasing rigidity.

a. AL 333
b. Asthenosphere
c. AL 129-1
d. AASHTO Soil Classification System

18. The _____ is the rigid outermost shell of a rocky planet.

In the Earth, the _____ includes the crust and the uppermost mantle, which constitute the hard and rigid outer layer of the planet. The _____ is underlain by the asthenosphere, the weaker, hotter, and deeper part of the upper mantle.

a. Nappe
b. Copperbelt Province
c. Continental crust
d. Lithosphere

19. A _____ is a vector field which surrounds magnets and electric currents, and is detected by the force it exerts on moving electric charges and on magnetic materials. When placed in a _____, magnetic dipoles tend to align their axes parallel to the _____. Magnetic fields also have their own energy with an energy density proportional to the square of the field intensity.

a. 1700 Cascadia earthquake
b. 1703 Genroku earthquake
c. Magnetic field
d. 1509 Istanbul earthquake

20. The _____, usually referred to as the Moho, is the boundary between the Earth's crust and the mantle. The Moho serves to separate both oceanic crust and continental crust from underlying mantle. The Moho mostly lies entirely within the lithosphere; only beneath mid-ocean ridges does it define the lithosphere-asthenosphere boundary.

a. Panthalassa
b. Mohorovičić discontinuity
c. Copperbelt Province
d. Gorda Ridge

21. A _____ is a large, slow-moving mass of ice, formed from compacted layers of snow, that slowly deforms and flows in response to gravity and high pressure.

_____ ice is the largest reservoir of fresh water on Earth, and second only to oceans as the largest reservoir of total water.

a. Little Ice Age
b. Greenhouse gases
c. Pacific Decadal Oscillation
d. Glacier

22. _____ is a type of potassic volcanic rock best known for sometimes containing diamonds. It is named after the town of Kimberley in South Africa, where the discovery of an 83.5 carats (16.7 g) diamond in 1871 spawned a diamond rush, eventually creating the Big Hole.

_____ occurs in the Earth's crust in vertical structures known as _____ pipes.

a. 1509 Istanbul earthquake
b. 1700 Cascadia earthquake
c. Kimberlite
d. 1703 Genroku earthquake

23. An _____ is a section of the Earth's oceanic crust and the underlying upper mantle that has been uplifted or emplaced to be exposed within continental crustal rocks. Ophio is Greek for 'snake', lite means 'stone' from the Greek lithos.

The term _____ was originally used by Alexandre Brongniart for an assemblage of green rocks (serpentine, diabase) in the Alps; Steinmann (1927) later modified its use to include serpentine, pillow lava, and chert ('Steinmann's trinity'), again based on occurrences in the Alps.

Chapter 10. Earth's Interior

a. Ophiolite
b. AL 129-1
c. AL 333
d. AASHTO Soil Classification System

24. A _____ is a dense, coarse-grained igneous rock, consisting mostly of the minerals olivine and pyroxene. _____ is ultramafic, as the rock contains less than 45% silica. It is high in magnesium, reflecting the high proportions of magnesium-rich olivine, with appreciable iron.

_____ is the dominant rock of the upper part of the Earth's mantle. The compositions of _____ nodules found in certain basalts and diamond pipes (kimberlites) are of special interest, because they provide samples of the Earth's Mantle roots of continents brought up from depths from about 30 km or so to depths at least as great as about 200 km.

a. 1509 Istanbul earthquake
b. 1700 Cascadia earthquake
c. 1703 Genroku earthquake
d. Peridotite

25. The _____ is part of the Earth's mantle, and is located between the lower mantle and the upper mantle, between a depth of 410 and 660 km. The Earth's mantle, including the _____, consists primarily of peridotite, a course grained, ultramafic, igneous rock.

The mantle was divided into the upper mantle, _____, and lower mantle as a result of sudden seismic-velocity discontinuities at depths of 410 and 660 km.

a. Cap carbonates
b. Palynomorph
c. Wave-cut platform
d. Transition zone

26. _____ is a common extrusive volcanic rock. It is usually grey to black and fine-grained due to rapid cooling of lava at the surface of a planet. It may be porphyritic containing larger crystals in a fine matrix, or vesicular, or frothy scoria.

a. 1700 Cascadia earthquake
b. 1509 Istanbul earthquake
c. 1703 Genroku earthquake
d. Basalt

27. _____ refers to a large group of dark, coarse-grained, intrusive igneous rocks chemically equivalent to basalt. The rocks are plutonic, formed when molten magma is trapped beneath the Earth's surface and cools into a crystalline mass.

The vast majority of the Earth's surface is underlain by _____ within the oceanic crust, produced by basalt magmatism at mid-ocean ridges.

a. 1703 Genroku earthquake
b. 1509 Istanbul earthquake
c. 1700 Cascadia earthquake
d. Gabbro

28. In geology, _____ refers to heat sources within the planet. _____ is technically an adjective (e.g., _____ energy) but in U.S. English the word has attained frequent use as a noun.

The planet's internal heat was originally generated during its accretion, due to gravitational binding energy, and since then additional heat has continued to be generated by decay heat from the radioactive decay of elements.

a. Cleavage
b. Geothermal
c. Combe
d. Stratification

29. The _____ is the rate of increase in temperature per unit depth in the Earth. It varies with location and is typically measured by determining the bottom open-hole temperature after borehole drilling. To achieve accuracy the drilling fluid needs time to reach the ambient temperature.
   a. Geothermal power
   b. Geothermal gradient
   c. Geothermal heat pump
   d. Hot Dry Rock Geothermal Energy

30. _____ is the transition of thermal energy or simply heat from a hotter object to a cooler object When an object or fluid is at a different temperature than its surroundings or another object, transfer of thermal energy or heat exchange, occurs in such a way that the body and the surroundings reach thermal equilibrium. _____ always occurs from a higher-temperature object to a cooler temperature one as described by the second law of thermodynamics or the Clausius statement.
   a. Heat transfer
   b. 1700 Cascadia earthquake
   c. 1509 Istanbul earthquake
   d. 1703 Genroku earthquake

31. The lithosphere is broken up into what are called _____. In the case of Earth, there are eight major and many minor plates The lithospheric plates ride on the asthenosphere. These plates move in relation to one another at one of three types of plate boundaries: convergent, or collisional boundaries; divergent boundaries, also called spreading centers; and transform boundaries.
   a. Tectonic plates
   b. Lithosphere
   c. Juan de Fuca Ridge
   d. Subduction

32. A _____ is an atom with an unstable nucleus, which is a nucleus characterized by excess energy which is available to be imparted either to a newly-created radiation particle within the nucleus, or else to an atomic electron . The _____, in this process, undergoes radioactive decay, and emits a gamma ray(s) and/or subatomic particles. These particles constitute ionizing radiation.
   a. 1700 Cascadia earthquake
   b. Half-life
   c. 1509 Istanbul earthquake
   d. Radionuclide

33. The _____ is a cosmological model of the initial conditions and subsequent development of the universe. It is supported by the most comprehensive and accurate explanations from current scientific evidence and observation. As used by cosmologists, the term _____ generally refers to the idea that the universe has expanded from a primordial hot and dense initial condition at some finite time in the past, and continues to expand to this day.
   a. 1700 Cascadia earthquake
   b. 1509 Istanbul earthquake
   c. 1703 Genroku earthquake
   d. Big Bang

34. A _____ or gravitometer, is an instrument used in gravimetry for measuring the local gravitational field of the Earth. A _____ is a type of accelerometer, specialized for measuring the constant downward acceleration of gravity. Though the essential principle of design is the same as in other accelerometers, _____s are typically designed to be much more sensitive in order to measure very tiny fractional changes within the Earth's gravity of 1 g, caused by nearby geologic structures or the shape of the Earth.
   a. 1509 Istanbul earthquake
   b. 1700 Cascadia earthquake
   c. 1703 Genroku earthquake
   d. Gravimeter

Chapter 10. Earth's Interior 117

35. Nuclear binding energy can be easily computed from the easily measurable difference in mass of a nucleus, and the sum of the masses of the number of free neutrons and protons that make up the nucleus. Once this mass difference, called the mass defect or _____, is known, Einstein's mass-energy equivalence formula $E = mc^2$ can be used to compute the binding energy of any nucleus. (As a historical note, early nuclear physicists used to refer to computing this value as a 'packing fraction' calculation.)

a. Decay product
b. 1509 Istanbul earthquake
c. Mass excess
d. Mass deficiency

36. The _____ of a nuclide is the difference between its actual mass and its mass number. It is not the same as binding energy, although the concepts are related. It is a useful quantity when deciding whether a radioactive decay will occur and, if it does, how much energy will be released. Radioactive decay processes will only occur if the _____ of the products is less than the _____ of the parent nuclide.

a. Decay product
b. Mass deficiency
c. 1509 Istanbul earthquake
d. Mass excess

37. The _____ are hemispheric-scale long but narrow topographic depressions of the sea floor. They are also the deepest parts of the ocean floor.

_____ define one of the most important natural boundaries on the Earth's solid surface, that lie between two lithospheric plates. There are three types of lithospheric plate boundaries: divergent (where lithosphere and oceanic crust is created at mid-ocean ridges), convergent (where one lithospheric plate sinks beneath another and returns to the mantle), and transform (where two lithospheric plates slide past each other).

a. AL 333
b. Oceanic trenches
c. AASHTO Soil Classification System
d. AL 129-1

38. A _____ is a type of structural dome formed when a thick bed of evaporite minerals found at depth intrudes vertically into surrounding rock strata, forming a diapir.

The salt that forms these domes was deposited within restricted marine basins. Due to restricted flow of water into a basin, evaporation occurs resulting in the precipitation of salts from solution, depositing evaporites.

a. Salt dome
b. 1703 Genroku earthquake
c. 1509 Istanbul earthquake
d. 1700 Cascadia earthquake

39. _____ is a term used in geology to refer to the state of gravitational equilibrium between the earth's lithosphere and asthenosphere such that the tectonic plates 'float' at an elevation which depends on their thickness and density. This concept is invoked to explain how different topographic heights can exist at the Earth's surface. When a certain area of lithosphere reaches the state of _____, it is said to be in isostatic equilibrium.

a. Isograd
b. Orientation Tensor
c. Economic geology
d. Isostasy

Chapter 10. Earth's Interior

40. The general term '_____' or, more precisely, 'glacial age' denotes a geological period of long-term reduction in the temperature of the Earth's surface and atmosphere, resulting in an expansion of continental ice sheets, polar ice sheets and alpine glaciers. Within a long-term _____, individual pulses of extra cold climate are termed 'glaciations'. Glaciologically, _____ implies the presence of extensive ice sheets in the northern and southern hemispheres; by this definition we are still in an _____
   a. AASHTO Soil Classification System
   b. AL 333
   c. AL 129-1
   d. Ice Age

41. _____ is the rise of land masses that were depressed by the huge weight of ice sheets during the last glacial period, through a process known as isostatic depression. It affects northern Europe (especially Scotland, Fennoscandia and northern Denmark), Siberia, Canada, and the Great Lakes of Canada and the United States.

During the last glacial period, much of northern Europe, Asia, North America, Greenland and Antarctica were covered by ice sheets. The ice was as thick as three kilometres during the last glacial maximum about 20,000 years ago. The enormous weight of this ice caused the surface of the crust to deform and downwarp under the ice load, forcing the fluid mantle material to flow away from the loaded area. At the end of the ice age when the glaciers retreated, the removal of the weight from the depressed land led to uplift or rebound of the land and the return flow of mantle material back under the deglaciated area.

   a. Cirque glacier
   b. Bergschrund
   c. Post-glacial rebound
   d. Glacial lake

42. An _____ is the result of a sudden release of energy in the Earth's crust that creates seismic waves. They are recorded with a seismometer or the related and mostly obsolete Richter magnitude, with a magnitude 3 or lower _____ being mostly imperceptible and magnitude 7 causing serious damage over large areas.
   a. AASHTO Soil Classification System
   b. Earthquake
   c. AL 129-1
   d. AL 333

43. The _____ at any point on the Earth is the angle between the local magnetic field -- the direction the north end of a compass points -- and true north. The declination is positive when the magnetic north is east of true north. The term magnetic variation is equivalent, and is more often used in aeronautical and other forms of navigation.
   a. 1703 Genroku earthquake
   b. 1700 Cascadia earthquake
   c. 1509 Istanbul earthquake
   d. Magnetic declination

44. A _____ is a scientific instrument used to measure the strength and/or direction of the magnetic field in the vicinity of the instrument. Magnetism varies from place to place and differences in Earth's magnetic field (the magnetosphere) can be caused by the differing nature of rocks and the interaction between charged particles from the Sun and the magnetosphere of a planet. _____s are often a frequent component instrument on spacecraft that explore planets.
   a. 1700 Cascadia earthquake
   b. 1509 Istanbul earthquake
   c. 1703 Genroku earthquake
   d. Magnetometer

45. _____ is the study of the record of the Earth's magnetic field preserved in various magnetic minerals through time. The study of _____ has demonstrated that the Earth's magnetic field varies substantially in both orientation and intensity through time. <

a. Stage
b. Radiometric dating
c. Lichenometry
d. Paleomagnetism

Chapter 11. The Seafloor

1. _____ are pillow-shaped structures sometimes seen in lavas and are attributed to the congealment of lava under water, or subaqeous extrusion. A pillow structure in certain extrusive igneous rock is characterized by discontinuous pillow-shaped masses, commonly up to 1 metre in diameter. _____ commonly occur at Constructive plate boundaries, forming part of a mid-ocean ridge.
   a. Metamorphic reaction
   b. Pillow lava
   c. Corrasion
   d. Compression

2. _____ is molten rock expelled by a volcano during eruption. When first expelled from a volcanic vent, it is a liquid at temperatures from 700 >°C to 1,200 >°C (1,300 >°F to 2,200 >°F.) Although _____ is quite viscous, with about 100,000 times the viscosity of water, it can flow great distances before cooling and solidifying, because of both its thixotropic and shear thinning properties.
   a. Pumice
   b. Cinder
   c. Lava
   d. Pyroclastic flow

3. _____ is a common extrusive volcanic rock. It is usually grey to black and fine-grained due to rapid cooling of lava at the surface of a planet. It may be porphyritic containing larger crystals in a fine matrix, or vesicular, or frothy scoria.
   a. 1703 Genroku earthquake
   b. 1700 Cascadia earthquake
   c. 1509 Istanbul earthquake
   d. Basalt

4. The _____ is the layer of igneous, sedimentary, and metamorphic rocks which form the continents and the areas of shallow seabed close to their shores, known as continental shelves. This layer is sometimes called sial due to more felsic, or granitic, bulk composition, which lies in contrast to the oceanic crust, called sima due to its mafic, or basaltic rock. (Based on the change in velocity of seismic waves, it is believed that at a certain depth sial becomes close in its physical properties to sima.
   a. Plate tectonics
   b. Divergent boundary
   c. Mirovia
   d. Continental crust

5. _____ refers to a large group of dark, coarse-grained, intrusive igneous rocks chemically equivalent to basalt. The rocks are plutonic, formed when molten magma is trapped beneath the Earth's surface and cools into a crystalline mass.

   The vast majority of the Earth's surface is underlain by _____ within the oceanic crust, produced by basalt magmatism at mid-ocean ridges.

   a. Gabbro
   b. 1703 Genroku earthquake
   c. 1700 Cascadia earthquake
   d. 1509 Istanbul earthquake

6. _____ is a term used in geology to refer to the state of gravitational equilibrium between the earth's lithosphere and asthenosphere such that the tectonic plates 'float' at an elevation which depends on their thickness and density. This concept is invoked to explain how different topographic heights can exist at the Earth's surface. When a certain area of lithosphere reaches the state of _____, it is said to be in isostatic equilibrium.
   a. Isograd
   b. Orientation Tensor
   c. Economic geology
   d. Isostasy

7. The _____ is a mid-ocean ridge, a divergent tectonic plate boundary located along the floor of the Atlantic Ocean, and the longest mountain range in the world. It separates the Eurasian Plate and North American Plate in the North Atlantic, and the African Plate from the South American Plate in the South Atlantic. The MAR extends from a junction with the Gakkel Ridge (Mid-Arctic Ridge) northeast of Greenland southward to the Bouvet Triple Junction in the South Atlantic.

| a. 1700 Cascadia earthquake | b. Mid-Atlantic Ridge |
| c. 1509 Istanbul earthquake | d. 1703 Genroku earthquake |

8. The _____, usually referred to as the Moho, is the boundary between the Earth's crust and the mantle. The Moho serves to separate both oceanic crust and continental crust from underlying mantle. The Moho mostly lies entirely within the lithosphere; only beneath mid-ocean ridges does it define the lithosphere-asthenosphere boundary.

| a. Panthalassa | b. Copperbelt Province |
| c. Gorda Ridge | d. Mohorovià iÄ‡ discontinuity |

9. _____ is the part of Earth's lithosphere that surfaces in the ocean basins. _____ is primarily composed of mafic rocks, or sima. It is thinner than continental crust, or sial, generally less than 10 kilometers thick, however it is denser, having a mean density of about 3.3 grams per cubic centimeter.

| a. AL 129-1 | b. AASHTO Soil Classification System |
| c. AL 333 | d. Oceanic crust |

10. The lithosphere is broken up into what are called _____. In the case of Earth, there are eight major and many minor plates The lithospheric plates ride on the asthenosphere. These plates move in relation to one another at one of three types of plate boundaries: convergent, or collisional boundaries; divergent boundaries, also called spreading centers; and transform boundaries.

| a. Subduction | b. Lithosphere |
| c. Tectonic plates | d. Juan de Fuca Ridge |

11. In geology, _____ is the process that takes place at convergent boundaries by which one tectonic plate moves under another tectonic plate, sinking into the Earth's mantle, as the plates converge. A _____ zone is an area on Earth where two tectonic plates move towards one another and _____ occurs. Rates of _____ are typically measured in centimeters per year, with the average rate of convergence being approximately 2 to 8 centimeters per year (about the rate a fingernail grows.)

| a. Forearc | b. Panthalassa |
| c. Subduction | d. Thrust fault |

12. The _____ is the zone of the ocean floor that separates the thin oceanic crust from thick continental crust. _____s constitute about 28% of the oceanic area.

The transition from continental to oceanic crust commonly occurs within the outer part of the margin, called continental rise.

| a. Longshore drift | b. 1509 Istanbul earthquake |
| c. Cuspate forelands | d. Continental margin |

13. The term _____ can be used to describe both the conduct of a survey for geological purposes and an institution holding geological information.

A _____ is the systematic investigation of the subsurface of a given piece of ground for the purpose of creating a geological map or model. A _____ employs techniques from the traditional walk-over survey, studying outcrops and landforms, to intrusive methods, such as hand augering and machine driven boreholes, to the use of geophysical techniques and remote sensing methods, such as aerial photography and satellite imagery.

a. Leaverite
b. Paralithic
c. Reading Prong
d. Geological Survey

14. An _____ is the result of a sudden release of energy in the Earth's crust that creates seismic waves. They are recorded with a seismometer or the related and mostly obsolete Richter magnitude, with a magnitude 3 or lower _____ being mostly imperceptible and magnitude 7 causing serious damage over large areas.
   a. AL 333
   b. AL 129-1
   c. AASHTO Soil Classification System
   d. Earthquake

15. A _____ or dyke in geology is a type of sheet intrusion referring to any geologic body that cuts discordantly across

- planar wall rock structures, such as bedding or foliation
- massive rock formations, like igneous/magmatic intrusions and salt diapirs.

They can therefore be either intrusive or sedimentary in origin.

An intrusive _____ is an igneous body with a very high aspect ratio, which means that its thickness is usually much smaller than the other two dimensions. Thickness can vary from sub-centimeter scale to many meters and the lateral dimensions can extend over many kilometers. A _____ is an intrusion into an opening cross-cutting fissure, shouldering aside other pre-existing layers or bodies of rock; this implies that a _____ is always younger than the rocks that contain it.

   a. Dike
   b. Schmidt hammer
   c. Fabric
   d. Haloclasty

16. In geology, a _____ or _____ line is a planar fracture in rock in which the rock on one side of the fracture has moved with respect to the rock on the other side. Large _____s within the Earth's crust are the result of differential or shear motion and active _____ zones are the causal locations of most earthquakes. Earthquakes are caused by energy release during rapid slippage along a _____.
   a. Fault
   b. Cohesion
   c. Geothermal
   d. Combe

17. _____ is molten rock that is found beneath the surface of the Earth, and may also exist on other terrestrial planets. Besides molten rock, _____ may also contain suspended crystals and gas bubbles. _____ often collects in a _____ chamber inside a volcano. _____ is capable of intrusion into adjacent rocks, extrusion onto the surface as lava, and explosive ejection as tephra to form pyroclastic rock.
   a. Magma
   b. Metavolcanic rock
   c. Rock cycle
   d. Vesicular texture

18. An _____ is a section of the Earth's oceanic crust and the underlying upper mantle that has been uplifted or emplaced to be exposed within continental crustal rocks. Ophio is Greek for 'snake', lite means 'stone' from the Greek lithos.

The term _____ was originally used by Alexandre Brongniart for an assemblage of green rocks (serpentine, diabase) in the Alps; Steinmann (1927) later modified its use to include serpentine, pillow lava, and chert ('Steinmann's trinity'), again based on occurrences in the Alps.

a. AL 333
b. AL 129-1
c. AASHTO Soil Classification System
d. Ophiolite

19. A _____ in geology is an intrusive igneous rock body that crystallized from a magma slowly cooling below the surface of the Earth. _____s include batholiths, dikes, sills, laccoliths, lopoliths, and other igneous bodies. In practice, '_____' usually refers to a distinctive mass of igneous rock, typically kilometers in dimension, without a tabular shape like those of dikes and sills.
    a. Pluton
    b. Metavolcanic rock
    c. Metamorphic rock
    d. Petrology

20. The _____ is a continental transform fault that runs a length of roughly 800 miles (1,300 km) through California in the United States. The fault's motion is right-lateral strike-slip (horizontal motion.) It forms the tectonic boundary between the Pacific Plate and the North American Plate.
    a. 1703 Genroku earthquake
    b. 1509 Istanbul earthquake
    c. San Andreas fault
    d. 1700 Cascadia earthquake

21. A _____ is a type of fault in which rocks of lower stratigraphic position are pushed up and over higher strata. They are often recognized because they place older rocks above younger. _____s are the result of compressional forces.
    a. Motagua Fault
    b. Supercontinent cycle
    c. Panthalassa
    d. Thrust fault

22. A _____ is a large emplacement of igneous intrusive rock that forms from cooled magma deep in the Earth's crust. they are almost always made mostly of felsic or intermediate rock-types, such as granite, quartz monzonite, or diorite

    Although they may appear uniform, _____s are in fact structures with complex histories and compositions.

    a. Tuff
    b. Batholith
    c. Scoria
    d. Great Dyke

23. In materials science, _____ is a change in the shape or size of an object due to an applied force. This can be a result of tensile (pulling) forces, compressive (pushing) forces, shear, bending or torsion (twisting.) _____ is often described as strain.
    a. Stack
    b. Combe
    c. Melange
    d. Deformation

24. A _____ is an opening in a planet's surface or crust, which allows hot, molten rock, ash, and gases to escape from below the surface. Volcanic activity involving the extrusion of rock tends to form mountains or features like mountains over a period of time.
    a. 1509 Istanbul earthquake
    b. 1703 Genroku earthquake
    c. Volcano
    d. 1700 Cascadia earthquake

25. The _____ is the extended perimeter of each continent and associated coastal plain, and was part of the continent during the glacial periods, but is undersea during interglacial periods such as the current epoch by relatively shallow seas (known as shelf seas) and gulfs.

The continental rise is below the slope, but landward of the abyssal plains. Its gradient is intermediate between the slope and the shelf, on the order of 0.5-1°.

a. Continental slope
c. Mud

b. Continental shelf
d. Surface runoff

26. A _____ is a large, slow-moving mass of ice, formed from compacted layers of snow, that slowly deforms and flows in response to gravity and high pressure.

_____ ice is the largest reservoir of fresh water on Earth, and second only to oceans as the largest reservoir of total water.

a. Pacific Decadal Oscillation
c. Little Ice Age

b. Greenhouse gases
d. Glacier

27. A _____ is a dense, coarse-grained igneous rock, consisting mostly of the minerals olivine and pyroxene. _____ is ultramafic, as the rock contains less than 45% silica. It is high in magnesium, reflecting the high proportions of magnesium-rich olivine, with appreciable iron.

_____ is the dominant rock of the upper part of the Earth's mantle. The compositions of _____ nodules found in certain basalts and diamond pipes (kimberlites) are of special interest, because they provide samples of the Earth's Mantle roots of continents brought up from depths from about 30 km or so to depths at least as great as about 200 km.

a. 1700 Cascadia earthquake
c. 1509 Istanbul earthquake

b. 1703 Genroku earthquake
d. Peridotite

28. The shelf usually ends at a point of decreasing slope (called the shelf break.) The sea floor below the break is the continental slope. Below the slope is the _____, which finally merges into the deep ocean floor, the abyssal plain.

a. Continental slope
c. Thermal pollution

b. Continental shelf
d. Continental rise

29. The shelf usually ends at a point of decreasing slope (called the shelf break.) The sea floor below the break is the _____. Below the slope is the continental rise, which finally merges into the deep ocean floor, the abyssal plain.

a. Continental shelf
c. Thermal pollution

b. Surface runoff
d. Continental slope

30. _____ is the geological process by which material is added to a landform or land mass. Fluids such as wind and water, as well as sediment gravity flows, transport previously eroded sediment, which, at the loss of enough kinetic energy in the fluid, is deposited, building up layers of sediment.

_____ occurs when the forces responsible for sediment transportation are no longer sufficient to overcome the forces of particle weight and friction, which resist motion.

Chapter 11. The Seafloor

a. Hydraulic action
b. Hydrothermal circulation
c. Stoping
d. Deposition

31. In geology, a _____ is one characterized by a systematic change in grain or clast size from the base of the bed to the top. Most commonly this takes the form of normal grading, with coarser sediments at the base, which grade upward into progressively finer ones. Normally _____s generally represent depositional environments which decrease in transport energy as time passes, but also form during rapid depositional events.

a. 1703 Genroku earthquake
b. 1509 Istanbul earthquake
c. 1700 Cascadia earthquake
d. Graded bed

32. _____ is any particulate matter that can be transported by fluid flow, and which eventually is deposited.

They are most often transported by water (fluvial processes) transported by wind (aeolian processes) and glaciers. Beach sands and river channel deposits are examples of fluvial transport and deposition, though _____ also often settles out of slow-moving or standing water in lakes and oceans.

a. Bovey Beds
b. Salt glacier
c. Quick clay
d. Sediment

33. _____ is the removal of solids (sediment, soil, rock and other particles) in the natural environment. It usually occurs due to transport by wind, water, or ice; by down-slope creep of soil and other material under the force of gravity; or by living organisms, such as burrowing animals, in the case of bioerosion.

_____ is distinguished from weathering, which is the process of chemical or physical breakdown of the minerals in the rocks, although the two processes may occur concurrently.

a. Erosion
b. AASHTO Soil Classification System
c. AL 333
d. AL 129-1

34. The _____ is an oceanic trench in the eastern Pacific Ocean, about 160 kilometers off the coast of Peru and Chile. It reaches a maximum depth of 8,065 meters below sea level in the Richards Deep and is approximately 5,900 kilometers long; its mean width is 64 kilometers and it covers an expanse of some 590,000 square kilometers

The trench is a result of the eastern edge of the Nazca Plate being subducted under the South American Plate.

a. Peru-Chile Trench
b. 1703 Genroku earthquake
c. 1509 Istanbul earthquake
d. 1700 Cascadia earthquake

35. A _____ is a steep-sided valley on the sea floor of the continental slope. Many _____s are found as extensions to large rivers; however there are many that have no such association. Canyons cutting the continental slopes have been found at depths greater than 2 km below sea level.

a. 1509 Istanbul earthquake
b. 1700 Cascadia earthquake
c. Submarine canyon
d. 1703 Genroku earthquake

Chapter 11. The Seafloor

36. _____ are flat or very gently sloping areas of the deep ocean basin floor. They are among the Earth's flattest and smoothest regions and the least explored. _____ cover approximately 40% of the ocean floor and reach depths between 2,200 and 5,500 m (7,200 and 18,000 ft.)
   a. Upwelling
   b. Overland flow
   c. Abyssal plains
   d. Eutrophication

37. The _____ are hemispheric-scale long but narrow topographic depressions of the sea floor. They are also the deepest parts of the ocean floor.

_____ define one of the most important natural boundaries on the Earth's solid surface, thatlie between two lithospheric plates. There are three types of lithospheric plate boundaries: divergent (where lithosphere and oceanic crust is created at mid-ocean ridges), convergent (where one lithospheric plate sinks beneath another and returns to the mantle), and transform (where two lithospheric plates slide past each other).

   a. AASHTO Soil Classification System
   b. AL 129-1
   c. AL 333
   d. Oceanic trenches

38. A _____ is a deep active seismic area in a subduction zone. Differential motion along the zone produces deep-seated earthquakes, the foci of which may be as deep as about 700 kilometres (435 miles.) They develop beneath volcanic island arcs and continental margins above active subduction zones.
   a. Pit crater
   b. Pumice
   c. Lava
   d. Wadati-Benioff zone

39. The _____ is a cosmological model of the initial conditions and subsequent development of the universe. It is supported by the most comprehensive and accurate explanations from current scientific evidence and observation. As used by cosmologists, the term _____ generally refers to the idea that the universe has expanded from a primordial hot and dense initial condition at some finite time in the past, and continues to expand to this day.
   a. 1509 Istanbul earthquake
   b. 1703 Genroku earthquake
   c. 1700 Cascadia earthquake
   d. Big Bang

40. The _____ is the deepest part of the world's oceans, and the deepest location on the surface of the Earth's crust. It has a maximum depth of about 10,911 meters (35,798 feet; 6.78 miles), and is located in the western North Pacific Ocean, to the east and south of the Mariana Islands, near Guam.

Part of the Izu-Bonin-Mariana Arc system, the trench forms the boundary between two tectonic plates, where the Pacific Plate is subducted beneath the small Mariana Plate.

   a. Mariana Trench
   b. 1703 Genroku earthquake
   c. 1700 Cascadia earthquake
   d. 1509 Istanbul earthquake

41. A _____ or sea vent, is a type of hydrothermal vent found on the ocean floor. They are formed in fields hundreds of meters wide when superheated water from below Earth's crust comes through the ocean floor. This water is rich in dissolved minerals from the crust, most notably sulfides.
   a. 1509 Istanbul earthquake
   b. Black smoker
   c. 1700 Cascadia earthquake
   d. 1703 Genroku earthquake

Chapter 11. The Seafloor

42. The _____ is a mid-oceanic ridge, a divergent tectonic plate boundary located along the floor of the Pacific Ocean. It separates the Pacific Plate to the west from (north to south) the North American Plate, the Rivera Plate, the Cocos Plate, the Nazca Plate, and the Antarctic Plate. It runs from an undefined point near Antarctica in the south northward to its termination at the northern end of the Gulf of California in the Salton Sea basin in southern California.
   a. Azores-Gibraltar Transform Fault
   b. Elastic rebound theory
   c. Obduction
   d. East Pacific Rise

43. _____ circulation in its most general sense is the circulation of hot water; 'hydros' in the Greek meaning water and 'thermos' meaning heat. _____ circulation occurs most often in the vicinity of sources of heat within the Earth's crust. This generally occurs near volcanic activity, but can occur in the deep crust related to the intrusion of granite, or as the result of orogeny or metamorphism.
   a. Hydrothermal
   b. Wave pounding
   c. Transgression
   d. Headward erosion

44. A _____ is a fissure in a planet's surface from which geothermally heated water issues. they are commonly found near volcanically active places, areas where tectonic plates are moving apart, ocean basins, and hotspots.

   They are locally very common because the earth is both geologically active and has large amounts of water on its surface and within its crust. Common land types include hot springs, fumaroles and geysers. The most famous _____ system on land is probably within Yellowstone National Park in the United States.

   a. Hydrothermal vent
   b. 1509 Istanbul earthquake
   c. 1703 Genroku earthquake
   d. 1700 Cascadia earthquake

45. The _____ is a tectonic spreading center located off the coasts of the state of Washington in the United States and the province of British Columbia in Canada. It runs northward from a transform boundary, the Blanco Fracture Zone, to a triple junction with the Nootka Fault and the Sovanco Fracture Zone. To its east is the Juan de Fuca Plate, which together with the Gorda Plate to its south and the Explorer Plate to its north, is what remains of the once-vast Farallon Plate which has been largely subducted under the North American Plate.
   a. Tectonic plates
   b. Thrust fault
   c. Gorda Ridge
   d. Juan de Fuca Ridge

46. _____ are natural conduits through which lava travels beneath the surface of a lava flow, expelled by a volcano during an eruption. They can be actively draining lava from a source, or can be extinct, meaning the lava flow has ceased and the rock has cooled and left a long, cave-like channel.

   _____ are formed when an active low-viscosity lava flow develops a continuous and hard crust, which thickens and forms a roof above the still-flowing lava stream.

   a. 1703 Genroku earthquake
   b. 1509 Istanbul earthquake
   c. 1700 Cascadia earthquake
   d. Lava tubes

47. The _____ is a divergent tectonic plate boundary located on the seafloor of the South Pacific Ocean, separating the Pacific Plate from the Antarctic Plate. It is regarded as the southern section of the East Pacific Rise in some usages, generally south of the Challenger Fracture Zone and stretching to the Macquarie Triple Junction south of New Zealand.

Stretching north-west from the _____ is a long line of seamounts called the Louisville seamount chain which is thought to have formed from the Pacific Plate sliding over a long-lived center of upwelling magma called the Louisville hotspot.

a. Pacific-Antarctic Ridge
c. Pacific-Kula Ridge
b. Pacific-Farallon Ridge
d. Kula-Farallon Ridge

48. In geology, a _____ is a place where the Earth's crust and lithosphere are being pulled apart and is an example of extensional tectonics.

Typical _____ features are a central linear downdropped fault segment, called a graben, with parallel normal faulting and _____-flank uplifts on either side forming a _____ valley, where the _____ remains above sea level. The axis of the _____ area commonly contains volcanic rocks and active volcanism is a part of many, but not all active _____ systems.

a. 1509 Istanbul earthquake
c. Rift
b. 1700 Cascadia earthquake
d. 1703 Genroku earthquake

49. _____ are a distinctive type of rock often found in primordial sedimentary rocks. The structures consist of repeated thin layers of iron oxides, either magnetite or hematite, alternating with bands of iron-poor shale and chert. Some of the oldest known rock formations, formed around three thousand million years before present, include banded iron layers, and the banded layers are a common feature in sediments for much of the Earth's early history.

a. Sandstone
c. Diatomaceous earth
b. Coquina
d. Banded Iron Formations

50. A _____ or sandstorm is a meteorological phenomenon common in arid and semi-arid regions and arises when a gust front passes or when the wind force exceeds the threshold value where loose sand and dust are removed from the dry surface. Particles are transported by saltation and suspension, causing soil erosion from one place and deposition in another. The Sahara and drylands around the Arabian peninsula are the main source of airborne dust, with some contributions from Iran, Pakistan and India into the Arabian Sea, and China's storms deposit dust in the Pacific.

a. 1700 Cascadia earthquake
c. 1703 Genroku earthquake
b. 1509 Istanbul earthquake
d. Dust storm

51. In geology the term _____ refers to a fracture in rock where there has been no lateral movement in the plane of the fracture (up, down or sideways) of one side relative to the other. This makes it different from a fault which is defined as a fracture in rock where one side slides laterally past to the other. _____s normally have a regular spacing related to either the mechanical properties of the individual rock or the thickness of the layer involved.

a. 1509 Istanbul earthquake
c. Joint
b. 1703 Genroku earthquake
d. 1700 Cascadia earthquake

52. _____, partially synonymous with microcontinents, are fragments of continents thought to have been broken off from the main continental mass forming distinct islands, possibly several hundred kilometers from their place of origin. All continents are fragments; the terms 'continental fragment' and 'microcontinent' are restricted to those smaller than Sahul (Australia-New Guinea.) Other than perhaps Zealandia, they are not known to contain a craton or fragment of a craton.

Chapter 11. The Seafloor

a. 1703 Genroku earthquake
b. 1509 Istanbul earthquake
c. 1700 Cascadia earthquake
d. Continental crustal fragments

53. A _____ is a mountain rising from the ocean seafloor that does not reach to the water's surface (sea level), and thus is not an island. These are typically formed from extinct volcanoes, that rise abruptly and are usually found rising from a seafloor of 1,000-4,000 meters depth. They are defined by oceanographers as independent features that rise to at least 1,000 meters above the seafloor.
a. 1700 Cascadia earthquake
b. 1509 Istanbul earthquake
c. 1703 Genroku earthquake
d. Seamount

54. A _____ or transform boundary is a fault which runs along the boundary of a tectonic plate. The relative motion of such plates is horizontal in either sinistral or dextral direction. Typically, some vertical motion may also exist, but the principal vectors in a _____ are oriented horizontally.
a. Syncline
b. Crenulation
c. Transform fault
d. Strike and dip

55. _____ is an ocean ridge in the southern Atlantic Ocean, extending for thousands of miles, off the coast of southwest Africa. Both it and the Rio Grande Rise originated from hotspot volcanism now occurring at the islands of Tristan da Cunha (the Tristan hotspot), 300 kilometres east of the crest of the Mid-Atlantic Ridge. The eastern section of the ridge is thought to have been created in the Middle Cretaceous period, between 120 and 80 million years ago.
a. 1703 Genroku earthquake
b. 1700 Cascadia earthquake
c. Walvis Ridge
d. 1509 Istanbul earthquake

56. Two important classifications of weathering processes exist -- physical and _____. Mechanical or physical weathering involves the breakdown of rocks and soils through direct contact with atmospheric conditions, such as heat, water, ice and pressure. The second classification, _____, involves the direct effect of atmospheric chemicals or biologically produced chemicals (also known as biological weathering) in the breakdown of rocks, soils and minerals.
a. 1509 Istanbul earthquake
b. Chemical weathering
c. Physical weathering
d. Frost disintegration

57. _____ is the decomposition of Earth rocks, soils and their minerals through direct contact with the planet's atmosphere. _____ occurs in situ, or 'with no movement', and thus should not be confused with erosion, which involves the movement of rocks and minerals by agents such as water, ice, wind and gravity.

Two important classifications of _____ processes exist -- physical and chemical _____.

a. Frost disintegration
b. 1509 Istanbul earthquake
c. Physical weathering
d. Weathering

58. _____ refers to a sediment, sedimentary rock, or soil type which is formed from or contains a high proportion of calcium carbonate in the form of calcite or aragonite.

It can also be used as an adjectival term applied to anatomical structures which are made of calcium carbonate in animals such as gastropods, when referring to such structures as the operculum, the clausilium, and the love dart.

130   Chapter 11. The Seafloor

_____ sediments are usually deposited in shallow water near land, since the carbonate is precipitated by marine organisms that need land-derived nutrients.

a. 1703 Genroku earthquake
c. 1509 Istanbul earthquake
b. 1700 Cascadia earthquake
d. Calcareous

59. _____ is the transport of various material by ice. Various objects deposited on ice may eventually become embedded in the ice. When the ice melts after a certain amount of drifting, these objects are deposited onto the bottom of the water body, e.g., onto a river bed or an ocean floor.

a. AASHTO Soil Classification System
c. AL 333
b. AL 129-1
d. Ice rafting

60. _____ are rock concretions on the sea bottom formed of concentric layers of iron and manganese hydroxides around a core. The core may be microscopically small and is sometimes completely transformed into manganese minerals by crystallization. When visible to the naked eye, it can be a small test of a microfossil, a phosphatized shark tooth, basalt debris or even fragments of earlier nodules.

a. 1703 Genroku earthquake
c. 1700 Cascadia earthquake
b. 1509 Istanbul earthquake
d. Polymetallic nodules

61. _____ are those that accumulate in the abyssal plain of the deep ocean, far away from terrestrial sources that provide terrigenous sediments; the latter are primarily limited to the continental shelf, and deposited by rivers. _____ that are mixed with terrigenous sediments are known as hemipelagic.

There are three main types of _____:

1.) Siliceous oozes
2.) Calcareous oozes
3.) Red clays

a. Mudstone
c. Shale
b. Sedimentary deposits
d. Pelagic sediments

62. _____s (also radiolaria) are amoeboid protozoa that produce intricate mineral skeletons, typically with a central capsule dividing the cell into inner and outer portions, called endoplasm and ectoplasm. They are found as zooplankton throughout the ocean, and their skeletal remains cover large portions of the ocean bottom as _____ ooze. Due to their rapid turn-over of species, they represent an important diagnostic fossil found from the Cambrian onwards.

a. 1700 Cascadia earthquake
c. 1703 Genroku earthquake
b. 1509 Istanbul earthquake
d. Radiolarian

63. _____ is composed of the debris of plankton with silica shells, such as diatoms and radiolaria. This ooze is limited to areas with high biological productivity, such as the polar oceans, and upwelling zones near the equator. The least common type of sediment, it covers only 15% of the ocean floor.

a. Teilzone
c. Transition zone
b. Siliceous ooze
d. Palynomorph

64. _____ is a naturally occurring material composed primarily of fine-grained minerals, which show plasticity through a variable range of water content, and which can be hardened when dried and/or fired. _____ deposits are mostly composed of _____ minerals (phyllosilicate minerals), minerals which impart plasticity and harden when fired and/or dried, and variable amounts of water trapped in the mineral structure by polar attraction. Organic materials which do not impart plasticity may also be a part of _____ deposits.
   a. 1703 Genroku earthquake
   b. 1700 Cascadia earthquake
   c. 1509 Istanbul earthquake
   d. Clay

65. A _____ in petrology or mineralogy is a secondary structure, generally spherical or irregularly rounded in shape. They are typically solid replacement bodies of chert or iron oxides formed during diagenesis of a sedimentary rock. They may be hollow as geodes or vugs or filled with crystals and intricate geometric shrinkage patterns as in septarian _____s.
   a. Heavy metal
   b. Stratification
   c. Tarn
   d. Nodule

66. In organic chemistry, a _____ is an organic compound consisting entirely of hydrogen and carbon. With relation to chemical terminology, aromatic _____s or arenes, alkanes, alkenes and alkyne-based compounds composed entirely of carbon or hydrogen are referred to as 'pure' _____s, whereas other _____s with bonded compounds or impurities of sulfur or nitrogen, are referred to as 'impure', and remain somewhat erroneously referred to as _____s.

_____s are referred to as consisting of a 'backbone' or 'skeleton' composed entirely of carbon and hydrogen and other bonded compounds, and have a functional group that generally facilitates combustion.

   a. 1703 Genroku earthquake
   b. 1509 Istanbul earthquake
   c. 1700 Cascadia earthquake
   d. Hydrocarbon

67. _____ is a sedimentary rock composed largely of the mineral calcite (calcium carbonate: $CaCO_3$.) The deposition of _____ strata is often a by-product and indicator of biological activity in the geologic record. Calcium (along with nitrogen, phosphorus, and potassium) is a key mineral to plant nutrition: soils overlying _____ bedrock tend to be pre-fertilized with calcium.
   a. 1700 Cascadia earthquake
   b. 1703 Genroku earthquake
   c. 1509 Istanbul earthquake
   d. Limestone

68. Under the law of the sea, an _____ is a seazone over which a state has special rights over the exploration and use of marine resources. It stretches from the edge of the state's territorial sea out to 200 nautical miles from its coast. In casual use, the term may include the territorial sea and even the continental shelf beyond the 200 mile limit.
   a. AL 129-1
   b. Exclusive Economic Zone
   c. AL 333
   d. AASHTO Soil Classification System

69. _____ is a gas consisting primarily of methane. It is found associated with fossil fuels, in coal beds, as methane clathrates, and is created by methanogenic organisms in marshes, bogs, and landfills. It is an important fuel source, a major feedstock for fertilizers, and a potent greenhouse gas.
   a. Natural gas
   b. 1700 Cascadia earthquake
   c. 1509 Istanbul earthquake
   d. 1703 Genroku earthquake

Chapter 11. The Seafloor

70. _____ is a term used in inorganic chemistry and organic chemistry to indicate that a substance contains water. The chemical state of the water varies widely between _____s, some of which were so labeled before their chemical structure was understood.

In organic chemistry, a _____ is a compound formed by the addition of water or its elements to a host molecule.

   a. 1703 Genroku earthquake   b. 1509 Istanbul earthquake
   c. Hydrate   d. 1700 Cascadia earthquake

71. _____ are crystalline water-based solids physically resembling ice, in which small non polar molecules (typically gases) are trapped inside 'cages' of hydrogen bonded water molecules. In other words, _____ are clathrate compounds in which the host molecule is water and the guest molecule is typically a gas.

   a. 1703 Genroku earthquake   b. Clathrate hydrates
   c. 1700 Cascadia earthquake   d. 1509 Istanbul earthquake

72. An _____ is an oceanographic phenomenon that involves wind-driven motion of dense, cooler, and usually nutrient-rich water towards the ocean surface, replacing the warmer, usually nutrient-depleted surface water. There are at least five types of _____: coastal _____, large-scale wind-driven _____ in the ocean interior, _____ associated with eddies, topographically-associated _____, and broad-diffusive _____ in the ocean interior.

Coastal _____ is the best known type of _____, and the most closely related to human activities as it supports some of the most productive fisheries in the world, like small pelagics (sardines, anchovies, etc.).

   a. Overland flow   b. Eutrophication
   c. Intertidal   d. Upwelling

73. _____ is the process of accumulation and sinking of higher density material beneath lower density material, such as cold or saline water beneath warmer or fresher water or cold air beneath warm air. It is the sinking limb of a convection cell. Upwelling is the opposite process and together these two forces are responsible in the oceans for the thermohaline circulation.

   a. Downwelling   b. 1700 Cascadia earthquake
   c. 1703 Genroku earthquake   d. 1509 Istanbul earthquake

74. _____ or phosphorite is a general description applied to several kinds of rock which contain significant concentrations of phosphate minerals, which are minerals that contain the phosphate ion in their chemical structure.

Many kinds of rock contain mineral components containing phosphate or other phosphorus compounds in small amounts. However, rocks which contain phosphate in quantity and concentration which are economic to mine as ore for their phosphate content are not particularly common.

   a. Slyne-Erris Trough   b. Skarn
   c. Diapir   d. Phosphate rock

Chapter 12. Plate Tectonics: A Unifying Theory

1. The _____ is a tectonic plate covering the continent of South America and extending eastward to the Mid-Atlantic Ridge.

The easterly side is a divergent boundary with the African Plate forming the southern part of the Mid-Atlantic Ridge. The southerly side is a complex boundary with the Antarctic Plate and the Scotia Plate.

- a. Sunda Plate
- b. South American plate
- c. Somali Plate
- d. Kermadec Plate

2. _____ is the movement of the Earth's continents relative to each other. The hypothesis that continents 'drift' was first put forward by Abraham Ortelius in 1596 and was fully developed by Alfred Wegener in 1912. However, it was not until the development of the theory of plate tectonics in the 1960s, that a sufficient geological explanation of that movement was found.
- a. Mirovia
- b. Subduction
- c. Nappe
- d. Continental drift

3. In geology, _____ is transported rock debris overlying the solid bedrock. The term is also sometimes refers to organic debris so-transported. In the largest sense, it refers to the material left behind by retreating continental glaciers.
- a. Geostrophic current
- b. Detritus
- c. Contact metamorphism
- d. Drift

4. An _____ is the result of a sudden release of energy in the Earth's crust that creates seismic waves. They are recorded with a seismometer or the related and mostly obsolete Richter magnitude, with a magnitude 3 or lower _____ being mostly imperceptible and magnitude 7 causing serious damage over large areas.
- a. AL 333
- b. AASHTO Soil Classification System
- c. AL 129-1
- d. Earthquake

5. A _____ is a large, slow-moving mass of ice, formed from compacted layers of snow, that slowly deforms and flows in response to gravity and high pressure.

_____ ice is the largest reservoir of fresh water on Earth, and second only to oceans as the largest reservoir of total water.

- a. Greenhouse gases
- b. Glacier
- c. Pacific Decadal Oscillation
- d. Little Ice Age

6. _____ describes the large scale motions of Earth's lithosphere. The theory encompasses the older concepts of continental drift, developed during the first decades of the 20th century by Alfred Wegener, and seafloor spreading, understood during the 1960s.

The outermost part of the Earth's interior is made up of two layers: the lithosphere and the asthenosphere.

- a. Supercontinent cycle
- b. Plate tectonics
- c. Copperbelt Province
- d. Lithosphere

7. The _____ is the zone of the ocean floor that separates the thin oceanic crust from thick continental crust. _____ s constitute about 28% of the oceanic area.

The transition from continental to oceanic crust commonly occurs within the outer part of the margin, called continental rise.

a. Continental margin
b. 1509 Istanbul earthquake
c. Cuspate forelands
d. Longshore drift

8. The _____ is the extended perimeter of each continent and associated coastal plain, and was part of the continent during the glacial periods, but is undersea during interglacial periods such as the current epoch by relatively shallow seas (known as shelf seas) and gulfs.

The continental rise is below the slope, but landward of the abyssal plains. Its gradient is intermediate between the slope and the shelf, on the order of 0.5-1°.

a. Continental slope
b. Surface runoff
c. Continental shelf
d. Mud

9. _____ is the largest and best-known genus of the extinct order of seed ferns known as Glossopteridales (or in some cases as Arberiales or Dictyopteridiales.)

The Glossopteridales arose around the beginning of the Permian on the great southern continent of Gondwana. These plants went on to become the dominant elements of the southern flora through the rest of the Permian but disappeared in almost all places at the end of the Permian.

a. 1509 Istanbul earthquake
b. Pteridospermatophyta
c. Petrified wood
d. Glossopteris

10. _____, originally Gondwanaland, is the name given to a southern precursor-supercontinent and then as a remnant separated from Laurasia 180-200 million years ago during the breakup of the Pangaea supercontinent that existed about 500 to 200 Ma ago into two large segments. While the corresponding northern hemisphere continent Laurasia moved further north, the nearly equal in area _____ included most of the landmasses in today's southern hemisphere, including Antarctica, South America, Africa, Madagascar, Australia-New Guinea, and New Zealand, as well as Arabia and the Indian subcontinent, which have now moved into the Northern Hemisphere.

a. Laurasia
b. Gondwana
c. 1700 Cascadia earthquake
d. 1509 Istanbul earthquake

11. The _____ is a mid-ocean ridge, a divergent tectonic plate boundary located along the floor of the Atlantic Ocean, and the longest mountain range in the world. It separates the Eurasian Plate and North American Plate in the North Atlantic, and the African Plate from the South American Plate in the South Atlantic. The MAR extends from a junction with the Gakkel Ridge (Mid-Arctic Ridge) northeast of Greenland southward to the Bouvet Triple Junction in the South Atlantic.

a. 1700 Cascadia earthquake
b. 1703 Genroku earthquake
c. 1509 Istanbul earthquake
d. Mid-Atlantic Ridge

12. _____ was the supercontinent that is theorized to have existed during the Paleozoic and Mesozoic eras about 250 million years ago, before the component continents were separated into their current configuration.

Chapter 12. Plate Tectonics: A Unifying Theory   135

The name was first used by the German originator of the continental drift theory, Alfred Wegener, in the 1920 edition of his book The Origin of Continents and Oceans , in which a postulated supercontinent _____ played a key role.

The single enormous ocean which surrounded Pangaea is known as Panthalassa.

a. 1703 Genroku earthquake
b. 1700 Cascadia earthquake
c. 1509 Istanbul earthquake
d. Pangea

13. The _____ is a chronologic schema (or idealized model) relating stratigraphy to time that is used by geologists, paleontologists and other earth scientists to describe the timing and relationships between events that have occurred during the history of the Earth. The table of geologic time spans presented here agrees with the dates and nomenclature proposed by the International Commission on Stratigraphy, and uses the standard color codes of the United States Geological Survey.

Evidence from radiometric dating indicates that the Earth is about 4.570 billion years old.

a. 1703 Genroku earthquake
b. Geologic time scale
c. 1700 Cascadia earthquake
d. 1509 Istanbul earthquake

14. The shelf usually ends at a point of decreasing slope (called the shelf break.) The sea floor below the break is the _____. Below the slope is the continental rise, which finally merges into the deep ocean floor, the abyssal plain.
a. Thermal pollution
b. Surface runoff
c. Continental slope
d. Continental shelf

15. _____ was a supercontinent that most recently existed as a part of the split of the Pangaean supercontinent in the late Mesozoic era. It included most of the landmasses which make up today's continents of the northern hemisphere, chiefly Laurentia (the name given to the North American craton), Baltica, Siberia, Kazakhstania, and the North China and East China cratons.
a. Rodinia
b. 1509 Istanbul earthquake
c. Laurasia
d. 1700 Cascadia earthquake

16. Alpine glaciers form high on the mountain slopes and are niche, slope or cirque glaciers. As a mountain glacier increases in size it can begin to flow down valley, and are referred to as _____.
a. Star dunes
b. Valley glaciers
c. Strike-slip faults
d. Tertiary

17. The _____ a natural area in New York State northwest of New York City and southwest of Albany, are a mature dissected plateau, an uplifted region that was subsequently eroded into sharp relief. They are an eastward continuation, and the highest representation, of the Allegheny Plateau.

The history of the _____ is a geologic story come full circle, from erosion, deposition and uplift back to erosion. The _____ are more of a dissected plateau than a series of mountain ranges. The sediments that make up the rocks in the Catskills were deposited when the ancient Acadian Mountains in the east were rising and subsequently eroding. The sediments traveled westward and formed a great delta into the sea that was in the area at that time.

a. 1509 Istanbul earthquake
b. Catskill Mountains
c. 1700 Cascadia earthquake
d. 1703 Genroku earthquake

18. In geology, _____ refers to inclined sedimentary structures in a horizontal unit of rock. These tilted structures are deposits from bedforms such as ripples and dunes, and they indicate that the depositional environment contained a flowing fluid (typically, water or wind.) This is a case in geology when original depositional layering is tilted, and that the tilting is not a result of post-depositional deformation.
   a. Perched coastline
   b. Paralithic
   c. Geopetal
   d. Cross-bedding

19. The _____ is a British rock formation of considerable importance to early paleontology. Hutton's angular unconformity at Siccar Point where 345 million year old Devonian _____ overlies 425 million year old Silurian greywacke.

The _____ describes a suite of rocks deposited in a variety of environments during the Devonian period but extending back into the late Silurian period and forward into the earliest part of the Carboniferous period.

   a. Old Red Sandstone
   b. AL 129-1
   c. AASHTO Soil Classification System
   d. AL 333

20. _____ is a sedimentary rock composed mainly of sand-size mineral or rock grains. Most _____ is composed of quartz and/or feldspar because these are the most common minerals in the Earth's crust. Like sand, _____ may be any color, but the most common colors are tan, brown, yellow, red, gray and white.
   a. Porcellanite
   b. Dolostone
   c. Sandstone
   d. Dolomite

21. _____ are the preserved remains or traces of animals, plants, and other organisms from the remote past. The totality of _____, both discovered and undiscovered, and their placement in fossiliferous rock formations and sedimentary layers (strata) is known as the fossil record. The study of _____ across geological time, how they were formed, and the evolutionary relationships between taxa (phylogeny) are some of the most important functions of the science of paleontology.
   a. 1700 Cascadia earthquake
   b. 1703 Genroku earthquake
   c. Fossils
   d. 1509 Istanbul earthquake

22. _____ was a metre-long predator of the Lower Triassic. It was one of the more mammal-like of the 'mammal-like reptiles', a member of a grouping called Eucynodontia. The genus _____ had an almost worldwide distribution.
   a. Cynognathus
   b. 1703 Genroku earthquake
   c. 1700 Cascadia earthquake
   d. 1509 Istanbul earthquake

23. _____ was a genus of Late Permian and Early Triassic Period dicynodont therapsids, which lived around 250 million years ago in what is now Antarctica, India and South Africa. At present 4 to 6 species are recognized, although from the 1930s to 1970s the number of species was thought to be much higher.

Being a dicynodont, _____ had only two teeth, a pair of tusk-like canines, and is thought to have had a horny beak that was used for biting off pieces of vegetation.

Chapter 12. Plate Tectonics: A Unifying Theory

a. 1700 Cascadia earthquake
b. Lystrosaurus
c. 1703 Genroku earthquake
d. 1509 Istanbul earthquake

24. A _____ is a vector field which surrounds magnets and electric currents, and is detected by the force it exerts on moving electric charges and on magnetic materials. When placed in a _____, magnetic dipoles tend to align their axes parallel to the _____. Magnetic fields also have their own energy with an energy density proportional to the square of the field intensity.
    a. 1703 Genroku earthquake
    b. 1700 Cascadia earthquake
    c. 1509 Istanbul earthquake
    d. Magnetic field

25. _____ is molten rock expelled by a volcano during eruption. When first expelled from a volcanic vent, it is a liquid at temperatures from 700 >°C to 1,200 >°C (1,300 >°F to 2,200 >°F.) Although _____ is quite viscous, with about 100,000 times the viscosity of water, it can flow great distances before cooling and solidifying, because of both its thixotropic and shear thinning properties.
    a. Pyroclastic flow
    b. Cinder
    c. Lava
    d. Pumice

26. The _____, usually referred to as the Moho, is the boundary between the Earth's crust and the mantle. The Moho serves to separate both oceanic crust and continental crust from underlying mantle. The Moho mostly lies entirely within the lithosphere; only beneath mid-ocean ridges does it define the lithosphere-asthenosphere boundary.
    a. MohoroviÄ iÄ‡ discontinuity
    b. Gorda Ridge
    c. Copperbelt Province
    d. Panthalassa

27. _____ is the study of the record of the Earth's magnetic field preserved in various magnetic minerals through time. The study of _____ has demonstrated that the Earth's magnetic field varies substantially in both orientation and intensity through time. <
    a. Radiometric dating
    b. Lichenometry
    c. Stage
    d. Paleomagnetism

28. _____ occurs at mid-ocean ridges, where new oceanic crust is formed through volcanic activity and then gradually moves away from the ridge. _____ helps explain continental drift in the theory of plate tectonics.

Earlier theories (e.g., by Alfred Wegener) of continental drift were that continents 'plowed' through the sea. The idea that the seafloor itself moves (and carries the continents with it) as it expands from a central axis was proposed by Harry Hess from Princeton University in the 1960s. The theory is well-accepted now, and the phenomenon is known to be caused by convection currents in the plastic, very weak upper mantle, or asthenosphere.

    a. Seafloor spreading
    b. Headward erosion
    c. Downcutting
    d. Deposition

29. The lithosphere is broken up into what are called _____. In the case of Earth, there are eight major and many minor plates The lithospheric plates ride on the asthenosphere. These plates move in relation to one another at one of three types of plate boundaries: convergent, or collisional boundaries; divergent boundaries, also called spreading centers; and transform boundaries.

a. Subduction
b. Tectonic plates
c. Juan de Fuca Ridge
d. Lithosphere

30. A _____ is an opening in a planet's surface or crust, which allows hot, molten rock, ash, and gases to escape from below the surface. Volcanic activity involving the extrusion of rock tends to form mountains or features like mountains over a period of time.
a. 1703 Genroku earthquake
b. 1509 Istanbul earthquake
c. Volcano
d. 1700 Cascadia earthquake

31. _____ is the part of Earth's lithosphere that surfaces in the ocean basins. _____ is primarily composed of mafic rocks, or sima. It is thinner than continental crust, or sial, generally less than 10 kilometers thick, however it is denser, having a mean density of about 3.3 grams per cubic centimeter.
a. AL 129-1
b. AL 333
c. AASHTO Soil Classification System
d. Oceanic crust

32. A _____ column (or _____) is a column of rising air in the lower altitudes of the Earth's atmosphere. They are created by the uneven heating of the Earth's surface from solar radiation, and an example of convection. The Sun warms the ground, which in turn warms the air directly above it.
a. 1509 Istanbul earthquake
b. 1700 Cascadia earthquake
c. 1703 Genroku earthquake
d. Thermal

33. A _____ is a phenomenon of fluid dynamics that occurs in situations where there are temperature differences within a body of liquid or gas.

Fluids are materials that exhibit the property of flow. Both gases and liquids have fluid properties, and in sufficient quantity, even particulate solids such as salt, grain, and gravel show some fluid properties. When a volume of fluid is heated, it expands and becomes less dense and thus more buoyant than the surrounding fluid. The colder, denser fluid settles underneath the warmer, less dense fluid and forces it to rise. Such movement is called convection, and the moving body of liquid is referred to as a _____.

a. 1700 Cascadia earthquake
b. 1703 Genroku earthquake
c. Convection cell
d. 1509 Istanbul earthquake

34. The _____ is the mechanically weak ductily-deforming region of the upper mantle of the Earth. It lies below the lithosphere, at depths between 100 and 200 km (~ 62 and 124 miles) below the surface, but perhaps extending as deep as 400 km (~ 249 miles.)

The _____ is a portion of the upper mantle just below the lithosphere that is involved in plate movements and isostatic adjustments. In spite of its heat, pressures keep it plastic, and it has a relatively low density. Seismic waves pass relatively slowly through the _____, compared to the overlying lithospheric mantle, thus it has been called the low-velocity zone. This was the observation that originally alerted seismologists to its presence and gave some information about its physical properties, as the speed of seismic waves decreases with decreasing rigidity.

a. AL 129-1
b. AASHTO Soil Classification System
c. Asthenosphere
d. AL 333

35. The _____ is the layer of igneous, sedimentary, and metamorphic rocks which form the continents and the areas of shallow seabed close to their shores, known as continental shelves. This layer is sometimes called sial due to more felsic, or granitic, bulk composition, which lies in contrast to the oceanic crust, called sima due to its mafic, or basaltic rock. (Based on the change in velocity of seismic waves, it is believed that at a certain depth sial becomes close in its physical properties to sima.

a. Mirovia
b. Divergent boundary
c. Plate tectonics
d. Continental crust

36. _____ is the geological process by which material is added to a landform or land mass. Fluids such as wind and water, as well as sediment gravity flows, transport previously eroded sediment, which, at the loss of enough kinetic energy in the fluid, is deposited, building up layers of sediment.

_____ occurs when the forces responsible for sediment transportation are no longer sufficient to overcome the forces of particle weight and friction, which resist motion.

a. Deposition
b. Hydrothermal circulation
c. Stoping
d. Hydraulic action

37. The _____ is a tectonic plate arising from the Juan de Fuca Ridge, and subducting under the northerly portion of the western side of the North American Plate at the Cascadia subduction zone. It is bounded on the south by the Blanco Fracture Zone, on the north by the Nootka Fault, and along the west by the Pacific Plate. The _____ was originally part of the once-vast Farallon Plate, now largely subducted under the North American Plate, and has since fractured into three pieces.

a. South Bismarck Plate
b. Lhasa Plate
c. Banda Sea Plate
d. Juan de Fuca plate

38. The _____ is the rigid outermost shell of a rocky planet.

In the Earth, the _____ includes the crust and the uppermost mantle, which constitute the hard and rigid outer layer of the planet. The _____ is underlain by the asthenosphere, the weaker, hotter, and deeper part of the upper mantle.

a. Copperbelt Province
b. Lithosphere
c. Nappe
d. Continental crust

39. The _____ are hemispheric-scale long but narrow topographic depressions of the sea floor. They are also the deepest parts of the ocean floor.

_____ define one of the most important natural boundaries on the Earth's solid surface, thatlie between two lithospheric plates. There are three types of lithospheric plate boundaries: divergent (where lithosphere and oceanic crust is created at mid-ocean ridges), convergent (where one lithospheric plate sinks beneath another and returns to the mantle), and transform (where two lithospheric plates slide past each other).

a. AL 129-1
b. AASHTO Soil Classification System
c. Oceanic trenches
d. AL 333

40. _____ is any particulate matter that can be transported by fluid flow, and which eventually is deposited.

They are most often transported by water (fluvial processes) transported by wind (aeolian processes) and glaciers. Beach sands and river channel deposits are examples of fluvial transport and deposition, though _____ also often settles out of slow-moving or standing water in lakes and oceans.

a. Bovey Beds
b. Salt glacier
c. Quick clay
d. Sediment

41. _____ refers to natural mountain building, and may be studied as a tectonic structural event, (b) as a geographical event, and (c) a chronological event. Orogenic events (a) cause distinctive structural phenomena and related tectonic activity, (b) affect certain regions of rocks and crust, and (c) happen within a specific period of time.
a. Orogenesis
b. Antler orogeny
c. Alice Springs Orogeny
d. Orogeny

42. In geology, a _____ is a landmass comprising more than one continental core, or craton. The assembly of cratons and accreted terranes that form Eurasia qualifies as a _____ today.

Most commonly, paleogeographers employ the term _____ to refer to a single landmass consisting of all the modern continents.

a. 1703 Genroku earthquake
b. 1509 Istanbul earthquake
c. 1700 Cascadia earthquake
d. Supercontinent

43. The _____ describes the quasi-periodic aggregation and dispersal of Earth's continental crust. There are varying opinions as to whether Earth's budget of continental crust is increasing, decreasing, or remaining about constant, but it is agreed that this inventory is constantly being reconfigured. One complete _____ is said to take 300 to 500 million years to occur.
a. Mirovia
b. Subduction
c. Convergent boundary
d. Supercontinent cycle

44. A _____ is a large emplacement of igneous intrusive rock that forms from cooled magma deep in the Earth's crust. they are almost always made mostly of felsic or intermediate rock-types, such as granite, quartz monzonite, or diorite

Although they may appear uniform, _____s are in fact structures with complex histories and compositions.

a. Tuff
b. Scoria
c. Batholith
d. Great Dyke

Chapter 12. Plate Tectonics: A Unifying Theory

45. A _____ or dyke in geology is a type of sheet intrusion referring to any geologic body that cuts discordantly across

- planar wall rock structures, such as bedding or foliation
- massive rock formations, like igneous/magmatic intrusions and salt diapirs.

They can therefore be either intrusive or sedimentary in origin.

An intrusive _____ is an igneous body with a very high aspect ratio, which means that its thickness is usually much smaller than the other two dimensions. Thickness can vary from sub-centimeter scale to many meters and the lateral dimensions can extend over many kilometers. A _____ is an intrusion into an opening cross-cutting fissure, shouldering aside other pre-existing layers or bodies of rock; this implies that a _____ is always younger than the rocks that contain it.

a. Schmidt hammer
b. Haloclasty
c. Fabric
d. Dike

46. The _____ is part of the larger Great Rift Valley. It is a continental rift zone that appears to be a developing divergent tectonic plate boundary. The rift is a narrow zone in which the African Plate is in the process of splitting into two new plates called the Nubian and Somalian subplates or protoplates.

a. East African Rift
b. AL 333
c. AASHTO Soil Classification System
d. AL 129-1

47. In geology, a _____ or _____ line is a planar fracture in rock in which the rock on one side of the fracture has moved with respect to the rock on the other side. Large _____s within the Earth's crust are the result of differential or shear motion and active _____ zones are the causal locations of most earthquakes. Earthquakes are caused by energy release during rapid slippage along a _____.

a. Combe
b. Geothermal
c. Cohesion
d. Fault

48. In geology the term _____ refers to a fracture in rock where there has been no lateral movement in the plane of the fracture (up, down or sideways) of one side relative to the other. This makes it different from a fault which is defined as a fracture in rock where one side slides laterally past to the other. _____s normally have a regular spacing related to either the mechanical properties of the individual rock or the thickness of the layer involved.

a. 1700 Cascadia earthquake
b. 1703 Genroku earthquake
c. 1509 Istanbul earthquake
d. Joint

49. _____ are pillow-shaped structures sometimes seen in lavas and are attributed to the congealment of lava under water, or subaqeous extrusion. A pillow structure in certain extrusive igneous rock is characterized by discontinuous pillow-shaped masses, commonly up to 1 metre in diameter. _____ commonly occur at Constructive plate boundaries, forming part of a mid-ocean ridge.

a. Metamorphic reaction
b. Pillow lava
c. Compression
d. Corrasion

Chapter 12. Plate Tectonics: A Unifying Theory

50. A _____ in geology is an intrusive igneous rock body that crystallized from a magma slowly cooling below the surface of the Earth. _____s include batholiths, dikes, sills, laccoliths, lopoliths, and other igneous bodies. In practice, '_____' usually refers to a distinctive mass of igneous rock, typically kilometers in dimension, without a tabular shape like those of dikes and sills.
   a. Metavolcanic rock
   b. Petrology
   c. Metamorphic rock
   d. Pluton

51. In geology, a _____ is a place where the Earth's crust and lithosphere are being pulled apart and is an example of extensional tectonics.

   Typical _____ features are a central linear downdropped fault segment, called a graben, with parallel normal faulting and _____-flank uplifts on either side forming a _____ valley, where the _____ remains above sea level. The axis of the _____ area commonly contains volcanic rocks and active volcanism is a part of many, but not all active _____ systems.

   a. 1700 Cascadia earthquake
   b. 1509 Istanbul earthquake
   c. 1703 Genroku earthquake
   d. Rift

52. A _____ is a linear-shaped lowland between highlands or mountain ranges created by the action of a geologic rift or fault. This action is manifest as crustal extension, a spreading apart of the surface which is subsequently further deepened by the forces of erosion. When the tensional forces are strong enough to cause the plate to split apart it will do so such that a center block will drop down relative to its flanking blocks.
   a. 1703 Genroku earthquake
   b. 1700 Cascadia earthquake
   c. Rift Valley
   d. 1509 Istanbul earthquake

53. Two important classifications of weathering processes exist -- physical and _____. Mechanical or physical weathering involves the breakdown of rocks and soils through direct contact with atmospheric conditions, such as heat, water, ice and pressure. The second classification, _____, involves the direct effect of atmospheric chemicals or biologically produced chemicals (also known as biological weathering) in the breakdown of rocks, soils and minerals.
   a. Physical weathering
   b. Frost disintegration
   c. 1509 Istanbul earthquake
   d. Chemical weathering

54. _____ is the decomposition of Earth rocks, soils and their minerals through direct contact with the planet's atmosphere. _____ occurs in situ, or 'with no movement', and thus should not be confused with erosion, which involves the movement of rocks and minerals by agents such as water, ice, wind and gravity.

   Two important classifications of _____ processes exist -- physical and chemical _____.

   a. Weathering
   b. Physical weathering
   c. 1509 Istanbul earthquake
   d. Frost disintegration

55. A _____ is the topographic expression of faulting attributed to the displacement of the land surface by movement along the fault. It can be caused by differential erosion along an old inactive geologic fault (a sort of old rupture) with hard and weak rock, or by a movement on an active fault. In many cases, bluffs form from the upthrown block and can be very steep.

Chapter 12. Plate Tectonics: A Unifying Theory

a. Fault scarp
b. Shutter ridge
c. Stream gradient
d. Gravitational erosion

56. A _____ is a sand- to boulder-sized particle of debris in the Solar System. The visible path of a _____ that enters Earth's (or another body's) atmosphere is called a meteor, or commonly a 'shooting star' or 'falling star.' If a _____ reaches the ground, it is then called a meteorite. Many meteors are part of a meteor shower.
   a. 1509 Istanbul earthquake
   b. 1700 Cascadia earthquake
   c. Meteoroid
   d. 1703 Genroku earthquake

57. The _____ is a continental transform fault that runs a length of roughly 800 miles (1,300 km) through California in the United States. The fault's motion is right-lateral strike-slip (horizontal motion.) It forms the tectonic boundary between the Pacific Plate and the North American Plate.
   a. 1509 Istanbul earthquake
   b. 1700 Cascadia earthquake
   c. San Andreas fault
   d. 1703 Genroku earthquake

58. _____, is the process of coastal sediments returning to the visible portion of a beach or foreshore following a submersion event. A sustainable beach or foreshore often goes through a cycle of submersion during rough weather then _____ during calmer periods. If a coastline is not in a healthy sustainable condition, then erosion can be more serious and _____ does not fully restore the original volume of the visible beach or foreshore leading to permanent beach or foreshore loss.
   a. AASHTO Soil Classification System
   b. AL 129-1
   c. AL 333
   d. Accretion

59. _____s, sometimes called minor planets or planetoids, are small Solar System bodies in orbit around the Sun, especially in the inner Solar System; they are smaller than planets but larger than meteoroids. The term '_____' has historically been applied primarily to bodies in the inner Solar System since the outer Solar System was poorly known when it came into common usage. The distinction between _____s and comets is made on visual appearance: Comets show a perceptible coma while _____s do not.
   a. AASHTO Soil Classification System
   b. AL 333
   c. Asteroid
   d. AL 129-1

60. In materials science, _____ is a change in the shape or size of an object due to an applied force. This can be a result of tensile (pulling) forces, compressive (pushing) forces, shear, bending or torsion (twisting.) _____ is often described as strain.
   a. Melange
   b. Deformation
   c. Combe
   d. Stack

61. An _____ is an ice mass that covers less than 50 000 km^2 of land area (usually covering a highland area.) Masses of ice covering more than 50 000 km^2 are termed an ice sheet.

They are not constrained by topographical features (i.e., they will lie over the top of mountains) but their dome is usually centred on the highest point of a massif.

   a. AL 129-1
   b. AL 333
   c. AASHTO Soil Classification System
   d. Ice cap

62. A _____ is a deep active seismic area in a subduction zone. Differential motion along the zone produces deep-seated earthquakes, the foci of which may be as deep as about 700 kilometres (435 miles.) They develop beneath volcanic island arcs and continental margins above active subduction zones.
   a. Pit crater
   b. Lava
   c. Wadati-Benioff zone
   d. Pumice

63. The _____ is a name given in the late 19th century by British explorer John Walter Gregory to the continuous geographic trough, approximately 6,000 kilometres (3,700 mi) in length, that runs from northern Syria in Southwest Asia to central Mozambique in East Africa. The name continues in some usages, although it is today considered geologically imprecise as it includes what are today regarded as separate, since 1869 due to the Suez Canal Company project, although related rift and fault systems. Today, the term is most often used to refer to the valley of the East African Rift, the divergent plate boundary which extends from the Afar Triple Junction southward across eastern Africa, and is in the process of splitting the African Plate into two new separate plates.
   a. Great Rift Valley
   b. 1703 Genroku earthquake
   c. 1700 Cascadia earthquake
   d. 1509 Istanbul earthquake

64. In geology, _____ is the process that takes place at convergent boundaries by which one tectonic plate moves under another tectonic plate, sinking into the Earth's mantle, as the plates converge. A _____ zone is an area on Earth where two tectonic plates move towards one another and _____ occurs. Rates of _____ are typically measured in centimeters per year, with the average rate of convergence being approximately 2 to 8 centimeters per year (about the rate a fingernail grows.)
   a. Panthalassa
   b. Subduction
   c. Thrust fault
   d. Forearc

65. _____ are geologic features, submarine basins associated with island arcs and subduction zones. They are found at some convergent plate boundaries, presently concentrated in the Western Pacific ocean. Most of them result from tensional forces caused by oceanic trench rollback and the collapse of the edge of the continent.
   a. Back-arc basins
   b. 1703 Genroku earthquake
   c. 1509 Istanbul earthquake
   d. 1700 Cascadia earthquake

66. A _____ is a mountain rising from the ocean seafloor that does not reach to the water's surface (sea level), and thus is not an island. These are typically formed from extinct volcanoes, that rise abruptly and are usually found rising from a seafloor of 1,000-4,000 meters depth. They are defined by oceanographers as independent features that rise to at least 1,000 meters above the seafloor.
   a. 1700 Cascadia earthquake
   b. 1509 Istanbul earthquake
   c. 1703 Genroku earthquake
   d. Seamount

67. The _____ is an oceanic tectonic plate in the eastern Pacific Ocean basin off the west coast of South America.

The eastern margin is a convergent boundary subduction zone under the South American Plate and the Andes Mountains, forming the Peru-Chile Trench. The southern side is a divergent boundary with the Antarctic Plate, the Chile Rise, where seafloor spreading permits magma to rise.

   a. South Bismarck Plate
   b. Sunda Plate
   c. Solomon Sea Plate
   d. Nazca plate

Chapter 12. Plate Tectonics: A Unifying Theory

68. The _____ is an oceanic trench in the eastern Pacific Ocean, about 160 kilometers off the coast of Peru and Chile. It reaches a maximum depth of 8,065 meters below sea level in the Richards Deep and is approximately 5,900 kilometers long; its mean width is 64 kilometers and it covers an expanse of some 590,000 square kilometers

The trench is a result of the eastern edge of the Nazca Plate being subducted under the South American Plate.

- a. 1700 Cascadia earthquake
- b. 1703 Genroku earthquake
- c. 1509 Istanbul earthquake
- d. Peru-Chile Trench

69. _____ is an igneous, volcanic rock, of intermediate composition, with aphanitic to porphyritic texture. The mineral assemblage is typically dominated by plagioclase plus pyroxene and/or hornblende. Magnetite, zircon, apatite, ilmenite, biotite, and garnet are common accessory minerals.
- a. AL 333
- b. AL 129-1
- c. AASHTO Soil Classification System
- d. Andesite

70. _____ is one of the three main rock types (the others being sedimentary and metamorphic rock.) _____ is formed by magma (molten rock) being cooled and becoming solid . They may form with or without crystallization, either below the surface as intrusive (plutonic) rocks or on the surface as extrusive (volcanic) rocks. They make up approximately 95% of the upper part of the Earth's crust, but their great abundance is hidden on the Earth's surface by a relatively thin but widespread layer of sedimentary and metamorphic rocks.
- a. AL 129-1
- b. AASHTO Soil Classification System
- c. Igneous rock
- d. AL 333

71. An _____ is a section of the Earth's oceanic crust and the underlying upper mantle that has been uplifted or emplaced to be exposed within continental crustal rocks. Ophio is Greek for 'snake', lite means 'stone' from the Greek lithos.

The term _____ was originally used by Alexandre Brongniart for an assemblage of green rocks (serpentine, diabase) in the Alps; Steinmann (1927) later modified its use to include serpentine, pillow lava, and chert ('Steinmann's trinity'), again based on occurrences in the Alps.

- a. AL 129-1
- b. AL 333
- c. AASHTO Soil Classification System
- d. Ophiolite

72. In geology, a _____ is a location on the Earth's surface that has experienced active volcanism for a long period of time.

J. Tuzo Wilson came up with the idea in 1963 that volcanic chains like the Hawaiian Islands result from the slow movement of a tectonic plate across a 'fixed' _____ deep beneath the surface of the planet.

- a. 1509 Istanbul earthquake
- b. 1700 Cascadia earthquake
- c. 1703 Genroku earthquake
- d. Hotspot

73. A _____ is an upwelling of abnormally hot rock within the Earth's mantle. As the heads of _____s can partly melt when they reach shallow depths, they are thought to be the cause of volcanic centers known as hotspots and probably also to have caused flood basalts. It is a secondary way that Earth loses heat, much less important in this regard than is heat loss at plate margins.

a. Seismic refraction
b. Strainmeter
c. Mazuku
d. Mantle plume

74. The _____ is a tectonic plate covering most of North America, Greenland and part of Siberia. It extends eastward to the Mid-Atlantic Ridge and westward to the Chersky Range in eastern Siberia. The plate includes both continental and oceanic crust. The interior of the main continental landmass includes an extensive granitic core called a craton. Along most of the edges of this craton are fragments of crustal material called terranes, accreted to the craton by tectonic actions over the long span of geologic time. It is believed that much of North America west of the Rockies is composed of such terranes.
   a. Conway Reef Plate
   b. North American plate
   c. New Hebrides Plate
   d. Nazca Plate

75. The _____ is an oceanic tectonic plate beneath the Pacific Ocean.

To the north the easterly side is a divergent boundary with the Explorer Plate, the Juan de Fuca Plate and the Gorda Plate forming respectively the Explorer Ridge, the Juan de Fuca Ridge and the Gorda Ridge. In the middle the easterly side is a transform boundary with the North American Plate along the San Andreas Fault and a boundary with the Cocos Plate.

   a. North American Plate
   b. South Bismarck Plate
   c. Juan de Fuca Plate
   d. Pacific plate

76. A _____ or transform boundary is a fault which runs along the boundary of a tectonic plate. The relative motion of such plates is horizontal in either sinistral or dextral direction. Typically, some vertical motion may also exist, but the principal vectors in a _____ are oriented horizontally.
   a. Syncline
   b. Transform fault
   c. Crenulation
   d. Strike and dip

77. _____ is the solid-state recrystallization of pre-existing rocks due to changes in physical and chemical conditions, primarily heat, pressure, and the introduction of chemically active fluids. Both mineralogical, chemical and crystallographic changes can occur during this process.

Three types of _____ exist: dynamic, contact and regional.

   a. Cross-bedding
   b. Dike
   c. Gradualism
   d. Metamorphism

78. The _____ is a large enclosed plain, approximately 50 miles (80 km) long and up to 15 miles (24 km) across, in southeastern San Luis Obispo County, California, about 100 miles (160 km) northwest of Los Angeles, California. The most prevalent geologic feature of the _____s is the San Andreas Fault. It is a right lateral fault which runs along the northeast of the Plain, at the base of the Elkhorn Scarp, and forms the boundary between the Pacific and North American Plates. Although the fault runs through California all the way from Cape Mendocino to just south of Los Angeles, the _____ remains one of the best places to study it.
   a. 1700 Cascadia earthquake
   b. 1509 Istanbul earthquake
   c. 1703 Genroku earthquake
   d. Carrizo Plain

Chapter 12. Plate Tectonics: A Unifying Theory

79. _____ circulation in its most general sense is the circulation of hot water; 'hydros' in the Greek meaning water and 'thermos' meaning heat. _____ circulation occurs most often in the vicinity of sources of heat within the Earth's crust. This generally occurs near volcanic activity, but can occur in the deep crust related to the intrusion of granite, or as the result of orogeny or metamorphism.
- a. Transgression
- b. Hydrothermal
- c. Wave pounding
- d. Headward erosion

80. An _____ is a type of rock that contains minerals such as gemstones and metals that can be extracted through mining and refined for use. Samples of _____ in the form of exceptionally beautiful crystals, exotic layering visible when sectioned or polished or metallic presentations such as large nuggets or crystalline formations of metals such as gold or copper may command a value far beyond their value as mere _____ or raw metal for subsequent reduction to utilitarian purposes.

The grade or concentration of an _____ mineral, or metal, as well as its form of occurrence, will directly affect the costs associated with mining the _____.

- a. Iron ores
- b. Ore
- c. AASHTO Soil Classification System
- d. Ore genesis

81. _____ are rocks and minerals from which metallic iron can be economically extracted. The ores are usually rich in iron oxides and vary in color from dark grey, bright yellow, deep purple, to rusty red. The iron itself is usually found in the form of magnetite (Fe_3O_4), haematite (Fe_2O_3), goethite, limonite or siderite.
- a. Ore genesis
- b. Ore
- c. AASHTO Soil Classification System
- d. Iron ores

1. _____ forms a group of medium-grade metamorphic rocks, chiefly notable for the preponderance of lamellar minerals such as micas, chlorite, talc, hornblende, graphite, and others. Quartz often occurs in drawn-out grains to such an extent that a particular form called quartz _____ is produced. By definition, _____ contains more than 50% platy and elongated minerals, often finely interleaved with quartz and feldspar.
   a. Foliation
   b. Schist
   c. Geothermobarometry
   d. Cataclasite

2. The _____ is the zone of the ocean floor that separates the thin oceanic crust from thick continental crust. _____s constitute about 28% of the oceanic area.

   The transition from continental to oceanic crust commonly occurs within the outer part of the margin, called continental rise.

   a. 1509 Istanbul earthquake
   b. Longshore drift
   c. Continental margin
   d. Cuspate forelands

3. In materials science, _____ is a change in the shape or size of an object due to an applied force. This can be a result of tensile (pulling) forces, compressive (pushing) forces, shear, bending or torsion (twisting.) _____ is often described as strain.
   a. Combe
   b. Melange
   c. Stack
   d. Deformation

4. The _____ is a chronologic schema (or idealized model) relating stratigraphy to time that is used by geologists, paleontologists and other earth scientists to describe the timing and relationships between events that have occurred during the history of the Earth. The table of geologic time spans presented here agrees with the dates and nomenclature proposed by the International Commission on Stratigraphy, and uses the standard color codes of the United States Geological Survey.

   Evidence from radiometric dating indicates that the Earth is about 4.570 billion years old.

   a. 1700 Cascadia earthquake
   b. 1703 Genroku earthquake
   c. 1509 Istanbul earthquake
   d. Geologic time scale

5. _____ is the solid-state recrystallization of pre-existing rocks due to changes in physical and chemical conditions, primarily heat, pressure, and the introduction of chemically active fluids. Both mineralogical, chemical and crystallographic changes can occur during this process.

   Three types of _____ exist: dynamic, contact and regional.

   a. Dike
   b. Cross-bedding
   c. Metamorphism
   d. Gradualism

6. _____ refers to natural mountain building, and may be studied as a tectonic structural event, (b) as a geographical event, and (c) a chronological event. Orogenic events (a) cause distinctive structural phenomena and related tectonic activity, (b) affect certain regions of rocks and crust, and (c) happen within a specific period of time.
   a. Orogeny
   b. Orogenesis
   c. Antler orogeny
   d. Alice Springs Orogeny

Chapter 13. Deformation, Mountain Building, and the Evolution of Continents 362

7. _____ is a gas consisting primarily of methane. It is found associated with fossil fuels, in coal beds, as methane clathrates, and is created by methanogenic organisms in marshes, bogs, and landfills. It is an important fuel source, a major feedstock for fertilizers, and a potent greenhouse gas.
   a. Natural gas
   b. 1703 Genroku earthquake
   c. 1509 Istanbul earthquake
   d. 1700 Cascadia earthquake

8. A _____ in geology is an intrusive igneous rock body that crystallized from a magma slowly cooling below the surface of the Earth. _____s include batholiths, dikes, sills, laccoliths, lopoliths, and other igneous bodies. In practice, '_____' usually refers to a distinctive mass of igneous rock, typically kilometers in dimension, without a tabular shape like those of dikes and sills.
   a. Metavolcanic rock
   b. Petrology
   c. Pluton
   d. Metamorphic rock

9. _____, is the process of coastal sediments returning to the visible portion of a beach or foreshore following a submersion event. A sustainable beach or foreshore often goes through a cycle of submersion during rough weather then _____ during calmer periods. If a coastline is not in a healthy sustainable condition, then erosion can be more serious and _____ does not fully restore the original volume of the visible beach or foreshore leading to permanent beach or foreshore loss.
   a. AL 333
   b. AL 129-1
   c. AASHTO Soil Classification System
   d. Accretion

10. A _____ is a large emplacement of igneous intrusive rock that forms from cooled magma deep in the Earth's crust. they are almost always made mostly of felsic or intermediate rock-types, such as granite, quartz monzonite, or diorite

Although they may appear uniform, _____s are in fact structures with complex histories and compositions.

   a. Tuff
   b. Great Dyke
   c. Batholith
   d. Scoria

11. The _____ is the extended perimeter of each continent and associated coastal plain, and was part of the continent during the glacial periods, but is undersea during interglacial periods such as the current epoch by relatively shallow seas (known as shelf seas) and gulfs.

The continental rise is below the slope, but landward of the abyssal plains. Its gradient is intermediate between the slope and the shelf, on the order of 0.5-1°.

   a. Continental shelf
   b. Continental slope
   c. Mud
   d. Surface runoff

12. An _____ is the result of a sudden release of energy in the Earth's crust that creates seismic waves. They are recorded with a seismometer or the related and mostly obsolete Richter magnitude, with a magnitude 3 or lower _____ being mostly imperceptible and magnitude 7 causing serious damage over large areas.
   a. AL 333
   b. AASHTO Soil Classification System
   c. AL 129-1
   d. Earthquake

Chapter 13. Deformation, Mountain Building, and the Evolution of Continents

13. The lithosphere is broken up into what are called _____. In the case of Earth, there are eight major and many minor plates The lithospheric plates ride on the asthenosphere. These plates move in relation to one another at one of three types of plate boundaries: convergent, or collisional boundaries; divergent boundaries, also called spreading centers; and transform boundaries.

    a. Juan de Fuca Ridge
    b. Lithosphere
    c. Tectonic plates
    d. Subduction

14. In geology the term _____ refers to the system of forces that tend to decrease the volume of or shorten rocks. Compressive strength refers to the maximum compressive stress that can be applied to a material before failure occurs. In tectonics, plates are always subjected to compressive stress.

    a. Compression
    b. Type locality
    c. Lake capture
    d. Pillow lava

15. Study of geological _____ is related to the study of structural geology, rock microstructure or rock texture and fault mechanics.

    _____ is the response of a rock to deformation usually by compressive stress and forms particular textures. _____ can be homogeneous or non-homogeneous, and may be pure _____ or simple _____.

    a. Syncline
    b. Petermann Orogeny
    c. Graben
    d. Shear

16. A _____, denoted τ (tau), is defined as a stress which is applied parallel or tangential to a face of a material, as opposed to a normal stress which is applied perpendicularly. In other words, considering that weight is a force, hanging something from a wall creates a _____ on the wall, since the weight of the object is acting parallel to the wall, as opposed to hanging something from the ceiling which creates a normal stress on the ceiling, since the weight is acting perpendicular to the ceiling.

    The formula to calculate average _____ is:

    $$\tau = \frac{F}{A}$$

    where

    τ = the _____
    F = the force applied
    A = the cross sectional area

    Beam shear is defined as the internal _____ of a beam caused by the shear force applied to the beam.

    a. Viscosity
    b. Tensile stress
    c. Shear stress
    d. Thixotropy

17. The _____ is an explanation for how energy is spread during earthquakes. As plates shift on opposite sides of a fault are subjected to force, they accumulate energy and slowly deform until their internal strength is exceeded. At that time, a sudden movement occurs along the fault, releasing the accumulated energy, and the rocks snap back to their original undeformed shape.
   a. Obduction
   b. Azores-Gibraltar Transform Fault
   c. East Pacific Rise
   d. Elastic rebound theory

18. In geology, a _____ or _____ line is a planar fracture in rock in which the rock on one side of the fracture has moved with respect to the rock on the other side. Large _____s within the Earth's crust are the result of differential or shear motion and active _____ zones are the causal locations of most earthquakes. Earthquakes are caused by energy release during rapid slippage along a _____.
   a. Geothermal
   b. Combe
   c. Cohesion
   d. Fault

19. In geology the term _____ refers to a fracture in rock where there has been no lateral movement in the plane of the fracture (up, down or sideways) of one side relative to the other. This makes it different from a fault which is defined as a fracture in rock where one side slides laterally past to the other. _____s normally have a regular spacing related to either the mechanical properties of the individual rock or the thickness of the layer involved.
   a. Joint
   b. 1703 Genroku earthquake
   c. 1509 Istanbul earthquake
   d. 1700 Cascadia earthquake

20. The _____ was proposed by the Danish geological pioneer Nicholas Steno (1638-1686.) This principle states that layers of sediment are originally deposited horizontally. The principle is important to the analysis of folded and tilted strata.
   a. Principle of original horizontality
   b. Bedrock
   c. Key bed
   d. Cyclostratigraphy

21. Two important classifications of weathering processes exist -- physical and _____. Mechanical or physical weathering involves the breakdown of rocks and soils through direct contact with atmospheric conditions, such as heat, water, ice and pressure. The second classification, _____, involves the direct effect of atmospheric chemicals or biologically produced chemicals (also known as biological weathering) in the breakdown of rocks, soils and minerals.
   a. 1509 Istanbul earthquake
   b. Chemical weathering
   c. Physical weathering
   d. Frost disintegration

22. _____ refer to the orientation or attitude of a geologic feature. The strike of a bed, fault, or other planar feature is a line representing the intersection of that feature with a horizontal plane. On a geologic map this is represented with a short straight line segment oriented parallel to the compass direction of the strike. Strike can be given as either a quadrant compass bearing (N25°E for example) in terms of east or west of north or south, a single three digit number representing the azimuth, where the lower number is usually given (where the example of N25°E would simply be 025, and the other value of 335 is discarded), or the azimuth number followed by the degree sign (example of N25°E would be 25° or 335°). The dip gives the angle below the horizontal of a tilted bed or feature, and is given by the number (0°-90°) as well as a letter (N,S,E,W) with rough direction in which the bed is dipping.
   a. Tectonites
   b. Crenulation
   c. Shear
   d. Strike and dip

23. _____ is the decomposition of Earth rocks, soils and their minerals through direct contact with the planet's atmosphere. _____ occurs in situ, or 'with no movement', and thus should not be confused with erosion, which involves the movement of rocks and minerals by agents such as water, ice, wind and gravity.

Two important classifications of _____ processes exist -- physical and chemical _____.

   a. Weathering
   b. Physical weathering
   c. 1509 Istanbul earthquake
   d. Frost disintegration

24. A _____ is a special-purpose map made to show geological features.

The stratigraphic contour lines are drawn on the surface of a selected deep stratum, so that they can show the topographic trends of the strata under the ground. It is not always possible to properly show this when the strata are extremely fractured, mixed, in some discontinuities, or where they are otherwise disturbed.

   a. 1703 Genroku earthquake
   b. 1700 Cascadia earthquake
   c. 1509 Istanbul earthquake
   d. Geologic map

25. In structural geology, an _____ is a fold that is convex up and has its oldest beds at its core. The term is not to be confused with antiform, which is a purely descriptive term for any fold that is convex up. Therefore if age relationships (i.e. younging direction) between various strata are unknown, the term antiform must be used.

   a. AASHTO Soil Classification System
   b. AL 333
   c. AL 129-1
   d. Anticline

26. In geology a _____ is the smallest division of a geologic formation or stratigraphic rock series marked by well-defined divisional planes (bedding planes) separating it from layers above and below. A _____ is the smallest lithostratigraphic unit, usually ranging in thickness from a centimeter to several meters and distinguishable from _____s above and below it. _____s can be differentiated in various ways, including rock or mineral type and particle size.

   a. Cyclostratigraphy
   b. Biozones
   c. Sequence stratigraphy
   d. Bed

27. The term _____ is used in geology when one or a stack of originally flat and planar surfaces, such as sedimentary strata, are bent or curved as a result of plastic (i.e. permanent) deformation. Synsedimentary _____s are those due to slumping of sedimentary material before it is lithified. _____s in rocks vary in size from microscopic crinkles to mountain-sized _____s.

   a. 1700 Cascadia earthquake
   b. 1703 Genroku earthquake
   c. 1509 Istanbul earthquake
   d. Fold

28. The _____ is a continental transform fault that runs a length of roughly 800 miles (1,300 km) through California in the United States. The fault's motion is right-lateral strike-slip (horizontal motion.) It forms the tectonic boundary between the Pacific Plate and the North American Plate.

   a. 1703 Genroku earthquake
   b. San Andreas fault
   c. 1509 Istanbul earthquake
   d. 1700 Cascadia earthquake

Chapter 13. Deformation, Mountain Building, and the Evolution of Continents 362

29. In structural geology, a _____ is a downward-curving fold, with layers that dip toward the center of the structure. A synclinorium is a large _____ with superimposed smaller folds.

On a geologic map, they are recognized by a sequence of rock layers that grow progressively younger, followed by the youngest layer at the fold's center or hinge, and by a reverse sequence of the same rock layers on the opposite side of the hinge.

a. Transform fault
c. Shear
b. Syncline
d. Sag pond

30. _____ is the removal of solids (sediment, soil, rock and other particles) in the natural environment. It usually occurs due to transport by wind, water, or ice; by down-slope creep of soil and other material under the force of gravity; or by living organisms, such as burrowing animals, in the case of bioerosion.

_____ is distinguished from weathering, which is the process of chemical or physical breakdown of the minerals in the rocks, although the two processes may occur concurrently.

a. AASHTO Soil Classification System
c. AL 129-1
b. AL 333
d. Erosion

31. In geology, a _____ is a large sheetlike body of rock that has been moved more than 2 km (1.2 miles) from its original position. _____s form during continental plate collisions, when folds are sheared so much that they fold back over on themselves and break apart. The resulting structure is a large-scale recumbent fold.

a. Forearc
c. Motagua Fault
b. Continental collision
d. Nappe

32. The _____ are a small, isolated mountain range rising from the Great Plains of North America in western South Dakota and extending into Wyoming, USA. Set off from the main body of the Rocky Mountains, the region is something of a geological anomaly--accurately described as an 'island of trees in a sea of grass'. The _____ encompass the _____ National Forest and are home to the tallest peaks of continental North America east of the Rockies.

a. Black Hills
c. Monument Valley
b. Rano Kau
d. Paleorrota

33. The _____ is a geologic basin centered on the Lower Peninsula of the US state of Michigan. The feature is represented by a nearly circular pattern of geologic sedimentary strata in the area with a nearly uniform structural dip toward the center of the peninsula.

The basin is centered in Gladwin County where the Precambrian basement rocks are 16,000 feet (4,900 m) deep. Around the margins, such as under Mackinaw City, Michigan, the Precambrian surface is around 4,000 feet (1,200 m) down. This 4,000-foot (1,200 m) contour on the bedrock clips the northern part of the lower peninsula and continues under Lake Michigan along the west.

a. Michigan Basin
c. 1700 Cascadia earthquake
b. 1703 Genroku earthquake
d. 1509 Istanbul earthquake

34. _____ can be again classified into the types 'reverse' and 'normal'. A normal fault occurs when the crust is extended. Alternatively such a fault can be called an extensional fault.
   a. Dip-slip faults
   b. 1509 Istanbul earthquake
   c. Reverse fault
   d. Fault plane

35. _____, or tectonic breccia is a breccia (a rock type consisting of angular clasts) that was formed by tectonic forces. _____ has no cohesion, it is normally an unconsolidated rock type, unless cementation took place at a later stage. Sometimes a distinction is made between fault gouge and _____, the first has a smaller grain size.
   a. Ventifacts
   b. 1509 Istanbul earthquake
   c. Fault breccia
   d. Coprolite

36. Since faults do not usually consist of a single, clean fracture, the term fault zone is used when referring to the zone of complex deformation that is associated with the _____. The two sides of a non-vertical fault are called the hanging wall and footwall. By definition, the hanging wall occurs above the fault and the footwall occurs below the fault.
   a. Reverse fault
   b. Hanging wall
   c. 1509 Istanbul earthquake
   d. Fault plane

37. A _____ is the topographic expression of faulting attributed to the displacement of the land surface by movement along the fault. It can be caused by differential erosion along an old inactive geologic fault (a sort of old rupture) with hard and weak rock, or by a movement on an active fault. In many cases, bluffs form from the upthrown block and can be very steep.
   a. Shutter ridge
   b. Stream gradient
   c. Fault scarp
   d. Gravitational erosion

38. Since faults do not usually consist of a single, clean fracture, the term fault zone is used when referring to the zone of complex deformation that is associated with the fault plane. The two sides of a non-vertical fault are called the _____ and footwall. By definition, the _____ occurs above the fault and the footwall occurs below the fault.
   a. Reverse fault
   b. Fault plane
   c. Hanging wall
   d. 1509 Istanbul earthquake

39. _____ or sheet joints are surface-parallel fracture systems in rock often leading to erosion of concentric slabs.
   a. AL 129-1
   b. AL 333
   c. Exfoliation joints
   d. AASHTO Soil Classification System

40. _____ is a rock composed of angular fragments of minerals or rocks in a matrix (cementing material), that may be similar or different in composition to the fragments. A _____ may have a variety of different origins, as indicated by the named types including sedimentary _____, tectonic _____, igneous _____, impact _____ and hydrothermal _____.

Sedimentary _____s are a type of clastic sedimentary rock which are composed of angular to subangular, randomly oriented clasts of other sedimentary rocks.

   a. Coprolite
   b. Ventifacts
   c. 1509 Istanbul earthquake
   d. Breccia

41. A _____ is the opposite of a normal fault -- the hanging wall moves up relative to the footwall. They are indicative of shortening of the crust. The dip of a _____ is relatively steep, greater than 45>°.

a. Hanging wall
b. Fault plane
c. 1509 Istanbul earthquake
d. Reverse fault

42. A _____ is a type of fault in which rocks of lower stratigraphic position are pushed up and over higher strata. They are often recognized because they place older rocks above younger. _____s are the result of compressional forces.
   a. Motagua Fault
   b. Panthalassa
   c. Thrust fault
   d. Supercontinent cycle

43. The fault surface of _____ is usually near vertical and the footwall moves either left or right or laterally with very little vertical motion. _____ with left-lateral motion are also known as sinistral faults. Those with right-lateral motion are also known as dextral faults.
   a. Loihi Seamount
   b. Strike-slip faults
   c. Tertiary
   d. Star dunes

44. A _____ is a large, slow-moving mass of ice, formed from compacted layers of snow, that slowly deforms and flows in response to gravity and high pressure.

_____ ice is the largest reservoir of fresh water on Earth, and second only to oceans as the largest reservoir of total water.

   a. Greenhouse gases
   b. Little Ice Age
   c. Pacific Decadal Oscillation
   d. Glacier

45. The _____ is a geologic fault structure of the Rocky Mountains within Glacier National Park in Montana, USA and Waterton Lakes National Park in Alberta, Canada, as well as into Lewis and Clark National Forest. It provides scientific insight into geologic processes happening in other parts of the world, like the Andes and the Himalaya Mountains. Scientific study of this region is practical because the original rock characteristics were well-preserved and recently sculptured by glaciers.
   a. 1509 Istanbul earthquake
   b. Lewis overthrust
   c. 1700 Cascadia earthquake
   d. 1703 Genroku earthquake

46. A _____ or transform boundary is a fault which runs along the boundary of a tectonic plate. The relative motion of such plates is horizontal in either sinistral or dextral direction. Typically, some vertical motion may also exist, but the principal vectors in a _____ are oriented horizontally.
   a. Crenulation
   b. Transform fault
   c. Strike and dip
   d. Syncline

47. In geology, a _____ is a location on the Earth's surface that has experienced active volcanism for a long period of time.

J. Tuzo Wilson came up with the idea in 1963 that volcanic chains like the Hawaiian Islands result from the slow movement of a tectonic plate across a 'fixed' _____ deep beneath the surface of the planet.

   a. 1700 Cascadia earthquake
   b. 1703 Genroku earthquake
   c. 1509 Istanbul earthquake
   d. Hotspot

48. A _____ is an elevated area of land with a flat top and sides that are usually steep cliffs. It takes its name from its characteristic table-top shape. It is a characteristic landform of arid environments, particularly the southwestern United States.

_____s form usually in areas where horizontally layered rocks are uplifted by tectonic activity, but may form also in its absence.

_____s are formed by weathering and erosion. Variations in the ability of different types of rock to resist weathering and erosion cause the weaker types of rocks to be eroded away, leaving the more resistant types of rocks topographically higher relative to their surroundings. This process is called differential erosion.

    a. 1509 Istanbul earthquake
    b. Palustrine
    c. Truncated spur
    d. Mesa

49. Alpine glaciers form high on the mountain slopes and are niche, slope or cirque glaciers. As a mountain glacier increases in size it can begin to flow down valley, and are referred to as _____.
    a. Tertiary
    b. Star dunes
    c. Strike-slip faults
    d. Valley glaciers

50. _____ is a geologic term for a type of topography characterized by a series of separate and parallel mountain ranges with broad valleys interposed, extending over a more or less wide area. It is typified by the topography found in the Great Basin in the western United States, which is part of a larger regional topography known as the _____ Province. _____ topography results from crustal extension.
    a. Slaty cleavage
    b. Lithostatic pressure
    c. Rill
    d. Basin and Range

51. The _____ is a large geologic province which includes parts of the southwestern United States and northwestern Mexico, typified by basin and range topography.

The topography of the _____ is a result of crustal extension within this part of the North American Plate. The cause of this extension is as yet not fully understood, although several hypotheses have been offered. The crust here has been stretched up to 100% of its original width. In fact, the crust underneath the _____, especially under the Great Basin, is some of the thinnest in the world.

    a. Basin and Range Province
    b. Musgrave Block
    c. Great Artesian Basin
    d. Gawler craton

52. The _____ is the layer of igneous, sedimentary, and metamorphic rocks which form the continents and the areas of shallow seabed close to their shores, known as continental shelves. This layer is sometimes called sial due to more felsic, or granitic, bulk composition, which lies in contrast to the oceanic crust, called sima due to its mafic, or basaltic rock. (Based on the change in velocity of seismic waves, it is believed that at a certain depth sial becomes close in its physical properties to sima.
    a. Mirovia
    b. Continental crust
    c. Divergent boundary
    d. Plate tectonics

53. A _____ is a depressed block of land bordered by parallel faults.

Chapter 13. Deformation, Mountain Building, and the Evolution of Continents 362

A _____ is the result of a block of land being downthrown producing a valley with a distinct scarp on each side.

_____ are produced from parallel normal faults, where the hanging wall is downthrown and the footwall is upthrown. The faults typically dip toward the center of the _____ from both sides.

a. Shear
b. Syncline
c. Strike and dip
d. Graben

54. _____ is the part of Earth's lithosphere that surfaces in the ocean basins. _____ is primarily composed of mafic rocks, or sima. It is thinner than continental crust, or sial, generally less than 10 kilometers thick, however it is denser, having a mean density of about 3.3 grams per cubic centimeter.
a. AL 129-1
b. AL 333
c. AASHTO Soil Classification System
d. Oceanic crust

55. _____ describes the large scale motions of Earth's lithosphere. The theory encompasses the older concepts of continental drift, developed during the first decades of the 20th century by Alfred Wegener, and seafloor spreading, understood during the 1960s.

The outermost part of the Earth's interior is made up of two layers: the lithosphere and the asthenosphere.

a. Lithosphere
b. Supercontinent cycle
c. Copperbelt Province
d. Plate tectonics

56. An _____ or accretionary prism is formed from sediments that are accreted onto the non-subducting tectonic plate at a convergent plate boundary. Most of the material in the _____ consists of marine sediments scraped off from the downgoing slab of oceanic crust but in some cases includes the erosional products of volcanic island arcs formed on the overriding plate.

The internal structure of an _____ is similar to that found in a thin-skinned foreland thrust belt.

a. AL 333
b. Accretionary wedge
c. AASHTO Soil Classification System
d. AL 129-1

57. _____ are geologic features, submarine basins associated with island arcs and subduction zones. They are found at some convergent plate boundaries, presently concentrated in the Western Pacific ocean. Most of them result from tensional forces caused by oceanic trench rollback and the collapse of the edge of the continent.
a. 1700 Cascadia earthquake
b. 1509 Istanbul earthquake
c. 1703 Genroku earthquake
d. Back-arc basins

58. _____ is a rock that forms by the metamorphism of basalt and rocks with similar composition at high pressures and low temperatures, approximately corresponding to a depth of 15 to 30 kilometers and 200 to ~500 degrees Celsius. The blue color of the rock comes from the presence of the mineral glaucophane.

They are typically found within orogenic belts as terranes of lithology in faulted contact with greenschist or rarely eclogite facies rocks.

a. Quartzite
b. Porphyroclast
c. Shock metamorphism
d. Blueschist

59. A _____ is a mountain rising from the ocean seafloor that does not reach to the water's surface (sea level), and thus is not an island. These are typically formed from extinct volcanoes, that rise abruptly and are usually found rising from a seafloor of 1,000-4,000 meters depth. They are defined by oceanographers as independent features that rise to at least 1,000 meters above the seafloor.

a. 1703 Genroku earthquake
b. 1700 Cascadia earthquake
c. Seamount
d. 1509 Istanbul earthquake

60. In geology, _____ are a body of rock with specified characteristics. Ideally, a _____ is a distinctive rock unit that forms under certain conditions of sedimentation, reflecting a particular process or environment.

The term _____ was introduced by the Swiss geologist Amanz Gressly in 1838 and was part of his significant contribution to the foundations of modern stratigraphy, [Cross and Homewood (1997)] which replaced the earlier notions of Neptunism.

a. Slate
b. Jadeitite
c. Porphyroblast
d. Facies

61. _____ is a term used in geology to refer to silicate minerals, magma, and rocks which are enriched in the lighter elements such as silicon, oxygen, aluminium, sodium, and potassium. _____ minerals are usually light in color and have specific gravities less than 3. Common _____ minerals include quartz, muscovite, orthoclase, and the sodium-rich plagioclase feldspars.

a. Laccolith
b. Felsic
c. Sedimentary rock
d. Phenocryst

62. The _____ is a mid-ocean ridge, a divergent tectonic plate boundary located along the floor of the Atlantic Ocean, and the longest mountain range in the world. It separates the Eurasian Plate and North American Plate in the North Atlantic, and the African Plate from the South American Plate in the South Atlantic. The MAR extends from a junction with the Gakkel Ridge (Mid-Arctic Ridge) northeast of Greenland southward to the Bouvet Triple Junction in the South Atlantic.

a. 1509 Istanbul earthquake
b. Mid-Atlantic Ridge
c. 1700 Cascadia earthquake
d. 1703 Genroku earthquake

63. _____ was the supercontinent that is theorized to have existed during the Paleozoic and Mesozoic eras about 250 million years ago, before the component continents were separated into their current configuration.

The name was first used by the German originator of the continental drift theory, Alfred Wegener, in the 1920 edition of his book The Origin of Continents and Oceans , in which a postulated supercontinent _____ played a key role.

The single enormous ocean which surrounded Pangaea is known as Panthalassa.

a. 1509 Istanbul earthquake
b. 1703 Genroku earthquake
c. 1700 Cascadia earthquake
d. Pangea

64. The _____ is an oceanic trench in the eastern Pacific Ocean, about 160 kilometers off the coast of Peru and Chile. It reaches a maximum depth of 8,065 meters below sea level in the Richards Deep and is approximately 5,900 kilometers long; its mean width is 64 kilometers and it covers an expanse of some 590,000 square kilometers

The trench is a result of the eastern edge of the Nazca Plate being subducted under the South American Plate.

a. Peru-Chile Trench
b. 1700 Cascadia earthquake
c. 1703 Genroku earthquake
d. 1509 Istanbul earthquake

65. The _____ is a tectonic plate covering the continent of South America and extending eastward to the Mid-Atlantic Ridge.

The easterly side is a divergent boundary with the African Plate forming the southern part of the Mid-Atlantic Ridge. The southerly side is a complex boundary with the Antarctic Plate and the Scotia Plate.

a. Sunda Plate
b. Somali Plate
c. Kermadec Plate
d. South American plate

66. In geology, _____ is the process that takes place at convergent boundaries by which one tectonic plate moves under another tectonic plate, sinking into the Earth's mantle, as the plates converge. A _____ zone is an area on Earth where two tectonic plates move towards one another and _____ occurs. Rates of _____ are typically measured in centimeters per year, with the average rate of convergence being approximately 2 to 8 centimeters per year (about the rate a fingernail grows.)
a. Thrust fault
b. Forearc
c. Panthalassa
d. Subduction

67. _____ is the movement of the Earth's continents relative to each other. The hypothesis that continents 'drift' was first put forward by Abraham Ortelius in 1596 and was fully developed by Alfred Wegener in 1912. However, it was not until the development of the theory of plate tectonics in the 1960s, that a sufficient geological explanation of that movement was found.
a. Nappe
b. Mirovia
c. Subduction
d. Continental drift

68. In geology, _____ is transported rock debris overlying the solid bedrock. The term is also sometimes refers to organic debris so-transported. In the largest sense, it refers to the material left behind by retreating continental glaciers.
a. Geostrophic current
b. Contact metamorphism
c. Detritus
d. Drift

69. _____ is molten rock that is found beneath the surface of the Earth, and may also exist on other terrestrial planets. Besides molten rock, _____ may also contain suspended crystals and gas bubbles. _____ often collects in a _____ chamber inside a volcano. _____ is capable of intrusion into adjacent rocks, extrusion onto the surface as lava, and explosive ejection as tephra to form pyroclastic rock.

a. Vesicular texture
b. Metavolcanic rock
c. Rock cycle
d. Magma

70. The _____ is one of three tectonic plates which have been moving northward over millions of years toward an inevitable collision with Eurasia. This is resulting in a mingling of plate pieces and mountain ranges extending in the west from the Pyrenees, crossing southern Europe and the Middle East, to the Himalayas and ranges of southeast Asia.

The _____ consists mostly of the Arabian peninsula; it extends northward to Turkey.

a. Okhotsk Plate
b. Easter Plate
c. Eurasian Plate
d. Arabian plate

71. The _____ is a tectonic plate that was originally a part of the ancient continent of Gondwanaland from which it split off, eventually becoming a major plate. About 50 to 55 million years ago, it fused with the adjacent Australian Plate. It is today part of the major Indo-Australian Plate, and includes the subcontinent of India and a portion of the basin under the Indian Ocean.

a. AASHTO Soil Classification System
b. AL 129-1
c. AL 333
d. Indian plate

72. A _____ in geology is a fragment of crustal material formed on one tectonic plate and accreted -- 'sutured' -- to crust lying on another plate. The crustal block or fragment preserves its own distinctive geologic history, which is different from that of the surrounding areas (hence the term 'exotic' _____). The suture zone between a _____ and the crust it attaches to is usually identifiable as a fault.

a. 1700 Cascadia earthquake
b. 1703 Genroku earthquake
c. 1509 Istanbul earthquake
d. Terrane

73. _____ is one of the three main rock types (the others being sedimentary and metamorphic rock.) _____ is formed by magma (molten rock) being cooled and becoming solid . They may form with or without crystallization, either below the surface as intrusive (plutonic) rocks or on the surface as extrusive (volcanic) rocks. They make up approximately 95% of the upper part of the Earth's crust, but their great abundance is hidden on the Earth's surface by a relatively thin but widespread layer of sedimentary and metamorphic rocks.

a. AL 129-1
b. Igneous rock
c. AL 333
d. AASHTO Soil Classification System

74. The _____ is a rock outcrop of Archaean tonalite gneiss in the Slave craton in Northwest Territories, Canada. The rock exposed in the outcrop formed just over four billion (4×10^9) years ago; an age based on radiometric dating of zircon crystals at 4.03 Ga, which were the oldest rocks in the world at that time. It was the oldest known rock outcrop in the world until a McGill University team reported a 4.28 billion year old outcrop on the eastern shores of Hudson Bay, 40 kilometres south of Inukjuak, Quebec, Canada.

a. AL 333
b. AL 129-1
c. AASHTO Soil Classification System
d. Acasta Gneiss

75. The _____ -- also called the Laurentian Plateau, or Bouclier Canadien -- is a massive geological shield covered by a thin layer of soil that forms the nucleus of the North American or Laurentia craton. It has a deep, common, joined bedrock region in eastern and central Canada and stretches North from the Great Lakes to the Arctic Ocean, covering over half of Canada; it also extends south into the northern reaches of the United States. Population is scarce, and industrial development is minimal, although the region has a large hydroelectric power potential.
   a. Yilgarn Craton
   b. Sahara pump theory
   c. Gawler craton
   d. Canadian Shield

76. A _____ is an old and stable part of the continental crust that has survived the merging and splitting of continents and supercontinents for at least 500 million years. Some are over two billion years old. They are generally found in the interiors of continents and are characteristically composed of ancient crystalline basement crust of lightweight felsic igneous rock such as granite.
   a. Craton
   b. Sebakwe proto-craton
   c. Kalahari craton
   d. Wyoming craton

77. _____ is a common and widely distributed type of rock formed by high-grade regional metamorphic processes from pre-existing formations that were originally either igneous or sedimentary rocks. Gneissic rocks are usually medium to coarse foliated and largely recrystallized but do not carry large quantities of micas, chlorite or other platy minerals. _____es that are metamorphosed igneous rocks or their equivalent are termed granite _____es, diorite _____es, etc.
   a. 1703 Genroku earthquake
   b. 1700 Cascadia earthquake
   c. 1509 Istanbul earthquake
   d. Gneiss

78. In geology, a _____ is a continental area covered by relatively flat or gently tilted, mainly sedimentary strata, which overlie a basement of consolidated igneous or metamorphic rocks of an earlier deformation. They as well as, shields and the basement rocks together constitute cratons.

It is also common practice to use the term _____ as a very general term for a sequence of shallow water carbonate _____.

   a. Streak
   b. Nodule
   c. Texture
   d. Platform

79. A _____ is generally a large area of exposed Precambrian crystalline igneous and high-grade metamorphic rocks that form tectonically stable areas. In all cases, the age of these rocks is greater than 570 million years and sometimes dates back 2 to 3.5 billion years. They have been little affected by tectonic events following the end of the Precambrian Era, and are relatively flat regions where mountain building, faulting, and other tectonic processes are greatly diminished compared with the activity that occurs at the margins of the _____s and the boundaries between tectonic plates.
   a. 1509 Istanbul earthquake
   b. Shield
   c. 1703 Genroku earthquake
   d. 1700 Cascadia earthquake

80. The _____ forms the core of both the North American continent and the Canadian Shield. It extends from Quebec in the east to eastern Manitoba in the west. The western margin extends from northern Minnesota through eastern Manitoba to northwestern Ontario.

The formation of the _____ is best explained within the context of 2.72-2.68 Ga accretion of small continental plates and trapped oceanic terranes in a tectonic regime resembling that of the rapidly changing southwestern Pacific Ocean. The craton is made up of a collage of small continental fragments of Mesoarchean age and Neoarchean oceanic plates and tracts of oceanic crust that consists of the following domains: Northern Superior, North Caribou, Winnipeg River, Marmion, Minnesota River Valley, Opatica, and Goudalie.

- a. Craton
- b. Wyoming craton
- c. Sebakwe proto-craton
- d. Superior Craton

81. The _____, was the major mountain building event that formed the Precambrian Canadian Shield, the North American craton, and the forging of the initial North American continent. It is the largest Paleoproterozoic orogenic belt in the world. It consists of a network of belts that were formed by Proterozoic crustal accretion and the collision of pre-existing Archean continents.

- a. Sevier orogeny
- b. Taconic orogeny
- c. Trans-Hudson orogeny
- d. Nevadan orogeny

82. The _____ is located in the west-central United States and west-central Canada -- more specifically, in Montana, Wyoming, southern Alberta, southern Saskatchewan, and parts of northern Utah. Also called the Wyoming province, it is the initial core of the continental crust of North America.

The _____ was sutured together with the Superior and Hearne-Rae cratons in the mountain-building episode that created the Trans-Hudson Suture Zone to form the core of North America (Laurentia.).

- a. Superior craton
- b. Craton
- c. Kalahari craton
- d. Wyoming Craton

83. _____ is a geological process occurring when areas of submerged seafloor are exposed above the sea level. The opposite event, marine transgression, occurs when flooding from the sea covers previously exposed land.

Evidence of _____ and transgression occurs throughout the fossil record, and these fluctuations are thought to have caused (or contributed to) several mass extinctions, among them the Permian-Triassic extinction event (250 million years ago) and Cretaceous-Tertiary extinction event (65 Ma.)

- a. 1700 Cascadia earthquake
- b. 1509 Istanbul earthquake
- c. 1703 Genroku earthquake
- d. Marine regression

84. A marine _____ is a geologic event during which sea level rises relative to the land and the shoreline moves toward higher ground, resulting in flooding. They can be caused either by the land sinking or the ocean basins filling with water (or decreasing in capacity.) Transgresssions and regressions may be caused by tectonic events such as orogenies, severe climate change such as ice ages or isostatic adjustments following removal of ice or sediment load.

- a. Hydrothermal circulation
- b. Hydraulic action
- c. Diagenesis
- d. Transgression

Chapter 14. Mass Wasting

1. The _____ is a cosmological model of the initial conditions and subsequent development of the universe. It is supported by the most comprehensive and accurate explanations from current scientific evidence and observation. As used by cosmologists, the term _____ generally refers to the idea that the universe has expanded from a primordial hot and dense initial condition at some finite time in the past, and continues to expand to this day.
   a. 1700 Cascadia earthquake
   b. 1509 Istanbul earthquake
   c. 1703 Genroku earthquake
   d. Big Bang

2. A _____ is a geological phenomenon which includes a wide range of ground movement, such as rock falls, deep failure of slopes and shallow debris flows, which can occur in offshore, coastal and onshore environments. Although the action of gravity is the primary driving force for a _____ to occur, there are other contributing factors affecting the original slope stability. Typically, pre-conditional factors build up specific sub-surface conditions that make the area/slope prone to failure, whereas the actual _____ often requires a trigger before being released.
   a. 1700 Cascadia earthquake
   b. Soil liquefaction
   c. 1509 Istanbul earthquake
   d. Landslide

3. _____ is the geomorphic process by which soil, regolith, and rock move downslope under the force of gravity. Types of _____ include creep, slides, flows, topples, and falls, each with its own characteristic features, and taking place over timescales from seconds to years. _____ occurs on both terrestrial and submarine slopes, and has been observed on Earth, Mars, and Venus.
   a. 1509 Istanbul earthquake
   b. Soil liquefaction
   c. 1700 Cascadia earthquake
   d. Mass wasting

4. _____ is the decomposition of Earth rocks, soils and their minerals through direct contact with the planet's atmosphere. _____ occurs in situ, or 'with no movement', and thus should not be confused with erosion, which involves the movement of rocks and minerals by agents such as water, ice, wind and gravity.

   Two important classifications of _____ processes exist -- physical and chemical _____.

   a. Physical weathering
   b. Weathering
   c. 1509 Istanbul earthquake
   d. Frost disintegration

5. An _____ is the result of a sudden release of energy in the Earth's crust that creates seismic waves. They are recorded with a seismometer or the related and mostly obsolete Richter magnitude, with a magnitude 3 or lower _____ being mostly imperceptible and magnitude 7 causing serious damage over large areas.
   a. AL 333
   b. AASHTO Soil Classification System
   c. AL 129-1
   d. Earthquake

6. The _____ is an engineering property of granular materials. The _____ is the maximum angle of a stable slope determined by friction, cohesion and the shapes of the particles.

   When bulk granular materials are poured onto a horizontal surface, a conical pile will form. The internal angle between the surface of the pile and the horizontal surface is known as the _____ and is related to the density, surface area, and coefficient of friction of the material.

   a. Angle of repose
   b. AL 333
   c. AL 129-1
   d. AASHTO Soil Classification System

Chapter 14. Mass Wasting

7. A system in _____ is a particular example of a system in a steady state. In a steady state the rate of inputs is equal to the rate of outputs so that the composition of the system is unchanging in time. For example, a lake is in a steady state when water flows in at the same rate as water flows out.
   a. Dynamic equilibrium
   b. 1700 Cascadia earthquake
   c. 1509 Istanbul earthquake
   d. 1703 Genroku earthquake

8. Study of geological _____ is related to the study of structural geology, rock microstructure or rock texture and fault mechanics.

   _____ is the response of a rock to deformation usually by compressive stress and forms particular textures. _____ can be homogeneous or non-homogeneous, and may be pure _____ or simple _____.

   a. Shear
   b. Graben
   c. Syncline
   d. Petermann Orogeny

9. _____ in reference to soil is a term used to describe the maximum strength of soil at which point significant plastic deformation or yielding occurs due to an applied shear stress. There is no definitive '_____' of a soil as it depends on a number of factors affecting the soil at any given time and on the frame of reference, in particular the rate at which the shearing occurs.

   Two theories are commonly used to estimate the _____ of a soil depending on the rate of shearing as a frame of reference.

   a. Shear strength
   b. Groundwater-related subsidence
   c. Slope stability
   d. Critical state soil mechanics

10. In stratigraphy, _____ is the native consolidated rock underlying the surface of a terrestrial planet, usually the Earth. Above the _____ is usually an area of broken and weathered unconsolidated rock in the basal subsoil. The top of the _____ is known as rockhead and identifying this, via excavations, drilling or geophysical methods, is an important task in most civil engineering projects.
    a. Polystrate
    b. Biozones
    c. Bedrock
    d. Sequence stratigraphy

11. _____ is the removal of solids (sediment, soil, rock and other particles) in the natural environment. It usually occurs due to transport by wind, water, or ice; by down-slope creep of soil and other material under the force of gravity; or by living organisms, such as burrowing animals, in the case of bioerosion.

    _____ is distinguished from weathering, which is the process of chemical or physical breakdown of the minerals in the rocks, although the two processes may occur concurrently.

    a. AASHTO Soil Classification System
    b. AL 129-1
    c. AL 333
    d. Erosion

Chapter 14. Mass Wasting

12. _____ is a naturally occurring material composed primarily of fine-grained minerals, which show plasticity through a variable range of water content, and which can be hardened when dried and/or fired. _____ deposits are mostly composed of _____ minerals (phyllosilicate minerals), minerals which impart plasticity and harden when fired and/or dried, and variable amounts of water trapped in the mineral structure by polar attraction. Organic materials which do not impart plasticity may also be a part of _____ deposits.
    a. 1700 Cascadia earthquake
    b. Clay
    c. 1509 Istanbul earthquake
    d. 1703 Genroku earthquake

13. _____ is the geological process by which material is added to a landform or land mass. Fluids such as wind and water, as well as sediment gravity flows, transport previously eroded sediment, which, at the loss of enough kinetic energy in the fluid, is deposited, building up layers of sediment.

_____ occurs when the forces responsible for sediment transportation are no longer sufficient to overcome the forces of particle weight and friction, which resist motion.

    a. Hydraulic action
    b. Hydrothermal circulation
    c. Stoping
    d. Deposition

14. An _____ is a rapid flow of snow down a slope, from either natural triggers or human activity. Typically occurring in mountainous terrain, an _____ can mix air and water with the descending snow. Powerful _____s have the capability to entrain ice, rocks, trees, and other material on the slope; however _____s are always initiated in snow, are primarily composed of flowing snow, and are distinct from mudslides, rock slides, rock _____s, and serac collapses from an icefall.
    a. Avalanche
    b. AL 333
    c. AASHTO Soil Classification System
    d. AL 129-1

15. The field of _____ encompasses the analysis of static and dynamic stability of slopes of earth and rock-fill dams, slopes of other types of embankments, excavated slopes, and natural slopes in soil and soft rock.

Earthen slopes can develop a cut-spherical weakness zone. The probability of this happening can be calculated in advance using a simple 2-D circular analysis package. A primary difficulty with analysis is locating the most-probable slip plane for any given situation. Many landslides have only been analyzed after the fact.

    a. Groundwater-related subsidence
    b. Critical state soil mechanics
    c. Consolidation
    d. Slope stability

16. In geology a _____ is the smallest division of a geologic formation or stratigraphic rock series marked by well-defined divisional planes (bedding planes) separating it from layers above and below. A _____ is the smallest lithostratigraphic unit, usually ranging in thickness from a centimeter to several meters and distinguishable from _____s above and below it. _____s can be differentiated in various ways, including rock or mineral type and particle size.
    a. Biozones
    b. Sequence stratigraphy
    c. Bed
    d. Cyclostratigraphy

Chapter 14. Mass Wasting

17. Two important classifications of weathering processes exist -- physical and _____. Mechanical or physical weathering involves the breakdown of rocks and soils through direct contact with atmospheric conditions, such as heat, water, ice and pressure. The second classification, _____, involves the direct effect of atmospheric chemicals or biologically produced chemicals (also known as biological weathering) in the breakdown of rocks, soils and minerals.
    a. Physical weathering
    b. Frost disintegration
    c. 1509 Istanbul earthquake
    d. Chemical weathering

18. _____ can also be called frost shattering or frost-wedging. This type of weathering is common in mountain areas where the temperature is around freezing point. Frost induced weathering, although often attributed to the expansion of freezing water captured in cracks, is generally independent of the water-to-ice expansion. It has long been known that moist soils expand or frost heave upon freezing as a result of water migrating along from unfrozen areas via thin films to collect at growing ice lenses. This same phenomena occurs within pore spaces of rocks.
    a. Weathering
    b. Physical weathering
    c. 1509 Istanbul earthquake
    d. Frost disintegration

19. _____ is a term given to an accumulation of broken rock fragments at the base of crags, mountain cliffs, or valley shoulders. Landforms associated with these materials are sometimes called _____ slopes or talus piles. These deposits typically have a concave upwards form, while the maximum inclination of such deposits corresponds to the angle of repose of the mean debris size.
    a. 1703 Genroku earthquake
    b. 1509 Istanbul earthquake
    c. 1700 Cascadia earthquake
    d. Scree

20. In geology the term _____ refers to a fracture in rock where there has been no lateral movement in the plane of the fracture (up, down or sideways) of one side relative to the other. This makes it different from a fault which is defined as a fracture in rock where one side slides laterally past to the other. _____s normally have a regular spacing related to either the mechanical properties of the individual rock or the thickness of the layer involved.
    a. 1703 Genroku earthquake
    b. 1509 Istanbul earthquake
    c. Joint
    d. 1700 Cascadia earthquake

21. In materials science, _____ is a change in the shape or size of an object due to an applied force. This can be a result of tensile (pulling) forces, compressive (pushing) forces, shear, bending or torsion (twisting.) _____ is often described as strain.
    a. Deformation
    b. Combe
    c. Melange
    d. Stack

22. _____ refers to quantities of rock falling freely from a cliff face. A _____ is a fragment of rock (a block) detached by sliding, toppling, or falling, that falls along a vertical or sub-vertical cliff, proceeds down slope by bouncing and flying along ballistic trajectories or by rolling on talus or debris slopes,'e; (Varnes, 1978.) Alternatively, a '_____ is the natural downward motion of a detached block or series of blocks with a small volume involving free falling, bouncing, rolling, and sliding'.
    a. Geohazard
    b. Rockfall
    c. Solifluction
    d. Cryoseism

Chapter 14. Mass Wasting

23. _____ is a form of mass wasting event that occurs when loosely consolidated materials or rock layers move a short distance down a slope. The landmass and the surface it _____s upon is called a failure surface. When the movement occurs in soil, there is often a distinctive rotational movement to the mass, that cuts vertically through bedding planes (landslides take place along a bedding plane or fault). This rotational movement moves along a curved slip surface of regolith (the failure surface) which overlies bedrock. This results in internal deformation of the moving mass consisting chiefly of overturned folds called 'sheath folds.'
   a. Slump
   b. 1509 Istanbul earthquake
   c. Topsoil
   d. Soil

24. _____ is the area of geology that deals with the distribution and movement of groundwater in the soil and rocks of the Earth's crust, (commonly in aquifers). The term geohydrology is often used interchangeably. Some make the minor distinction between a hydrologist or engineer applying themselves to geology (geohydrology), and a geologist applying themselves to hydrology (_____).
   a. Hydrogeology
   b. 1703 Genroku earthquake
   c. 1509 Istanbul earthquake
   d. 1700 Cascadia earthquake

25. A _____ or sandstorm is a meteorological phenomenon common in arid and semi-arid regions and arises when a gust front passes or when the wind force exceeds the threshold value where loose sand and dust are removed from the dry surface. Particles are transported by saltation and suspension, causing soil erosion from one place and deposition in another. The Sahara and drylands around the Arabian peninsula are the main source of airborne dust, with some contributions from Iran, Pakistan and India into the Arabian Sea, and China's storms deposit dust in the Pacific.
   a. Dust storm
   b. 1703 Genroku earthquake
   c. 1509 Istanbul earthquake
   d. 1700 Cascadia earthquake

26. A _____ is a fast moving mass of unconsolidated, saturated debris that looks like flowing concrete. They differentiate from a mudflow by terms of the viscosity of the flow. Flows can carry clasts ranging in size from clay particles to boulders, and also often contains a large amount of woody debris.
   a. Solifluction
   b. Predator trap
   c. Debris flow
   d. Cryoseism

27. An _____ is a downslope viscous flow of fine grained materials that have been saturated with water, and moves under the pull of gravity. They are an intermediate type of mass wasting that is between downhill creep and mudflow. The types of materials that are susceptible to _____s are clay, fine sand and silt, and fine-grained pyroclastic material.
   a. AASHTO Soil Classification System
   b. AL 333
   c. AL 129-1
   d. Earthflow

28. A _____ or mudslide is the most rapid (up to 80 km/h, or 50 mph) and fluid type of downhill mass wasting. It is a rapid movement of a large mass of mud formed from loose earth and water. Similar terms are mudslide (not very liquid), mud stream, debris flow (e.g. in high mountains), j>ökulhlaup, and lahar
   a. 1700 Cascadia earthquake
   b. 1703 Genroku earthquake
   c. 1509 Istanbul earthquake
   d. Mudflow

29. _____ is a measure of the resistance of a fluid which is being deformed by either shear stress or extensional stress. In everyday terms (and for fluids only), _____ is 'thickness'. Thus, water is 'thin', having a lower _____, while honey is 'thick' having a higher _____.

Chapter 14. Mass Wasting

a. Thixotropy
c. Shear stress
b. Viscosity
d. Tensile stress

30. _____ is a unique form of highly sensitive marine clay, with the tendency to change from a relatively stiff condition to a liquid mass when it is disturbed.

Undisturbed _____ resembles a water-saturated gel. When a mass of _____ undergoes sufficient stress, however, it instantly turns into a flowing ooze, a process known as liquefaction.

a. Fech fech
c. Quick clay
b. Bovey Beds
d. Sediment

31. In geology, _____ or _____ soil is soil at or below the freezing point of water (0 >°C or 32 >°F) for two or more years. Ice is not always present, as may be in the case of nonporous bedrock, but it frequently occurs and it may be in amounts exceeding the potential hydraulic saturation of the ground material. Most _____ is located in high latitudes (i.e. land in close proximity to the North and South poles), but alpine _____ may exist at high altitudes in much lower latitudes.

a. 1700 Cascadia earthquake
c. 1509 Istanbul earthquake
b. 1703 Genroku earthquake
d. Permafrost

32. In geology, _____ is a type of mass wasting where waterlogged sediment slowly moves downslope over impermeable material. It can occur in any climate where the ground is saturated by water, though it is most often found in periglacial environments where the ground is permanently frozen, under which conditions the process is often called gelifluction. During warm seasonal periods the surface layer melts and slides over the frozen underlayer, slowly moving downslope due to frost heave that occurs normal to the slope.

a. Sturzstrom
c. Debris flow
b. Solifluction
d. Geohazard

33. _____ is the naturally occurring, unconsolidated or loose covering on the Earth's surface. _____ is composed of particles of broken rock that have been altered by chemical, biological and environmental processes including weathering and erosion. _____ is different from its parent rock(s) source(s), altered by interactions between the lithosphere, hydrosphere, atmosphere, and the biosphere.

a. Topsoil
c. Soil
b. 1509 Istanbul earthquake
d. Slump

34. A _____ is a structure that holds back soil or rock from a building, structure or area. _____s prevent downslope movement or erosion and provide support for vertical or near-vertical grade changes. Cofferdams and bulkheads, structures that hold back water, are sometimes also considered _____s.

a. 1703 Genroku earthquake
c. 1700 Cascadia earthquake
b. 1509 Istanbul earthquake
d. Retaining wall

35. A _____ is a long anchor bolt, for stabilizing rock excavations, which may be tunnels or rock cuts. It transfers load from the unstable exterior, to the confined (and much stronger) interior of the rock mass.

They were first used in mining starting in the 1890s, with systematic use documented at the St Joseph Lead Mine in the US in the 1920s.

a. Dynamic load testing
c. Rock bolt

b. Wave equation analysis
d. Nuclear Densometer Test

Chapter 15. Running Water

1. A _____ is a large, slow-moving mass of ice, formed from compacted layers of snow, that slowly deforms and flows in response to gravity and high pressure.

_____ ice is the largest reservoir of fresh water on Earth, and second only to oceans as the largest reservoir of total water.

  a. Pacific Decadal Oscillation
  b. Little Ice Age
  c. Greenhouse gases
  d. Glacier

2. _____s, sometimes called minor planets or planetoids, are small Solar System bodies in orbit around the Sun, especially in the inner Solar System; they are smaller than planets but larger than meteoroids. The term '_____' has historically been applied primarily to bodies in the inner Solar System since the outer Solar System was poorly known when it came into common usage. The distinction between _____s and comets is made on visual appearance: Comets show a perceptible coma while _____s do not.
  a. AL 333
  b. Asteroid
  c. AASHTO Soil Classification System
  d. AL 129-1

3. The _____ is a chronologic schema (or idealized model) relating stratigraphy to time that is used by geologists, paleontologists and other earth scientists to describe the timing and relationships between events that have occurred during the history of the Earth. The table of geologic time spans presented here agrees with the dates and nomenclature proposed by the International Commission on Stratigraphy, and uses the standard color codes of the United States Geological Survey.

Evidence from radiometric dating indicates that the Earth is about 4.570 billion years old.

  a. 1509 Istanbul earthquake
  b. 1700 Cascadia earthquake
  c. 1703 Genroku earthquake
  d. Geologic time scale

4. In physics, _____ is the rate at which work is performed or energy is transmitted, or the amount of energy required or expended for a given unit of time. As a rate of change of work done or the energy of a subsystem, _____ is:

$$P = \frac{W}{t}$$

where P is _____, W is work and t is time.

The average _____ (often simply called '_____' when the context makes it clear) is the average amount of work done or energy transferred per unit time.

  a. 1509 Istanbul earthquake
  b. Strong interaction
  c. Turbulent flow
  d. Power

5. The _____ describes the continuous movement of water on, above, and below the surface of the Earth. Since the _____ is truly a 'cycle,' there is no beginning or end. Water can change states among liquid, vapor, and ice at various places in the _____.
  a. Stream capacity
  b. Surface water
  c. Water cycle
  d. Hydraulic conductivity

Chapter 15. Running Water

6. _____ is the process by which water on the ground surface enters the soil. _____ rate in soil science is a measure of the rate at which soil is able to absorb rainfall or irrigation. It is measured in inches per hour or millimeters per hour.
   a. AASHTO Soil Classification System
   b. AL 129-1
   c. AL 333
   d. Infiltration

7. _____, sometimes known as streamline flow, occurs when a fluid flows in parallel layers, with no disruption between the layers. In fluid dynamics, _____ is a flow regime characterized by high momentum diffusion, low momentum convection, pressure and velocity independent from time. It is the opposite of turbulent flow.
   a. Laminar flow
   b. 1509 Istanbul earthquake
   c. 1703 Genroku earthquake
   d. 1700 Cascadia earthquake

8. In fluid dynamics, turbulence or _____ is a fluid regime characterized by chaotic, stochastic property changes. This includes low momentum diffusion, high momentum convection, and rapid variation of pressure and velocity in space and time. Flow that is not turbulent is called laminar flow.
   a. Power
   b. Strong interaction
   c. 1509 Istanbul earthquake
   d. Turbulent flow

9. _____ is a measure of the resistance of a fluid which is being deformed by either shear stress or extensional stress. In everyday terms (and for fluids only), _____ is 'thickness'. Thus, water is 'thin', having a lower _____, while honey is 'thick' having a higher _____.
   a. Viscosity
   b. Tensile stress
   c. Shear stress
   d. Thixotropy

10. The _____ is a cosmological model of the initial conditions and subsequent development of the universe. It is supported by the most comprehensive and accurate explanations from current scientific evidence and observation. As used by cosmologists, the term _____ generally refers to the idea that the universe has expanded from a primordial hot and dense initial condition at some finite time in the past, and continues to expand to this day.
    a. 1509 Istanbul earthquake
    b. Big Bang
    c. 1703 Genroku earthquake
    d. 1700 Cascadia earthquake

11. _____ is the removal of solids (sediment, soil, rock and other particles) in the natural environment. It usually occurs due to transport by wind, water, or ice; by down-slope creep of soil and other material under the force of gravity; or by living organisms, such as burrowing animals, in the case of bioerosion.

    _____ is distinguished from weathering, which is the process of chemical or physical breakdown of the minerals in the rocks, although the two processes may occur concurrently.

    a. AL 333
    b. AASHTO Soil Classification System
    c. AL 129-1
    d. Erosion

12. In fluid dynamics the _____ of a fluid is a vector field which is used to mathematically describe the motion of a fluid. The length of the _____ vector is the flow speed.

The _____ u of a fluid is a vector field

>

which gives the velocity of an element of fluid at a position ⬚> and time ⬚>.

   a. 1703 Genroku earthquake   b. Flow velocity
   c. 1509 Istanbul earthquake   d. 1700 Cascadia earthquake

13. _____ is water located beneath the ground surface in soil pore spaces and in the fractures of lithologic formations. A unit of rock or an unconsolidated deposit is called an aquifer when it can yield a usable quantity of water. The depth at which soil pore spaces or fractures and voids in rock become completely saturated with water is called the water table.
   a. 1700 Cascadia earthquake   b. Depression focused recharge
   c. 1509 Istanbul earthquake   d. Groundwater

14. A _____ is a narrow and shallow incision into soil resulting from erosion by overland flow that has been focused into a thin thread by soil surface roughness. Rilling, the process of _____ formation, is common on agricultural land and unvegetated ground.
   a. Transition zone   b. Cross-cutting relationships
   c. Fort Union Formation   d. Rill

15. _____ is the naturally occurring, unconsolidated or loose covering on the Earth's surface. _____ is composed of particles of broken rock that have been altered by chemical, biological and environmental processes including weathering and erosion. _____ is different from its parent rock(s) source(s), altered by interactions between the lithosphere, hydrosphere, atmosphere, and the biosphere.
   a. Topsoil   b. Slump
   c. 1509 Istanbul earthquake   d. Soil

16. _____ is the ratio of drop in a stream per unit distance, usually expressed as feet per mile or meters per kilometer. A high gradient indicates a steep slope and rapid flow of water (ie. more ability to erode); whereas a low gradient indicates a more nearly level stream bed and sluggishly moving water, that may be able to carry only small amounts of very fine sediment.
   a. Bradyseism   b. Stream gradient
   c. Coastal erosion   d. Fault-block

17. An _____ is a confined aquifer containing groundwater that will flow upward through a well without the need for pumping. Water may even reach the ground surface if the natural pressure is high enough, in which case the well is called a flowing artesian well. An aquifer provides the water for an artesian well.
   a. AL 333   b. Artesian aquifer
   c. AASHTO Soil Classification System   d. AL 129-1

18. _____ or moisture content is the quantity of water contained in a material, such as soil (called soil moisture), rock, ceramics, or wood on a volumetric or gravimetric basis. The property is used in a wide range of scientific and technical areas, and is expressed as a ratio, which can range from 0 (completely dry) to the value of the materials' porosity at saturation.

Volumetric _____, θ, is defined mathematically as:

$$\theta = \frac{V_w}{V_T}$$

where V_w is the volume of water and $V_T = V_s + V_v = V_s + V_w + V_a$ is the total volume (that is Soil Volume + Water Volume + Void Space.)

a. 1509 Istanbul earthquake
b. 1700 Cascadia earthquake
c. Trace element
d. Water content

19. _____ is the geological process by which material is added to a landform or land mass. Fluids such as wind and water, as well as sediment gravity flows, transport previously eroded sediment, which, at the loss of enough kinetic energy in the fluid, is deposited, building up layers of sediment.

_____ occurs when the forces responsible for sediment transportation are no longer sufficient to overcome the forces of particle weight and friction, which resist motion.

a. Deposition
b. Stoping
c. Hydraulic action
d. Hydrothermal circulation

20. The _____ of an object is the extra energy which it possesses due to its motion. It is defined as the work needed to accelerate a body of a given mass from rest to its current velocity. Having gained this energy during its acceleration, the body maintains this _____ unless its speed changes.

a. 1700 Cascadia earthquake
b. 1703 Genroku earthquake
c. 1509 Istanbul earthquake
d. Kinetic energy

21. _____ is any particulate matter that can be transported by fluid flow, and which eventually is deposited.

They are most often transported by water (fluvial processes) transported by wind (aeolian processes) and glaciers. Beach sands and river channel deposits are examples of fluvial transport and deposition, though _____ also often settles out of slow-moving or standing water in lakes and oceans.

a. Salt glacier
b. Quick clay
c. Bovey Beds
d. Sediment

22. _____ is mechanical scraping of a rock surface by friction between rocks and moving particles during their transport in wind, glacier, waves, gravity or running water, after friction, the moving particles dislodge loose and weak debris from the side of the rock, these particles can be dissolved in the water source.

The intensity of _____ depends on the hardness, concentration, velocity and mass of moving particles.

A virtually smooth marine platform cut by the ocean waves at a coastline.

a. AASHTO Soil Classification System
b. AL 129-1
c. AL 333
d. Abrasion

23. _____ is the term for material, especially ions from chemical weathering, that are carried in solution by a stream.
a. Salt tectonics
b. Dissolved load
c. Siliceous ooze
d. Palynomorph

24. _____ is a form of mechanical weathering caused by the force of moving water currents rushing into a crack in the rockface. The water compresses the air in the crack, pushing it right to the back. As the wave retreats, the highly pressurised air is suddenly released with explosive force, capable of chipping away the rockface over time.
a. Deposition
b. Hydrothermal circulation
c. Mid-ocean ridge
d. Hydraulic action

25. In geology a _____ is the smallest division of a geologic formation or stratigraphic rock series marked by well-defined divisional planes (bedding planes) separating it from layers above and below. A _____ is the smallest lithostratigraphic unit, usually ranging in thickness from a centimeter to several meters and distinguishable from _____s above and below it. _____s can be differentiated in various ways, including rock or mineral type and particle size.
a. Cyclostratigraphy
b. Bed
c. Sequence stratigraphy
d. Biozones

26. The term _____ describes particles in a flowing fluid (usually a river) that are transported along the bed. This is in opposition to suspended load and wash load which are carried entirely in suspension.

_____ moves by a variety of methods, including rolling, sliding, traction, and saltation.

a. Differential weathering
b. Shutter ridge
c. Bradyseism
d. Bed load

27. _____ is a naturally occurring material composed primarily of fine-grained minerals, which show plasticity through a variable range of water content, and which can be hardened when dried and/or fired. _____ deposits are mostly composed of _____ minerals (phyllosilicate minerals), minerals which impart plasticity and harden when fired and/or dried, and variable amounts of water trapped in the mineral structure by polar attraction. Organic materials which do not impart plasticity may also be a part of _____ deposits.
a. Clay
b. 1509 Istanbul earthquake
c. 1700 Cascadia earthquake
d. 1703 Genroku earthquake

28. _____ is rock that is of a specific particle size range. Specifically, it is any loose rock that is larger than two millimeters (2mm) in its largest dimension (about 1/12 of an inch) and no more than 64 millimeters (about 2.5 inches.) The next smaller size class in geology is sand, which is >0.0625 mm to 2 mm in size.

Chapter 15. Running Water

a. 1703 Genroku earthquake
c. Gravel
b. 1700 Cascadia earthquake
d. 1509 Istanbul earthquake

29. _____ is a term for a formation in rivers caused by a whirlpool eroding a hole into rock. The abrasion is mainly caused by the circular motion of small sediments such as small stones in the river. The interiors of _____s tend to be smooth and regular, unlike a plunge pool.

a. Pothole
c. Subsidence
b. 1700 Cascadia earthquake
d. 1509 Istanbul earthquake

30. In geology, _____ is a specific type of particle transport by fluids such as wind, or the denser fluid water. It occurs when loose material is removed from a bed and carried by the fluid, before being transported back to the surface. Examples include pebble transport by rivers, sand drift over desert surfaces, soil blowing over fields, or even snow drift over smooth surfaces such as those in the Arctic or Canadian Prairies.

a. Headward erosion
c. Seafloor spreading
b. Stoping
d. Saltation

31. _____ is a naturally occurring granular material composed of finely divided rock and mineral particles.

As the term is used by geologists, _____ particles range in diameter from 0.0625 (or $>^1\!/_{16}$ mm, or 62.5 micrometers) to 2 millimeters. An individual particle in this range size is termed a _____ grain.

a. 1700 Cascadia earthquake
c. 1703 Genroku earthquake
b. 1509 Istanbul earthquake
d. Sand

32. _____ is soil or rock derived granular material of a grain size between sand and clay. _____ may occur as a soil or as suspended sediment in a surface water body. It may also exist as soil deposited at the bottom of a water body.

a. 1700 Cascadia earthquake
c. 1703 Genroku earthquake
b. Silt
d. 1509 Istanbul earthquake

33. _____ is the term for the fine particles that are light enough to be carried in a stream without touching the stream bed. These particles are generally of the fine sand, silt and clay size, although they can be larger, especially in cases of high discharge, such as during floods. This is in contrast to bed load which is carried along the bottom of the stream.

a. Suspended load
c. Historical geology
b. Logarithmic Spiral Beach
d. Principle of inclusions and components

34. _____ is soil or sediments deposited by a river or other running water. _____ is typically made up of a variety of materials, including fine particles of silt and clay and larger particles of sand and gravel.

Flowing water associated with glaciers may also deposit _____, but deposits directly from ice are not _____.

a. AASHTO Soil Classification System
c. Alluvium
b. AL 333
d. AL 129-1

35. The _____ is the zone of the ocean floor that separates the thin oceanic crust from thick continental crust. _____s constitute about 28% of the oceanic area.

Chapter 15. Running Water

The transition from continental to oceanic crust commonly occurs within the outer part of the margin, called continental rise.

a. 1509 Istanbul earthquake
b. Cuspate forelands
c. Longshore drift
d. Continental margin

36. _____ is a geological term used to describe particles of rock derived from pre-existing rock through processes of weathering and erosion. Thesel particles can consist of lithic fragments (particles of recognisable rock), or of monomineralic fragments (mineral grains.) These particles are often transported through sedimentary processes into depositional systems such as riverbeds, lakes or the ocean forming sedimentary successions.
a. Detritus
b. Dispersion
c. Metamorphism
d. Perched coastline

37. A _____ is flat or nearly flat land adjacent to a stream or river that experiences occasional or periodic flooding. It includes the floodway, which consists of the stream channel and adjacent areas that carry flood flows, and the flood fringe, which are areas covered by the flood, but which do not experience a strong current.

They generally contain unconsolidated sediments, often extending below the bed of the stream.

a. 1509 Istanbul earthquake
b. 1703 Genroku earthquake
c. 1700 Cascadia earthquake
d. Floodplain

38. A _____ in general is a bend in a sinuous watercourse. A _____ is formed when the moving water in a river erodes the outer banks and widens its valley. A stream of any volume may assume a meandering course, alternatively eroding sediments from the outside of a bend and depositing them on the inside.
a. 1703 Genroku earthquake
b. Meander
c. 1509 Istanbul earthquake
d. 1700 Cascadia earthquake

39. _____, is the process of coastal sediments returning to the visible portion of a beach or foreshore following a submersion event. A sustainable beach or foreshore often goes through a cycle of submersion during rough weather then _____ during calmer periods. If a coastline is not in a healthy sustainable condition, then erosion can be more serious and _____ does not fully restore the original volume of the visible beach or foreshore leading to permanent beach or foreshore loss.
a. AL 129-1
b. AL 333
c. AASHTO Soil Classification System
d. Accretion

40. A _____, dike (or dyke), embankment, floodbank or stopbank is a natural or artificial slope or wall to regulate water levels. It is usually earthen and often parallel to the course of a river or the coast.
a. 1700 Cascadia earthquake
b. 1703 Genroku earthquake
c. 1509 Istanbul earthquake
d. Levee

41. A _____ is a stream that branches off and flows away from a main stream channel. They are a common feature of river deltas. The phenomenon is known as river bifurcation.

Chapter 15. Running Water

a. 1703 Genroku earthquake
c. Distributary

b. 1509 Istanbul earthquake
d. 1700 Cascadia earthquake

42. _____ is a gas consisting primarily of methane. It is found associated with fossil fuels, in coal beds, as methane clathrates, and is created by methanogenic organisms in marshes, bogs, and landfills. It is an important fuel source, a major feedstock for fertilizers, and a potent greenhouse gas.

a. 1703 Genroku earthquake
c. 1700 Cascadia earthquake

b. 1509 Istanbul earthquake
d. Natural gas

43. The _____ is the extended perimeter of each continent and associated coastal plain, and was part of the continent during the glacial periods, but is undersea during interglacial periods such as the current epoch by relatively shallow seas (known as shelf seas) and gulfs.

The continental rise is below the slope, but landward of the abyssal plains. Its gradient is intermediate between the slope and the shelf, on the order of 0.5-1°.

a. Mud
c. Continental slope

b. Surface runoff
d. Continental shelf

44. An _____ is a fan-shaped deposit formed where a fast flowing stream flattens, slows, and spreads typically at the exit of a canyon onto a flatter plain. A convergence of neighboring fans into a single apron of deposits against a slope is called a bajada, or compound _____.

a. AL 333
c. AASHTO Soil Classification System

b. AL 129-1
d. Alluvial fan

45. A _____ or mudslide is the most rapid (up to 80 km/h, or 50 mph) and fluid type of downhill mass wasting. It is a rapid movement of a large mass of mud formed from loose earth and water. Similar terms are mudslide (not very liquid), mud stream, debris flow (e.g. in high mountains), j>ökulhlaup, and lahar

a. 1509 Istanbul earthquake
c. 1703 Genroku earthquake

b. 1700 Cascadia earthquake
d. Mudflow

46. The _____ is the level at which the ground water pressure is equal to atmospheric pressure. It may be conveniently visualized as the 'surface' of the ground water in a given vicinity. It usually coincides with the phreatic surface, but can be many feet above it. As water infiltrates through pore spaces in the soil, it first passes through the zone of aeration, where the soil is unsaturated. At increasing depths water fills in more spaces, until the zone of saturation is reached. The relatively horizontal plane atop this zone constitutes the _____.

a. Crosshole sonic logging
c. Rock bolt

b. Shaft construction
d. Water table

47. The term _____ can be used to describe both the conduct of a survey for geological purposes and an institution holding geological information.

A _____ is the systematic investigation of the subsurface of a given piece of ground for the purpose of creating a geological map or model. A _____ employs techniques from the traditional walk-over survey, studying outcrops and landforms, to intrusive methods, such as hand augering and machine driven boreholes, to the use of geophysical techniques and remote sensing methods, such as aerial photography and satellite imagery.

a. Leaverite
b. Paralithic
c. Geological Survey
d. Reading Prong

48. An _____ is the result of a sudden release of energy in the Earth's crust that creates seismic waves. They are recorded with a seismometer or the related and mostly obsolete Richter magnitude, with a magnitude 3 or lower _____ being mostly imperceptible and magnitude 7 causing serious damage over large areas.

a. Earthquake
b. AL 333
c. AASHTO Soil Classification System
d. AL 129-1

49. In geomorphology, a _____ is the pattern formed by the streams, rivers, and lakes in a particular drainage basin. They are governed by the topography of the land, whether a particular region is dominated by hard or soft rocks, and the gradient of the land.

They can fall into one of several categories, depending on the topography and geology of the land:

Dendritic _____s are the most common form of _____.

a. Stratification
b. Nodule
c. Submersion
d. Drainage system

50. _____ is the natural or artificial removal of surface and sub-surface water from an area. Many agricultural soils need _____ to improve production or to manage water supplies.

The earliest archaeological record of an advanced system of _____ comes from the Indus Valley Civilization from around 3100 BC in what is now Pakistan and North India.

a. 1703 Genroku earthquake
b. 1509 Istanbul earthquake
c. 1700 Cascadia earthquake
d. Drainage

51. A _____ is an extent of land where water from rain or snow melt drains downhill into a body of water, such as a river, lake, reservoir, estuary, wetland, sea or ocean. The _____ includes both the streams and rivers that convey the water as well as the land surfaces from which water drains into those channels, and is separated from adjacent basins by a drainage divide.

The _____ acts like a funnel, collecting all the water within the area covered by the basin and channelling it into a waterway.

a. Drainage basin
b. 1700 Cascadia earthquake
c. 1703 Genroku earthquake
d. 1509 Istanbul earthquake

52. _____, also called erosional _____ or downward erosion or vertical erosion is a geological process that deepens the channel of a stream or valley by removing material from the stream's bed or the valley's floor. How fast _____ occurs depends on the stream's base level, which is the lowest point to which the stream can erode. Sea level is the ultimate base level, but many streams have a higher 'temporary' base level because they empty into another body of water that is above sea level or encounter bedrock that resists erosion.

a. Hydraulic action
b. Saltation
c. Permineralization
d. Downcutting

53. _____ is a fluvial process of erosion that lengthens a stream, a valley or a gully at its head and also enlarges its drainage basin. The stream erodes away at the rock and soil at its headwaters in the opposite direction that it flows. Once a stream has begun to cut back, the erosion is sped up by the steep gradient the water is flowing down. As water erodes a path from its headwaters to its mouth at a standing body of water, it tries to cut an ever-shallower path. This leads to increased erosion at the steepest parts, which is _____.
   a. Stoping
   b. Hydraulic action
   c. Headward erosion
   d. Diagenesis

54. _____ is the geomorphic process by which soil, regolith, and rock move downslope under the force of gravity. Types of _____ include creep, slides, flows, topples, and falls, each with its own characteristic features, and taking place over timescales from seconds to years. _____ occurs on both terrestrial and submarine slopes, and has been observed on Earth, Mars, and Venus.
   a. 1509 Istanbul earthquake
   b. 1700 Cascadia earthquake
   c. Mass wasting
   d. Soil liquefaction

55. In stratigraphy, _____ is the native consolidated rock underlying the surface of a terrestrial planet, usually the Earth. Above the _____ is usually an area of broken and weathered unconsolidated rock in the basal subsoil. The top of the _____ is known as rockhead and identifying this, via excavations, drilling or geophysical methods, is an important task in most civil engineering projects.
   a. Bedrock
   b. Polystrate
   c. Sequence stratigraphy
   d. Biozones

56. _____ refers to natural mountain building, and may be studied as a tectonic structural event, (b) as a geographical event, and (c) a chronological event. Orogenic events (a) cause distinctive structural phenomena and related tectonic activity, (b) affect certain regions of rocks and crust, and (c) happen within a specific period of time.
   a. Alice Springs Orogeny
   b. Orogenesis
   c. Antler orogeny
   d. Orogeny

57. In chronostratigraphy, a _____ is a succession of rock strata laid down in an single age on the geologic timescale, which usually represents millions of years of deposition. A given _____ of rock and the corresponding age of time will by convention have the same name, and the same boundaries.
   a. Relative dating
   b. Global Boundary Stratotype Section and Point
   c. Lichenometry
   d. Stage

Chapter 16. Groundwater

1. _____ is a sedimentary rock composed largely of the mineral calcite (calcium carbonate: $CaCO_3$.) The deposition of _____ strata is often a by-product and indicator of biological activity in the geologic record. Calcium (along with nitrogen, phosphorus, and potassium) is a key mineral to plant nutrition: soils overlying _____ bedrock tend to be pre-fertilized with calcium.
   a. 1703 Genroku earthquake
   b. 1700 Cascadia earthquake
   c. 1509 Istanbul earthquake
   d. Limestone

2. _____ in the earth sciences (commonly symbolized as κ a rock or k) is a measure of the ability of a material (typically unconsolidated material) to transmit fluids. It is of great importance in determining the flow characteristics of hydrocarbons in oil and gas reservoirs, and of groundwater in aquifers. It is typically measured in the lab by application of Darcy's law under steady state conditions or, more generally, by application of various solutions to the diffusion equation for unsteady flow conditions.
   a. Phreatic zone
   b. Permeability
   c. Saltwater intrusion
   d. Porosity

3. _____ is a measure of the void spaces in a material, and is measured as a fraction, between 0-1, or as a percentage between 0-100%. The term is used in multiple fields including ceramics, metallurgy, materials, manufacturing, earth sciences and construction.

   Used in geology, hydrogeology, soil science, and building science, the _____ of a porous medium (such as rock or sediment) describes the fraction of void space in the material, where the void may contain, for example, air or water.

   a. Permeability
   b. Phreatic zone
   c. Saltwater intrusion
   d. Porosity

4. _____ is one of the three main rock types (the others being igneous and metamorphic rock.) _____ is formed by deposition and consolidation of mineral and organic material and from precipitation of minerals from solution. The processes that form _____ occur at the surface of the Earth and within bodies of water.
   a. Groundmass
   b. Sedimentary rock
   c. Pluton
   d. Migmatite

5. An _____ is a confined aquifer containing groundwater that will flow upward through a well without the need for pumping. Water may even reach the ground surface if the natural pressure is high enough, in which case the well is called a flowing artesian well. An aquifer provides the water for an artesian well.
   a. AL 129-1
   b. AASHTO Soil Classification System
   c. AL 333
   d. Artesian aquifer

6. The _____ describes the continuous movement of water on, above, and below the surface of the Earth. Since the _____ is truly a 'cycle,' there is no beginning or end. Water can change states among liquid, vapor, and ice at various places in the _____.
   a. Surface water
   b. Hydraulic conductivity
   c. Stream capacity
   d. Water cycle

Chapter 16. Groundwater

7. An _____ is an underground layer of water-bearing permeable rock or unconsolidated materials (gravel, sand, silt, or clay) from which groundwater can be usefully extracted using a water well. The study of water flow in _____s and the characterization of _____s is called hydrogeology. Related terms include: an aquitard, which is an impermeable layer along an _____, and an aquiclude (or aquifuge), which is a solid, impermeable area beneath an _____.
   a. Aquifer
   b. AL 333
   c. AASHTO Soil Classification System
   d. AL 129-1

8. _____ is a naturally occurring material composed primarily of fine-grained minerals, which show plasticity through a variable range of water content, and which can be hardened when dried and/or fired. _____ deposits are mostly composed of _____ minerals (phyllosilicate minerals), minerals which impart plasticity and harden when fired and/or dried, and variable amounts of water trapped in the mineral structure by polar attraction. Organic materials which do not impart plasticity may also be a part of _____ deposits.
   a. Clay
   b. 1700 Cascadia earthquake
   c. 1509 Istanbul earthquake
   d. 1703 Genroku earthquake

9. _____ is a geological term used to describe particles of rock derived from pre-existing rock through processes of weathering and erosion. Thesel particles can consist of lithic fragments (particles of recognisable rock), or of monomineralic fragments (mineral grains.) These particles are often transported through sedimentary processes into depositional systems such as riverbeds, lakes or the ocean forming sedimentary successions.
   a. Metamorphism
   b. Perched coastline
   c. Detritus
   d. Dispersion

10. _____ or dolomite rock is a sedimentary carbonate rock that contains a high percentage of the mineral dolomite. In old U.S.G.S. publications it was referred to as magnesian limestone. Most _____ formed as a magnesium replacement of limestone or lime mud prior to lithification.
    a. Metasediment
    b. Pelagic sediments
    c. Sandstone
    d. Dolostone

11. In geology, a _____ or _____ line is a planar fracture in rock in which the rock on one side of the fracture has moved with respect to the rock on the other side. Large _____s within the Earth's crust are the result of differential or shear motion and active _____ zones are the causal locations of most earthquakes. Earthquakes are caused by energy release during rapid slippage along a _____.
    a. Geothermal
    b. Fault
    c. Cohesion
    d. Combe

12. '_____' is degraded organic material in soil, which causes some soil layers to be dark brown or black.

In soil science, _____ refers to any organic matter that has reached a point of stability, where it will break down no further and might, if conditions do not change, remain essentially as it is for centuries, if not millennia.

   a. 1700 Cascadia earthquake
   b. Humus
   c. 1703 Genroku earthquake
   d. 1509 Istanbul earthquake

13. _____ is one of the three main rock types (the others being sedimentary and metamorphic rock.) _____ is formed by magma (molten rock) being cooled and becoming solid . They may form with or without crystallization, either below the surface as intrusive (plutonic) rocks or on the surface as extrusive (volcanic) rocks. They make up approximately 95% of the upper part of the Earth's crust, but their great abundance is hidden on the Earth's surface by a relatively thin but widespread layer of sedimentary and metamorphic rocks.

   a. AL 129-1
   b. Igneous rock
   c. AASHTO Soil Classification System
   d. AL 333

14. In geology the term _____ refers to a fracture in rock where there has been no lateral movement in the plane of the fracture (up, down or sideways) of one side relative to the other. This makes it different from a fault which is defined as a fracture in rock where one side slides laterally past to the other. _____s normally have a regular spacing related to either the mechanical properties of the individual rock or the thickness of the layer involved.

   a. 1700 Cascadia earthquake
   b. 1703 Genroku earthquake
   c. Joint
   d. 1509 Istanbul earthquake

15. _____ is the result of the transformation of an existing rock type, the protolith, in a process called metamorphism, which means 'change in form'. The protolith is subjected to heat and pressure (temperatures greater than 150 to 200 >°C and pressures of 1500 bars) causing profound physical and/or chemical change. The protolith may be sedimentary rock, igneous rock or another older _____.

   a. Volcanic rock
   b. Metamorphic rock
   c. Phenocryst
   d. Sedimentary rock

16. _____ is a naturally occurring granular material composed of finely divided rock and mineral particles.

As the term is used by geologists, _____ particles range in diameter from 0.0625 (or $>^1\!\!>/_{16}$ mm, or 62.5 micrometers) to 2 millimeters. An individual particle in this range size is termed a _____ grain.

   a. 1509 Istanbul earthquake
   b. 1700 Cascadia earthquake
   c. 1703 Genroku earthquake
   d. Sand

17. _____ is a fine-grained sedimentary rock whose original constituents were clay minerals or muds. It is characterized by thin laminae breaking with an irregular curving fracture, often splintery and usually parallel to the often-indistinguishable bedding plane. This property is called fissility.

   a. Sandstone
   b. Diatomaceous earth
   c. Siltstone
   d. Shale

18. _____ is the decomposition of Earth rocks, soils and their minerals through direct contact with the planet's atmosphere. _____ occurs in situ, or 'with no movement', and thus should not be confused with erosion, which involves the movement of rocks and minerals by agents such as water, ice, wind and gravity.

Two important classifications of _____ processes exist -- physical and chemical _____.

   a. Frost disintegration
   b. 1509 Istanbul earthquake
   c. Physical weathering
   d. Weathering

19. Two important classifications of weathering processes exist -- physical and _____. Mechanical or physical weathering involves the breakdown of rocks and soils through direct contact with atmospheric conditions, such as heat, water, ice and pressure. The second classification, _____, involves the direct effect of atmospheric chemicals or biologically produced chemicals (also known as biological weathering) in the breakdown of rocks, soils and minerals.
   a. 1509 Istanbul earthquake
   b. Physical weathering
   c. Frost disintegration
   d. Chemical weathering

20. _____ is the geological process by which material is added to a landform or land mass. Fluids such as wind and water, as well as sediment gravity flows, transport previously eroded sediment, which, at the loss of enough kinetic energy in the fluid, is deposited, building up layers of sediment.

   _____ occurs when the forces responsible for sediment transportation are no longer sufficient to overcome the forces of particle weight and friction, which resist motion.

   a. Deposition
   b. Stoping
   c. Hydrothermal circulation
   d. Hydraulic action

21. The _____ is a cosmological model of the initial conditions and subsequent development of the universe. It is supported by the most comprehensive and accurate explanations from current scientific evidence and observation. As used by cosmologists, the term _____ generally refers to the idea that the universe has expanded from a primordial hot and dense initial condition at some finite time in the past, and continues to expand to this day.
   a. Big Bang
   b. 1703 Genroku earthquake
   c. 1700 Cascadia earthquake
   d. 1509 Istanbul earthquake

22. The _____ is the subsurface layer in which groundwater seeps up from a water table by capillary action to fill pores. Pores at the base of the _____ are filled with water due to tension saturation. This saturated portion of the _____ is less than total capillary rise because of the presence of a mix in pore size.
   a. Strike-slip faults
   b. Historical geology
   c. Capillary fringe
   d. Tertiary

23. The _____ is the level at which the ground water pressure is equal to atmospheric pressure. It may be conveniently visualized as the 'surface' of the ground water in a given vicinity. It usually coincides with the phreatic surface, but can be many feet above it. As water infiltrates through pore spaces in the soil, it first passes through the zone of aeration, where the soil is unsaturated. At increasing depths water fills in more spaces, until the zone of saturation is reached. The relatively horizontal plane atop this zone constitutes the _____.
   a. Water table
   b. Shaft construction
   c. Rock bolt
   d. Crosshole sonic logging

24. The _____ is the area in an aquifer, below the water table, in which relatively all pores and fractures are saturated with water. The _____ may fluctuate with changes of season and during wet and dry periods.
   a. Saltwater intrusion
   b. Porosity
   c. Phreatic zone
   d. Permeability

25. A _____ is a large, slow-moving mass of ice, formed from compacted layers of snow, that slowly deforms and flows in response to gravity and high pressure.

_____ ice is the largest reservoir of fresh water on Earth, and second only to oceans as the largest reservoir of total water.

   a. Greenhouse gases
   b. Little Ice Age
   c. Pacific Decadal Oscillation
   d. Glacier

26. _____ is water located beneath the ground surface in soil pore spaces and in the fractures of lithologic formations. A unit of rock or an unconsolidated deposit is called an aquifer when it can yield a usable quantity of water. The depth at which soil pore spaces or fractures and voids in rock become completely saturated with water is called the water table.
   a. 1509 Istanbul earthquake
   b. Groundwater
   c. Depression focused recharge
   d. 1700 Cascadia earthquake

27. The _____ are a small, isolated mountain range rising from the Great Plains of North America in western South Dakota and extending into Wyoming, USA. Set off from the main body of the Rocky Mountains, the region is something of a geological anomaly--accurately described as an 'island of trees in a sea of grass'. The _____ encompass the _____ National Forest and are home to the tallest peaks of continental North America east of the Rockies.
   a. Paleorrota
   b. Monument Valley
   c. Rano Kau
   d. Black Hills

28. A _____ occurs in an aquifer when groundwater is pumped from a well. In an unconfined (water table) aquifer, this is an actual depression of the water levels. In confined (artesian) aquifers, the _____ is a reduction in the pressure head surrounding the pumped well.
   a. Specific storage
   b. Cone of depression
   c. Stream capacity
   d. Hydraulic conductivity

29. The _____ is a general term for an ill-defined early Cretaceous formation of the Rocky Mountains and Great Plains. It consists of sandy, shallow-marine deposits with intermittent mud flat sediments, and occasional stream deposits. It is an important aquifer in some areas of the Great Plains. It is made of porous sandstone more than 30 meters thick.
   a. 1700 Cascadia earthquake
   b. Dakota Sandstone
   c. 1509 Istanbul earthquake
   d. Potomac Formation

30. _____ is the change in population over time, and can be quantified as the change in the number of individuals in a population using 'per unit time' for measurement. The term _____ can technically refer to any species, but almost always refers to humans, and it is often used informally for the more specific demographic term _____ rate , and is often used to refer specifically to the growth of the population of the world.

Simple models of _____ include the Malthusian Growth Model and the logistic model.

   a. 1703 Genroku earthquake
   b. 1700 Cascadia earthquake
   c. 1509 Istanbul earthquake
   d. Population growth

31. _____ is a sedimentary rock composed mainly of sand-size mineral or rock grains. Most _____ is composed of quartz and/or feldspar because these are the most common minerals in the Earth's crust. Like sand, _____ may be any color, but the most common colors are tan, brown, yellow, red, gray and white.

a. Dolomite
b. Dolostone
c. Porcellanite
d. Sandstone

32. _____ in geology is a landform sunken or depressed below the surrounding area. _____s may be formed by various mechanisms, and may be referred to by a variety of technical terms.

- A basin may be any large sediment filled _____. In tectonics, it may refer specifically to a circular, syncline-like _____: a geologic basin; while in sedimentology, it may refer to an area thickly filled with sediment: sedimentary basin.

- A blowout is a _____ created by wind erosion typically in either a desert sand or dry soil (such as a post-glacial loess environment.)

- A graben is a down dropped and typically linear _____ or basin created by rifting in a region under tensional tectonic forces.

- An impact crater is a _____ created by an impact such as a meteorite crater.
- A pit crater is a _____ formed by a sinking, or caving in, of the ground surface lying over a void.
- A kettle is left behind when a piece of ice left behind in glacial deposits melts.

- A _____ may be an area of subsidence caused by the collapse of an underlying structure. Examples include sinkholes above caves in karst topography, or calderas.

a. Drainage system
b. Stratification
c. Depression
d. Platform

33. _____ is the removal of solids (sediment, soil, rock and other particles) in the natural environment. It usually occurs due to transport by wind, water, or ice; by down-slope creep of soil and other material under the force of gravity; or by living organisms, such as burrowing animals, in the case of bioerosion.

_____ is distinguished from weathering, which is the process of chemical or physical breakdown of the minerals in the rocks, although the two processes may occur concurrently.

a. AASHTO Soil Classification System
b. AL 333
c. AL 129-1
d. Erosion

34. _____ is a landscape shaped by the dissolution of a layer or layers of soluble bedrock, usually carbonate rock such as limestone or dolomite.

Due to subterranean drainage, there may be very limited surface water, even to the absence of all rivers and lakes. Many karst regions display distinctive surface features, with sinkholes or dolines being the most common.

a. Karst topography
b. Amblypoda
c. Ambulocetus
d. Andrija Mohorović ić

35. A _____ is a natural depression or hole in the surface topography caused by the removal of soil or bedrock, often both, by water. They may vary in size from less than a meter to several hundred meters both in diameter and depth, and vary in form from soil-lined bowls to bedrock-edged chasms. They may be formed gradually or suddenly, and are found worldwide.
   a. Sinkhole
   b. 1700 Cascadia earthquake
   c. 1509 Istanbul earthquake
   d. 1703 Genroku earthquake

36. A _____ is a type of speleothem (secondary mineral) that hangs from the ceiling or wall of limestone caves. It is sometimes referred to as dripstone.

They are formed by the deposition of calcium carbonate and other minerals, which is precipitated from mineralized water solutions.

   a. Stalactite
   b. 1703 Genroku earthquake
   c. 1509 Istanbul earthquake
   d. 1700 Cascadia earthquake

37. _____ is a sedimentary rock. It is a natural chemical precipitate of carbonate minerals; typically aragonite, but often recrystallized to, or primarily, calcite.

_____ forms as calcium carbonate is deposited from the water of mineral springs or rivulets that are saturated with dissolved calcium bicarbonate. The spring water from which the calcium carbonate precipitates can be hot, warm or cold. The rate of deposition increases with the temperature of the water, or alternatively, when biotic material accelerates the process of precipitation.

   a. Travertine
   b. 1509 Istanbul earthquake
   c. 1703 Genroku earthquake
   d. 1700 Cascadia earthquake

38. The _____ is a vast yet shallow underground water table aquifer located beneath the Great Plains in the United States. One of the world's largest aquifers, it covers an area of approximately 174,000 mi^2 in portions of the eight states of South Dakota, Nebraska, Wyoming, Colorado, Kansas, Oklahoma, New Mexico, and Texas. It was named in 1898 by N.H. Darton from its type locality near the town of Ogallala, Nebraska.
   a. Ogallala Aquifer
   b. AASHTO Soil Classification System
   c. AL 333
   d. AL 129-1

39. A _____ is a type of speleothem that rises from the floor of a limestone cave due to the dripping of mineralized solutions and the deposition of calcium carbonate.

The corresponding formation on the ceiling of a cave is known as a stalactite. If these formations grow together, the result is known as a column.

   a. 1509 Istanbul earthquake
   b. 1703 Genroku earthquake
   c. 1700 Cascadia earthquake
   d. Stalagmite

40. In geology, engineering, and surveying, _____ is the motion of a surface (usually, the Earth's surface) as it shifts downward relative to a datum such as sea-level. The opposite of _____ is uplift, which results in an increase in elevation. There are several types of _____.

Chapter 16. Groundwater

a. 1700 Cascadia earthquake
b. Subsidence
c. Pothole
d. 1509 Istanbul earthquake

41. A _____, commonly known as a cave formation, is a secondary mineral deposit formed in a cave. They are typically formed in limestone or dolostone solutional caves.

Water seeping through cracks in a cave's surrounding bedrock may dissolve certain compounds, usually calcite and aragonite , or gypsum (calcium sulfate.)

a. 1509 Istanbul earthquake
b. 1703 Genroku earthquake
c. Speleothem
d. 1700 Cascadia earthquake

42. The _____ is the extended perimeter of each continent and associated coastal plain, and was part of the continent during the glacial periods, but is undersea during interglacial periods such as the current epoch by relatively shallow seas (known as shelf seas) and gulfs.

The continental rise is below the slope, but landward of the abyssal plains. Its gradient is intermediate between the slope and the shelf, on the order of 0.5-1°.

a. Surface runoff
b. Continental slope
c. Mud
d. Continental shelf

43. The term _____ can be used to describe both the conduct of a survey for geological purposes and an institution holding geological information.

A _____ is the systematic investigation of the subsurface of a given piece of ground for the purpose of creating a geological map or model. A _____ employs techniques from the traditional walk-over survey, studying outcrops and landforms, to intrusive methods, such as hand augering and machine driven boreholes, to the use of geophysical techniques and remote sensing methods, such as aerial photography and satellite imagery.

a. Paralithic
b. Leaverite
c. Reading Prong
d. Geological Survey

44. An _____ is the result of a sudden release of energy in the Earth's crust that creates seismic waves. They are recorded with a seismometer or the related and mostly obsolete Richter magnitude, with a magnitude 3 or lower _____ being mostly imperceptible and magnitude 7 causing serious damage over large areas.
a. AL 129-1
b. AL 333
c. Earthquake
d. AASHTO Soil Classification System

45. _____ is the physical, chemical and biological characteristics of water. It is most frequently used by reference to a set of standards against which compliance can be assessed. The most common standards used to assess _____ relate to drinking water, safety of human contact, and for health of ecosystems.
a. 1509 Istanbul earthquake
b. Soft water
c. Hydraulic head
d. Water quality

188 Chapter 16. Groundwater

46. In geology, _____ refers to heat sources within the planet. _____ is technically an adjective (e.g., _____ energy) but in U.S. English the word has attained frequent use as a noun.

The planet's internal heat was originally generated during its accretion, due to gravitational binding energy, and since then additional heat has continued to be generated by decay heat from the radioactive decay of elements.

- a. Combe
- b. Cleavage
- c. Stratification
- d. Geothermal

47. The _____ is the rate of increase in temperature per unit depth in the Earth. It varies with location and is typically measured by determining the bottom open-hole temperature after borehole drilling. To achieve accuracy the drilling fluid needs time to reach the ambient temperature.

- a. Geothermal power
- b. Hot Dry Rock Geothermal Energy
- c. Geothermal heat pump
- d. Geothermal gradient

48. _____ is water that has high mineral content (mainly calcium and magnesium ions) (in contrast with soft water.) _____ minerals primarily consist of calcium (Ca^{2+}), and magnesium (Mg^{2+}) metal cations, and sometimes other dissolved compounds such as bicarbonates and sulfates. Calcium usually enters the water as either calcium carbonate ($CaCO_3$), in the form of limestone and chalk, or calcium sulfate ($CaSO_4$), in the form of other mineral deposits.

- a. 1509 Istanbul earthquake
- b. Hard water
- c. Water quality
- d. Soft water

49. _____ circulation in its most general sense is the circulation of hot water; 'hydros' in the Greek meaning water and 'thermos' meaning heat. _____ circulation occurs most often in the vicinity of sources of heat within the Earth's crust. This generally occurs near volcanic activity, but can occur in the deep crust related to the intrusion of granite, or as the result of orogeny or metamorphism.

- a. Hydrothermal
- b. Wave pounding
- c. Transgression
- d. Headward erosion

50. _____ is a liquid or semi-liquid mixture of water and some combination of soil, silt, and clay. Ancient _____ deposits harden over geological time to form sedimentary rock such as siltstone or solid, mudrock lutites. When geological deposits of _____ are formed in estuaries the resultant layers are termed bay _____s.

- a. Continental slope
- b. Surface runoff
- c. Mud
- d. Continental shelf

51. A _____, mud pool or paint pot is a sort of hot spring or fumarole consisting of a pool of usually bubbling mud. The mud is generally of white to greyish color, but is sometimes stained with reddish or pink spots from iron compounds. When the slurry is particularly colorful, the feature is then called a paint pot.

- a. 1703 Genroku earthquake
- b. Mudpot
- c. 1509 Istanbul earthquake
- d. 1700 Cascadia earthquake

52. _____ the term used to describe types of water that contain few or no calcium or magnesium metal cations. The term is usually related to hard water, which does contain significant amounts of these ions.

_____ usually comes from peat or igneous rock sources, such as granite but may also derive from sandstone sources, since such sedimentary rocks are usually low in calcium and magnesium.

Chapter 16. Groundwater

a. Water quality
b. Soft water
c. 1509 Istanbul earthquake
d. Hydraulic head

53. _____ refers to a sediment, sedimentary rock, or soil type which is formed from or contains a high proportion of calcium carbonate in the form of calcite or aragonite.

It can also be used as an adjectival term applied to anatomical structures which are made of calcium carbonate in animals such as gastropods, when referring to such structures as the operculum, the clausilium, and the love dart.

_____ sediments are usually deposited in shallow water near land, since the carbonate is precipitated by marine organisms that need land-derived nutrients.

a. 1509 Istanbul earthquake
b. 1703 Genroku earthquake
c. 1700 Cascadia earthquake
d. Calcareous

54. _____ is power extracted from heat stored in the earth. This geothermal energy originates from the original formation of the planet, from radioactive decay of minerals, and from solar energy absorbed at the surface. It has been used for space heating and bathing since ancient roman times, but is now better known for generating electricity.
a. Geothermal desalination
b. Geothermal power
c. Geothermal gradient
d. Geothermal heat pump

55. _____ is a form of opaline silica that is often found around hot springs and geysers. Botryoidal _____ is known as fiorite.
a. 1700 Cascadia earthquake
b. 1509 Istanbul earthquake
c. Quartz
d. Geyserite

56. In physics, _____ is the rate at which work is performed or energy is transmitted, or the amount of energy required or expended for a given unit of time. As a rate of change of work done or the energy of a subsystem, _____ is:

$$P = \frac{W}{t}$$

where P is _____, W is work and t is time.

The average _____ (often simply called '_____' when the context makes it clear) is the average amount of work done or energy transferred per unit time.

a. 1509 Istanbul earthquake
b. Turbulent flow
c. Strong interaction
d. Power

Chapter 17. Glaciers and Glaciation

1. The terms _____ and icehouse Earth refer to the prevailing global climate on a timescale of millions of years.

During a _____ Earth period, the planet's atmosphere contains sufficient _____ gases such as carbon dioxide and methane for ice to be entirely absent from the planet's surface.

During icehouse periods, glaciers are present in fluctuating amounts; variations in the Earth's orbit may result in many ice ages, glacials, and interglacials.

   a. 1509 Istanbul earthquake
   b. Greenhouse
   c. 1703 Genroku earthquake
   d. 1700 Cascadia earthquake

2. The general term '_____' or, more precisely, 'glacial age' denotes a geological period of long-term reduction in the temperature of the Earth's surface and atmosphere, resulting in an expansion of continental ice sheets, polar ice sheets and alpine glaciers. Within a long-term _____, individual pulses of extra cold climate are termed 'glaciations'. Glaciologically, _____ implies the presence of extensive ice sheets in the northern and southern hemispheres; by this definition we are still in an _____.

   a. AASHTO Soil Classification System
   b. AL 333
   c. Ice Age
   d. AL 129-1

3. The _____ was a period of cooling occurring after a warmer North Atlantic era known as the Medieval Warm Period. While not a true ice age, the term was introduced into scientific literature by Fran>çois E. Matthes in 1939. Climatologists and historians working with local records no longer expect to agree on either the start or end dates of this period, which varied according to local conditions.

   a. Greenhouse gases
   b. Pacific Decadal Oscillation
   c. Glacier
   d. Little Ice Age

4. A _____ is a large, slow-moving mass of ice, formed from compacted layers of snow, that slowly deforms and flows in response to gravity and high pressure.

_____ ice is the largest reservoir of fresh water on Earth, and second only to oceans as the largest reservoir of total water.

   a. Greenhouse gases
   b. Pacific Decadal Oscillation
   c. Little Ice Age
   d. Glacier

5. In materials science, _____ is a change in the shape or size of an object due to an applied force. This can be a result of tensile (pulling) forces, compressive (pushing) forces, shear, bending or torsion (twisting.) _____ is often described as strain.

   a. Melange
   b. Stack
   c. Combe
   d. Deformation

6. _____ is the removal of solids (sediment, soil, rock and other particles) in the natural environment. It usually occurs due to transport by wind, water, or ice; by down-slope creep of soil and other material under the force of gravity; or by living organisms, such as burrowing animals, in the case of bioerosion.

_____ is distinguished from weathering, which is the process of chemical or physical breakdown of the minerals in the rocks, although the two processes may occur concurrently.

Chapter 17. Glaciers and Glaciation

a. AL 333
b. AASHTO Soil Classification System
c. AL 129-1
d. Erosion

7. _____ is partially-compacted n>év>é, a type of snow that has been left over from past seasons and has been recrystallized into a substance denser than n>év>é. It is ice that is at an intermediate stage between snow and glacial ice. _____ has the appearance of wet sugar, but has a hardness that makes it extremely resistant to shovelling. It generally has a density greater than 550 kg/mÅ³ and is often found underneath the snow that accumulates at the head of a glacier.
 a. Bull Lake glaciation
 b. Terminal moraine
 c. Glacial striations
 d. Firn

8. The _____ describes the continuous movement of water on, above, and below the surface of the Earth. Since the _____ is truly a 'cycle,' there is no beginning or end. Water can change states among liquid, vapor, and ice at various places in the _____.
 a. Hydraulic conductivity
 b. Surface water
 c. Stream capacity
 d. Water cycle

9. _____ is an active glaciated andesitic stratovolcano in the Cascade Volcanic Arc and the North Cascades of Washington State in the United States. It is the second-most active volcano in the range after Mount Saint Helens. It is about 31 miles (50 km) due east of the city of Bellingham, Whatcom County, making it the northernmost volcano in the Cascade Range but not the northernmost of the Cascade Volcanic Arc, which extends north into the Coast Mountains.
 a. Stratovolcano
 b. Broken Top
 c. Nevado Sajama
 d. Mount Baker

10. Alpine glaciers form high on the mountain slopes and are niche, slope or cirque glaciers. As a mountain glacier increases in size it can begin to flow down valley, and are referred to as _____.
 a. Valley glaciers
 b. Tertiary
 c. Strike-slip faults
 d. Star dunes

11. An _____ is an ice mass that covers less than 50 000 km² of land area (usually covering a highland area.) Masses of ice covering more than 50 000 km² are termed an ice sheet.

They are not constrained by topographical features (i.e., they will lie over the top of mountains) but their dome is usually centred on the highest point of a massif.

 a. AL 129-1
 b. AASHTO Soil Classification System
 c. AL 333
 d. Ice Cap

12. _____ are the largest glaciers, enormous masses of ice that are not visibly affected by the landscape and that cover the entire surface beneath them, except possibly on the margins where they are thinnest. Antarctica and Greenland are the only places where continental _____ currently exist. These regions contain vast quantities of fresh water.
 a. AL 129-1
 b. AASHTO Soil Classification System
 c. AL 333
 d. Ice sheets

13. The _____ is a vast body of ice covering 1.71 million km², roughly 80% of the surface of Greenland. It is the second largest ice body in the World, after the Antarctic Ice Sheet. The ice sheet is almost 2,400 kilometers long in a north-south direction, and its greatest width is 1,100 kilometers at a latitude of 77>°N, near its northern margin.

a. 1509 Istanbul earthquake
b. 1703 Genroku earthquake
c. 1700 Cascadia earthquake
d. Greenland ice sheet

14. A _____ is a huge crack formed by two glaciers colliding. Accelerations in glacier speed cause extension and can initiate a _____. Crevasses often have vertical or near-vertical walls, which can then melt and create seracs, arches, etc.; these walls sometimes expose layers that represent the glacier's stratigraphy.
   a. Crevasse
   b. Solifluction
   c. Predator trap
   d. Sturzstrom

15. In fluid dynamics the _____ of a fluid is a vector field which is used to mathematically describe the motion of a fluid. The length of the _____ vector is the flow speed.

The _____ u of a fluid is a vector field

which gives the velocity of an element of fluid at a position and time.

   a. 1509 Istanbul earthquake
   b. 1700 Cascadia earthquake
   c. 1703 Genroku earthquake
   d. Flow velocity

16. _____ is the geological process by which material is added to a landform or land mass. Fluids such as wind and water, as well as sediment gravity flows, transport previously eroded sediment, which, at the loss of enough kinetic energy in the fluid, is deposited, building up layers of sediment.

_____ occurs when the forces responsible for sediment transportation are no longer sufficient to overcome the forces of particle weight and friction, which resist motion.

   a. Hydraulic action
   b. Hydrothermal circulation
   c. Stoping
   d. Deposition

17. _____ is a tidewater glacier in the U.S. state of Alaska and the Yukon Territory of Canada. From its source in the Yukon, the glacier stretches 122 km (76 mi) to the sea at Yakutat Bay and Disenchantment Bay. It is the longest tidewater glacier in Alaska, with an open calving face over ten kilometers (6 mi) wide.
   a. 1509 Istanbul earthquake
   b. 1703 Genroku earthquake
   c. 1700 Cascadia earthquake
   d. Hubbard Glacier

18. An _____ is a region of an ice sheet that moves significantly faster than the surrounding ice. They are significant features of the Antarctic where they account for 10% of the volume of the ice. They are up to 50 km wide, 2 km thick, can stretch for hundreds of kilometres, and account for most of the ice leaving the ice sheet.
   a. AASHTO Soil Classification System
   b. AL 129-1
   c. AL 333
   d. Ice stream

19. _____ is any particulate matter that can be transported by fluid flow, and which eventually is deposited.

They are most often transported by water (fluvial processes) transported by wind (aeolian processes) and glaciers. Beach sands and river channel deposits are examples of fluvial transport and deposition, though _____ also often settles out of slow-moving or standing water in lakes and oceans.

   a. Bovey Beds
   b. Quick clay
   c. Sediment
   d. Salt glacier

20. _____ is mechanical scraping of a rock surface by friction between rocks and moving particles during their transport in wind, glacier, waves, gravity or running water, after friction, the moving particles dislodge loose and weak debris from the side of the rock, these particles can be dissolved in the water source.

The intensity of _____ depends on the hardness, concentration, velocity and mass of moving particles.

A virtually smooth marine platform cut by the ocean waves at a coastline.

   a. Abrasion
   b. AASHTO Soil Classification System
   c. AL 129-1
   d. AL 333

21. In stratigraphy, _____ is the native consolidated rock underlying the surface of a terrestrial planet, usually the Earth. Above the _____ is usually an area of broken and weathered unconsolidated rock in the basal subsoil. The top of the _____ is known as rockhead and identifying this, via excavations, drilling or geophysical methods, is an important task in most civil engineering projects.
   a. Sequence stratigraphy
   b. Polystrate
   c. Bedrock
   d. Biozones

22. _____ is a characteristic of rock surfaces where glaciers have passed over bedrock, typically granite or other hard igneous or metamorphic rock. Moving ice will carry pebbles and sand grains removed from upper levels which in turn grind a smooth or groved surface upon the underlying rock. The presence of such polish indicates that the glaciation was relatively recent (in geologic time scale) or was subsequently protected by deposition, as such polish will be subsequently lost due to weathering processes (such as exfoliation).
   a. Bull Lake glaciation
   b. Glacial striations
   c. Bramertonian Stage
   d. Glacial polish

23. _____ or glacial grooves are scratches or gouges cut into bedrock by process of glacial abrasion. _____ usually occur as multiple straight, parallel grooves representing the movement of the sediment-loaded base of the glacier. Large amounts of coarse gravel and boulders carried along underneath the glacier provide the abrasive power to cut the grooves, and finer sediments also in the base of the moving glacier further scour and polish the bedrock.
   a. Terminal moraine
   b. Firn
   c. Bramertonian Stage
   d. Glacial striations

24. _____ consists of clay-sized particles of rock, generated by glacial erosion or by artificial grinding to a similar size. Because the material is very small, it becomes suspended in river water making the water appear cloudy.

If the river flows into a glacial lake, the lake may appear turquoise in color as a result.

a. Drumlin field
b. Cordilleran Ice Sheet
c. Rock flour
d. Post-glacial rebound

25. _____ is the geomorphic process by which soil, regolith, and rock move downslope under the force of gravity. Types of _____ include creep, slides, flows, topples, and falls, each with its own characteristic features, and taking place over timescales from seconds to years. _____ occurs on both terrestrial and submarine slopes, and has been observed on Earth, Mars, and Venus.
   a. Mass wasting
   b. 1509 Istanbul earthquake
   c. 1700 Cascadia earthquake
   d. Soil liquefaction

26. A _____ is an amphitheatre-like valley formed at the head of a glacier by erosion. A _____ is also known as a coombe or coomb in England, a combe or comb in America, a corrie in Scotland and Ireland, and a cwm in Wales, although these terms apply to a specific feature of which several may be found in a _____. The term 'comb' is often found at the end of placenames such as Newcomb and Maycomb, where it is pronounced /kÉ™m/.
   a. 1509 Istanbul earthquake
   b. 1700 Cascadia earthquake
   c. Cirque
   d. 1703 Genroku earthquake

27. Geologically, a _____ is a long, narrow inlet with steep sides, created in a valley carved by glacial activity.

The seeds of a _____ are laid when a glacier cuts a U-shaped valley through abrasion of the surrounding bedrock by the sediment it carries. Many such valleys were formed during the recent ice age.

   a. 1700 Cascadia earthquake
   b. 1509 Istanbul earthquake
   c. 1703 Genroku earthquake
   d. Fjord

28. _____ can also be called frost shattering or frost-wedging. This type of weathering is common in mountain areas where the temperature is around freezing point. Frost induced weathering, although often attributed to the expansion of freezing water captured in cracks, is generally independent of the water-to-ice expansion. It has long been known that moist soils expand or frost heave upon freezing as a result of water migrating along from unfrozen areas via thin films to collect at growing ice lenses. This same phenomena occurs within pore spaces of rocks.
   a. Physical weathering
   b. Weathering
   c. Frost disintegration
   d. 1509 Istanbul earthquake

29. A _____ is a tributary valley with the floor at a higher relief than the main channel into which it flows. They are most commonly associated with U-shaped valleys when a tributary glacier flows into a glacier of larger volume. The main glacier erodes a deep U-shaped valley with nearly vertical sides while the tributary glacier, with a smaller volume of ice, makes a shallower U-shaped valley.
   a. 1703 Genroku earthquake
   b. 1700 Cascadia earthquake
   c. Hanging valley
   d. 1509 Istanbul earthquake

30. The _____ is the epoch from 1.8 million to 11550 years BP covering the world's recent period of repeated glaciations. The _____ epoch follows the Pliocene epoch and is followed by the Holocene epoch. The _____ is the third epoch of the Neogene period or 6th epoch of the Cenozoic Era. The end of the _____ corresponds with the retreat of the last continental glacier. It also corresponds with the end of the Paleolithic age used in archaeology.

Chapter 17. Glaciers and Glaciation

a. Sicilian Stage
b. Late Pleistocene
c. Pleistocene
d. Tyrrhenian

31. A _____ is a mountain lake or pool, formed in a cirque excavated by a glacier. A moraine may form a natural dam below a _____. A corrie may be called a cirque.
   a. Cohesion
   b. Nodule
   c. Heavy metal
   d. Tarn

32. A _____ occurs when the action of a glacier does not follow the original course of the river that wound round interlocking spurs, but, as the force of a glacier is much more powerful and cannot flow as freely around corners, it can carve its way though the rock cutting off the edges of interlocking spurs to form _____s. Hanging valleys are found in between _____s from a side view as the Hanging valleys join the main glacier from an angle.
   a. 1509 Istanbul earthquake
   b. Mesa
   c. Palustrine
   d. Truncated spur

33. The term _____ can be used to describe both the conduct of a survey for geological purposes and an institution holding geological information.

A _____ is the systematic investigation of the subsurface of a given piece of ground for the purpose of creating a geological map or model. A _____ employs techniques from the traditional walk-over survey, studying outcrops and landforms, to intrusive methods, such as hand augering and machine driven boreholes, to the use of geophysical techniques and remote sensing methods, such as aerial photography and satellite imagery.

   a. Paralithic
   b. Geological Survey
   c. Leaverite
   d. Reading Prong

34. The _____ is a geologic fault structure of the Rocky Mountains within Glacier National Park in Montana, USA and Waterton Lakes National Park in Alberta, Canada, as well as into Lewis and Clark National Forest. It provides scientific insight into geologic processes happening in other parts of the world, like the Andes and the Himalaya Mountains. Scientific study of this region is practical because the original rock characteristics were well-preserved and recently sculptured by glaciers.
   a. 1703 Genroku earthquake
   b. 1509 Istanbul earthquake
   c. Lewis overthrust
   d. 1700 Cascadia earthquake

35. An _____ is the result of a sudden release of energy in the Earth's crust that creates seismic waves. They are recorded with a seismometer or the related and mostly obsolete Richter magnitude, with a magnitude 3 or lower _____ being mostly imperceptible and magnitude 7 causing serious damage over large areas.
   a. AL 129-1
   b. AL 333
   c. AASHTO Soil Classification System
   d. Earthquake

36. The _____ -- also called the Laurentian Plateau, or Bouclier Canadien -- is a massive geological shield covered by a thin layer of soil that forms the nucleus of the North American or Laurentia craton. It has a deep, common, joined bedrock region in eastern and central Canada and stretches North from the Great Lakes to the Arctic Ocean, covering over half of Canada; it also extends south into the northern reaches of the United States. Population is scarce, and industrial development is minimal, although the region has a large hydroelectric power potential.

Chapter 17. Glaciers and Glaciation

a. Canadian Shield
b. Gawler craton
c. Sahara pump theory
d. Yilgarn Craton

37. A _____ is a piece of rock that differs from the size and type of rock native to the area in which it rests. They are carried by glacial ice, often over distances of hundreds of kilometres and can range in size from pebbles to large boulders such as Big Rock (16,500 tons) in Alberta.
 a. 1703 Genroku earthquake
 b. 1509 Istanbul earthquake
 c. 1700 Cascadia earthquake
 d. Glacial erratic

38. _____ is rock that is of a specific particle size range. Specifically, it is any loose rock that is larger than two millimeters (2mm) in its largest dimension (about 1/12 of an inch) and no more than 64 millimeters (about 2.5 inches.) The next smaller size class in geology is sand, which is >0.0625 mm to 2 mm in size.
 a. 1700 Cascadia earthquake
 b. 1509 Istanbul earthquake
 c. 1703 Genroku earthquake
 d. Gravel

39. _____ is a naturally occurring granular material composed of finely divided rock and mineral particles.

As the term is used by geologists, _____ particles range in diameter from 0.0625 (or $>^1\!\!/_{16}$ mm, or 62.5 micrometers) to 2 millimeters. An individual particle in this range size is termed a _____ grain.

 a. 1700 Cascadia earthquake
 b. 1509 Istanbul earthquake
 c. Sand
 d. 1703 Genroku earthquake

40. A _____ is generally a large area of exposed Precambrian crystalline igneous and high-grade metamorphic rocks that form tectonically stable areas. In all cases, the age of these rocks is greater than 570 million years and sometimes dates back 2 to 3.5 billion years. They have been little affected by tectonic events following the end of the Precambrian Era, and are relatively flat regions where mountain building, faulting, and other tectonic processes are greatly diminished compared with the activity that occurs at the margins of the _____ s and the boundaries between tectonic plates.
 a. Shield
 b. 1700 Cascadia earthquake
 c. 1703 Genroku earthquake
 d. 1509 Istanbul earthquake

41. _____ is unsorted glacial sediment. Glacial drift is a general term for the coarsely graded and extremely heterogeneous sediments of glacial origin. Glacial _____ is that part of glacial drift which was deposited directly by the glacier. In cases where _____ has been indurated or lithified by subsequent burial into solid rock, it is known as the sedimentary rock tillite.
 a. 1509 Istanbul earthquake
 b. 1703 Genroku earthquake
 c. 1700 Cascadia earthquake
 d. Till

42. _____ is the natural or artificial removal of surface and sub-surface water from an area. Many agricultural soils need _____ to improve production or to manage water supplies.

The earliest archaeological record of an advanced system of _____ comes from the Indus Valley Civilization from around 3100 BC in what is now Pakistan and North India.

a. 1509 Istanbul earthquake
b. Drainage
c. 1703 Genroku earthquake
d. 1700 Cascadia earthquake

43. In geology, _____ is transported rock debris overlying the solid bedrock. The term is also sometimes refers to organic debris so-transported. In the largest sense, it refers to the material left behind by retreating continental glaciers.
    a. Detritus
    b. Geostrophic current
    c. Contact metamorphism
    d. Drift

44. In the earth sciences and geology sub-fields, a _____ or physical feature comprises a geomorphological unit, and is largely defined by its surface form and location in the landscape, as part of the terrain, and as such, is typically an element of topography. _____ elements also include seascape and oceanic waterbody interface features such as bays, peninsulas, seas and so forth, including sub-surface terrain features such as submersed mountain ranges, volcanoes, and the great ocean basins under the thin skin of water, for the whole earth is the province and domain of geology. This panorama in Great Smoky Mountains National Park has the readily identifiable physical features of a rolling plain, actually part of a broad valley, distant foothills, and a backdrop of the old much weathered Appalachian mountain range.

_____s are categorised by characteristic physical attributes such as elevation, slope, orientation, stratification, rock exposure, and soil type.

    a. 1509 Istanbul earthquake
    b. 1700 Cascadia earthquake
    c. Landform
    d. 1703 Genroku earthquake

45. A _____ is a moraine that forms at the end of the glacier called the snout.

They mark the maximum advance of the glacier. An end moraine is at the present boundary of the glacier. They are one of the most prominent types of moraines in the Arctic. One famous _____ is the Giant's Wall in Norway.

    a. Glacial striations
    b. Firn
    c. Terminal moraine
    d. Glacial polish

46. A _____ is any glacially formed accumulation of unconsolidated glacial debris (soil and rock) which can occur in currently glaciated and formerly glaciated regions, such as those areas acted upon by a past ice age. This debris may have been plucked off the valley floor as a glacier advanced or it may have fallen off the valley walls as a result of frost wedging. _____s may be composed of silt like glacial flour to large boulders.
    a. 1700 Cascadia earthquake
    b. 1509 Istanbul earthquake
    c. 1703 Genroku earthquake
    d. Moraine

47. An _____ is the place where a glacier thins and ends. The _____'s position changes as the glacier moves or melts.
    a. AL 333
    b. Ice front
    c. AASHTO Soil Classification System
    d. AL 129-1

Chapter 17. Glaciers and Glaciation

48. A _____ is a mountain rising from the ocean seafloor that does not reach to the water's surface (sea level), and thus is not an island. These are typically formed from extinct volcanoes, that rise abruptly and are usually found rising from a seafloor of 1,000-4,000 meters depth. They are defined by oceanographers as independent features that rise to at least 1,000 meters above the seafloor.
   a. Seamount
   b. 1700 Cascadia earthquake
   c. 1509 Istanbul earthquake
   d. 1703 Genroku earthquake

49. A _____ is an elongated whale-shaped hill formed by glacial action. Its long axis is parallel with the movement of the ice, with the blunter end facing into the glacial movement. They may be more than 45 m (150 ft) high and more than 0.8 km (1/2 mile) long, and are often in _____ fields of similarly shaped, sized and oriented hills. They usually have layers indicating that the material was repeatedly added to a core, which may be of rock or glacial till.
   a. Sandur
   b. 1509 Istanbul earthquake
   c. Rogen moraine
   d. Drumlin

50. A _____ is a cauldron-like volcanic feature usually formed by the collapse of land following a volcanic eruption such as the one at Yellowstone National Park. They are sometimes confused with volcanic craters.
   a. 1703 Genroku earthquake
   b. 1700 Cascadia earthquake
   c. Caldera
   d. 1509 Istanbul earthquake

51. A _____ is a cluster of dozens to hundreds of similarly shaped, sized and oriented drumlins, also called a drumlin swarm. Drumlins are one type of landform that indicate continental ice sheet glaciation. The total depth of glacial deposits may be hundreds of feet deep.
   a. Post-glacial rebound
   b. Quaternary glaciation
   c. Rock flour
   d. Drumlin field

52. _____ is the water released by the melting of snow or ice, including glacial ice and ice shelfs over oceans. _____ is often found in the ablation zone of glaciers, where the rate of snow cover is reducing. _____ can be produced during volcanic eruptions, in a similar way in which the more dangerous lahars form.
   a. Meltwater
   b. 1509 Istanbul earthquake
   c. 1700 Cascadia earthquake
   d. 1703 Genroku earthquake

53. A _____ is a glacial outwash plain formed of sediments deposited by meltwater at the terminus of a glacier.

   _____ are found in glaciated areas, such as Svalbard, Kerguelen Islands, and Iceland. Glaciers and icecaps contain large amounts of silt and sediment, picked up as they erode the underlying rocks when they move slowly downhill, and at the snout of the glacier, meltwater can carry this sediment away from the glacier and deposit it on a broad plain.

   a. Rogen moraine
   b. Monadnock
   c. 1509 Istanbul earthquake
   d. Sandur

54. An _____ is a long winding ridge of stratified sand and gravel, examples of which occur in glaciated and formerly glaciated regions of Europe and North America. They are frequently several miles long and, because of their peculiar uniform shape, are somewhat like railroad embankments.

Most are believed to form in ice-walled tunnels by streams which flowed within (englacial) and under (subglacial) glaciers.

a. AL 333
b. Esker
c. AASHTO Soil Classification System
d. AL 129-1

55. The _____ is the level at which the ground water pressure is equal to atmospheric pressure. It may be conveniently visualized as the 'surface' of the ground water in a given vicinity. It usually coincides with the phreatic surface, but can be many feet above it. As water infiltrates through pore spaces in the soil, it first passes through the zone of aeration, where the soil is unsaturated. At increasing depths water fills in more spaces, until the zone of saturation is reached. The relatively horizontal plane atop this zone constitutes the _____.

a. Shaft construction
b. Water table
c. Crosshole sonic logging
d. Rock bolt

56. A _____ is a lake with origins in a melted glacier.

_____s can be green as a result of pulverized minerals (rock flour) that support a large population of algae.

A retreating glacier often leaves behind large deposits of ice in hollows between drumlins or hills. As the ice age ends, these will melt to create lakes.

a. Drumlin field
b. Glacial lake
c. Rock flour
d. Pastonian Stage

57. A _____ is an annual layer of sediment or sedimentary rock. Initially, _____ was used to describe the separate components of annual layers in glacial lake sediments, but at the 1910 Geological Congress, the Swedish geologist Gerard De Geer (1858-1943) proposed a new formal definition where _____ described the whole of any annual sedimentary layer.

a. Varve
b. 1703 Genroku earthquake
c. 1700 Cascadia earthquake
d. 1509 Istanbul earthquake

58. _____ are isolated fragments of rock found within finer-grained water-deposited sedimentary rocks. They range in size from small pebbles to boulders. The critical distinguishing feature is that there is evidence that they were not transported by normal water currents, but rather dropped in vertically through the water column.

a. 1700 Cascadia earthquake
b. 1509 Istanbul earthquake
c. Dropstones
d. 1703 Genroku earthquake

59. The _____ describes the documented cooling trend in the Earth's climate during the Holocene, following the retreat of the Wisconsin glaciation, the most recent glacial period. _____ has followed the hypsithermal or Holocene Climatic Optimum, the warmest point in the Earth's climate during the current interglacial stage. The _____ has no well-marked universal beginning: local conditions and ecological inertia affected the onset of detectably cooler (and wetter) conditions.

a. 1700 Cascadia earthquake
b. Holocene glacial retreat
c. 1509 Istanbul earthquake
d. Neoglaciation

60. In geology and climatology, a _____ was an extended period of abundant rainfall lasting many thousands of years. The term is especially applied to such periods during the Pleistocene Epoch. A minor, short _____ may be termed a 'subpluvial'.

   a. 1509 Istanbul earthquake
   b. 1700 Cascadia earthquake
   c. 1703 Genroku earthquake
   d. Pluvial

61. A _____ is a lake that experiences significant increase in depth and extent as a result of increased precipitation and reduced evaporation. Such lakes are likely to be endorheic.

They represent changes in the hydrological cycle -- wet cycles generate large lakes, whereas dry cycles cause the lakes to dry up leaving large flat plains.

   a. 1509 Istanbul earthquake
   b. 1700 Cascadia earthquake
   c. 1703 Genroku earthquake
   d. Pluvial lake

62. _____ was an immense glacial lake located in the center of North America. Fed by glacial runoff at the end of the last glacial period, its area was larger than all of the modern Great Lakes combined, and held more water than contained by all lakes in the world today.

During the last Ice Age, northern North America was covered by a glacier, which alternately advanced and decayed with variations in the climate. This continental ice sheet formed during the period now know as the Wisconsin glaciation, and covered much of central North America between 30,000 and 10,000 years ago. As the ice sheet decayed, it created at its front an immense glacial lake, formed from its meltwaters.

   a. 1703 Genroku earthquake
   b. 1700 Cascadia earthquake
   c. 1509 Istanbul earthquake
   d. Lake Agassiz

63. The Channeled _____ are unique geological erosion features in the U.S. state of Washington. They were created by the cataclysmic Missoula Floods that swept periodically across eastern Washington and down the Columbia River Plateau during the Pleistocene epoch. Geologist J Harlen Bretz coined the term in a series of papers in the 1920s. Debate over the origin of the _____ raged for four decades and is one of the great debates in the history of earth science.

River valleys formed by erosion normally have a 'V' cross section, and glaciers leave a 'U' cross section. The channeled _____ have a rectangular cross section and are spread over immense areas of eastern Washington. They exhibit a unique drainage pattern that appears to have an entrance in the northeast and an exit in the southwest.

   a. Scablands
   b. 1703 Genroku earthquake
   c. 1700 Cascadia earthquake
   d. 1509 Istanbul earthquake

Chapter 17. Glaciers and Glaciation

64. In geology, _____ are sedimentary structures that indicate agitation by water (current or waves) or wind. _____ formed by water consist of two basic types:

1. Current _____ are asymmetrical in profile, with a gentle up-current slope and a steeper down-current slope. The down-current slope depends on the shape of the sediment, with 33>° being typical.
2. Wave-formed _____ have a symmetrical, almost sinusoidal profile; they indicate an environment with weak currents where water motion is dominated by wave oscillations.

Ripples will not form in sediment larger than course sand.

a. 1703 Genroku earthquake
c. 1509 Istanbul earthquake
b. 1700 Cascadia earthquake
d. Ripple marks

65. _____ is a term used in geology to refer to the state of gravitational equilibrium between the earth's lithosphere and asthenosphere such that the tectonic plates 'float' at an elevation which depends on their thickness and density. This concept is invoked to explain how different topographic heights can exist at the Earth's surface. When a certain area of lithosphere reaches the state of _____, it is said to be in isostatic equilibrium.

a. Isograd
c. Isostasy
b. Orientation Tensor
d. Economic geology

66. _____ is the rise of land masses that were depressed by the huge weight of ice sheets during the last glacial period, through a process known as isostatic depression. It affects northern Europe (especially Scotland, Fennoscandia and northern Denmark), Siberia, Canada, and the Great Lakes of Canada and the United States.

During the last glacial period, much of northern Europe, Asia, North America, Greenland and Antarctica were covered by ice sheets. The ice was as thick as three kilometres during the last glacial maximum about 20,000 years ago. The enormous weight of this ice caused the surface of the crust to deform and downwarp under the ice load, forcing the fluid mantle material to flow away from the loaded area. At the end of the ice age when the glaciers retreated, the removal of the weight from the depressed land led to uplift or rebound of the land and the return flow of mantle material back under the deglaciated area.

a. Cirque glacier
c. Glacial lake
b. Bergschrund
d. Post-glacial rebound

67. In astronomy, _____ is the inclination angle of a planet's rotational axis in relation to its orbital plane. It is also called axial inclination or obliquity. The _____ is expressed as the angle made by the planet's axis and a line drawn through the planet's center perpendicular to the orbital plane.

a. Axial tilt
c. AL 333
b. AASHTO Soil Classification System
d. AL 129-1

68. _____ are the collective effect of changes in the Earth's movements upon its climate axial tilt, and precession of the Earth's orbit determined climatic patterns on Earth, resulting in 100,000-year ice age cycles of the Quaternary glaciation over the last few million years. The Earth's axis completes one full cycle of precession approximately every 26,000 years. At the same time, the elliptical orbit rotates, more slowly, leading to a 23,000-year cycle between the seasons and the orbit.

a. Chronostratigraphy
b. Global Standard Stratigraphic Age
c. Milankovitch theory
d. Paleomagnetism

69. _____ refers to natural mountain building, and may be studied as a tectonic structural event, (b) as a geographical event, and (c) a chronological event. Orogenic events (a) cause distinctive structural phenomena and related tectonic activity, (b) affect certain regions of rocks and crust, and (c) happen within a specific period of time.

a. Orogeny
b. Alice Springs Orogeny
c. Antler orogeny
d. Orogenesis

70. _____ include a variety of substances given off by active (or, at times, by dormant) volcanoes. These include gases trapped in cavities (vesicles) in volcanic rocks, dissolved or dissociated gases in magma and lava, or gases emanating directly from lava or indirectly through ground water heated by volcanic action.

The sources of _____ on Earth include:

- primordial and recycled constituents from the Earth's mantle,
- assimilated constituents from the Earth's crust,
- groundwater and the Earth's atmosphere.

Substances that may become gaseous or give off gases when heated are termed volatile substances.

Gases are released from magma through volatile constituents reaching such high concentrations in the base magma that they evaporate.

a. Volcanic gases
b. Cinder
c. Volcanic ash
d. Pit crater

Chapter 18. The Work of Wind and Deserts

1. In geology a _____ is the smallest division of a geologic formation or stratigraphic rock series marked by well-defined divisional planes (bedding planes) separating it from layers above and below. A _____ is the smallest lithostratigraphic unit, usually ranging in thickness from a centimeter to several meters and distinguishable from _____s above and below it. _____s can be differentiated in various ways, including rock or mineral type and particle size.
   a. Sequence stratigraphy
   b. Biozones
   c. Cyclostratigraphy
   d. Bed

2. The term _____ describes particles in a flowing fluid (usually a river) that are transported along the bed. This is in opposition to suspended load and wash load which are carried entirely in suspension.

   _____ moves by a variety of methods, including rolling, sliding, traction, and saltation.

   a. Bed load
   b. Differential weathering
   c. Shutter ridge
   d. Bradyseism

3. _____ is a naturally occurring material composed primarily of fine-grained minerals, which show plasticity through a variable range of water content, and which can be hardened when dried and/or fired. _____ deposits are mostly composed of _____ minerals (phyllosilicate minerals), minerals which impart plasticity and harden when fired and/or dried, and variable amounts of water trapped in the mineral structure by polar attraction. Organic materials which do not impart plasticity may also be a part of _____ deposits.
   a. 1509 Istanbul earthquake
   b. 1700 Cascadia earthquake
   c. 1703 Genroku earthquake
   d. Clay

4. _____ is the geological process by which material is added to a landform or land mass. Fluids such as wind and water, as well as sediment gravity flows, transport previously eroded sediment, which, at the loss of enough kinetic energy in the fluid, is deposited, building up layers of sediment.

   _____ occurs when the forces responsible for sediment transportation are no longer sufficient to overcome the forces of particle weight and friction, which resist motion.

   a. Stoping
   b. Hydrothermal circulation
   c. Deposition
   d. Hydraulic action

5. _____ is the removal of solids (sediment, soil, rock and other particles) in the natural environment. It usually occurs due to transport by wind, water, or ice; by down-slope creep of soil and other material under the force of gravity; or by living organisms, such as burrowing animals, in the case of bioerosion.

   _____ is distinguished from weathering, which is the process of chemical or physical breakdown of the minerals in the rocks, although the two processes may occur concurrently.

   a. AL 333
   b. AL 129-1
   c. AASHTO Soil Classification System
   d. Erosion

Chapter 18. The Work of Wind and Deserts

6. _____ is the change in population over time, and can be quantified as the change in the number of individuals in a population using 'per unit time' for measurement. The term _____ can technically refer to any species, but almost always refers to humans, and it is often used informally for the more specific demographic term _____ rate , and is often used to refer specifically to the growth of the population of the world.

Simple models of _____ include the Malthusian Growth Model and the logistic model.

   a. 1700 Cascadia earthquake
   b. 1509 Istanbul earthquake
   c. 1703 Genroku earthquake
   d. Population growth

7. In geology, _____ is a specific type of particle transport by fluids such as wind, or the denser fluid water. It occurs when loose material is removed from a bed and carried by the fluid, before being transported back to the surface. Examples include pebble transport by rivers, sand drift over desert surfaces, soil blowing over fields, or even snow drift over smooth surfaces such as those in the Arctic or Canadian Prairies.
   a. Headward erosion
   b. Stoping
   c. Seafloor spreading
   d. Saltation

8. _____ is a naturally occurring granular material composed of finely divided rock and mineral particles.

As the term is used by geologists, _____ particles range in diameter from 0.0625 (or $>^1\!\!/\!_{16}$ mm, or 62.5 micrometers) to 2 millimeters. An individual particle in this range size is termed a _____ grain.

   a. 1509 Istanbul earthquake
   b. 1703 Genroku earthquake
   c. 1700 Cascadia earthquake
   d. Sand

9. _____ is any particulate matter that can be transported by fluid flow, and which eventually is deposited.

They are most often transported by water (fluvial processes) transported by wind (aeolian processes) and glaciers. Beach sands and river channel deposits are examples of fluvial transport and deposition, though _____ also often settles out of slow-moving or standing water in lakes and oceans.

   a. Sediment
   b. Bovey Beds
   c. Salt glacier
   d. Quick clay

10. _____ is soil or rock derived granular material of a grain size between sand and clay. _____ may occur as a soil or as suspended sediment in a surface water body. It may also exist as soil deposited at the bottom of a water body.
    a. 1703 Genroku earthquake
    b. 1509 Istanbul earthquake
    c. Silt
    d. 1700 Cascadia earthquake

11. _____ is the naturally occurring, unconsolidated or loose covering on the Earth's surface. _____ is composed of particles of broken rock that have been altered by chemical, biological and environmental processes including weathering and erosion. _____ is different from its parent rock(s) source(s), altered by interactions between the lithosphere, hydrosphere, atmosphere, and the biosphere.

a. Slump
b. Topsoil
c. 1509 Istanbul earthquake
d. Soil

12. _____ is the term for the fine particles that are light enough to be carried in a stream without touching the stream bed. These particles are generally of the fine sand, silt and clay size, although they can be larger, especially in cases of high discharge, such as during floods. This is in contrast to bed load which is carried along the bottom of the stream.
   a. Logarithmic Spiral Beach
   b. Historical geology
   c. Principle of inclusions and components
   d. Suspended load

13. _____s, sometimes called minor planets or planetoids, are small Solar System bodies in orbit around the Sun, especially in the inner Solar System; they are smaller than planets but larger than meteoroids. The term '_____' has historically been applied primarily to bodies in the inner Solar System since the outer Solar System was poorly known when it came into common usage. The distinction between _____s and comets is made on visual appearance: Comets show a perceptible coma while _____s do not.
   a. AL 129-1
   b. AASHTO Soil Classification System
   c. AL 333
   d. Asteroid

14. A _____ is a large, slow-moving mass of ice, formed from compacted layers of snow, that slowly deforms and flows in response to gravity and high pressure.

_____ ice is the largest reservoir of fresh water on Earth, and second only to oceans as the largest reservoir of total water.

   a. Little Ice Age
   b. Pacific Decadal Oscillation
   c. Greenhouse gases
   d. Glacier

15. _____ in the French school of pedology are two regressive evolution processes associated with the loss of equilibrium of a stable soil. Retrogression is primarily due to erosion and corresponds to a phenomenon where succession reverts back to pioneer conditions (such as bare ground.) Degradation is an evolution, different of natural evolution, related to the locale climate and vegetation.
   a. 1700 Cascadia earthquake
   b. 1509 Istanbul earthquake
   c. 1703 Genroku earthquake
   d. Soils retrogression and degradation

16. _____ is mechanical scraping of a rock surface by friction between rocks and moving particles during their transport in wind, glacier, waves, gravity or running water, after friction, the moving particles dislodge loose and weak debris from the side of the rock, these particles can be dissolved in the water source.

The intensity of _____ depends on the hardness, concentration, velocity and mass of moving particles.

A virtually smooth marine platform cut by the ocean waves at a coastline.

   a. AL 333
   b. Abrasion
   c. AASHTO Soil Classification System
   d. AL 129-1

Chapter 18. The Work of Wind and Deserts

17. The _____ or the Dirty Thirties was a period of severe dust storms causing major ecological and agricultural damage to American and Canadian prairie lands from 1930 to 1936 (in some areas until 1940.) The phenomenon was caused by severe drought coupled with decades of extensive farming without crop rotation or other techniques to prevent erosion. Deep plowing of the virgin topsoil of the Great Plains had killed the natural grasses that normally kept the soil in place and trapped moisture even during periods of drought and high winds.
   - a. 1509 Istanbul earthquake
   - b. 1703 Genroku earthquake
   - c. 1700 Cascadia earthquake
   - d. Dust Bowl

18. A _____ or sandstorm is a meteorological phenomenon common in arid and semi-arid regions and arises when a gust front passes or when the wind force exceeds the threshold value where loose sand and dust are removed from the dry surface. Particles are transported by saltation and suspension, causing soil erosion from one place and deposition in another. The Sahara and drylands around the Arabian peninsula are the main source of airborne dust, with some contributions from Iran, Pakistan and India into the Arabian Sea, and China's storms deposit dust in the Pacific.
   - a. Dust storm
   - b. 1700 Cascadia earthquake
   - c. 1703 Genroku earthquake
   - d. 1509 Istanbul earthquake

19. _____ are rocks that have been abraded, pitted, etched, grooved, or polished by wind-driven sand or ice crystals. These geomorphic features are most typically found in arid environments where there is little vegetation to interfere with aeolian particle transport, where there are frequently strong winds, and where there is a steady but not overwhelming supply of sand.

    _____ can be abraded to eye-catching natural sculptures.

   - a. Ventifacts
   - b. Fault breccia
   - c. Coprolite
   - d. 1509 Istanbul earthquake

20. A _____ is a wind-abraded ridge found in a desert environment. They are elongate features typically three or more times longer than they are wide, and when viewed from above, resemble the hull of a boat. Facing the wind is a steep, blunt face that gradually gets lower and narrower toward the lee end.
   - a. 1700 Cascadia earthquake
   - b. Yardang
   - c. 1703 Genroku earthquake
   - d. 1509 Istanbul earthquake

21. The _____ is the level at which the ground water pressure is equal to atmospheric pressure. It may be conveniently visualized as the 'surface' of the ground water in a given vicinity. It usually coincides with the phreatic surface, but can be many feet above it. As water infiltrates through pore spaces in the soil, it first passes through the zone of aeration, where the soil is unsaturated. At increasing depths water fills in more spaces, until the zone of saturation is reached. The relatively horizontal plane atop this zone constitutes the _____.
   - a. Rock bolt
   - b. Water table
   - c. Shaft construction
   - d. Crosshole sonic logging

22. _____ are sandy depressions in a sand dune ecosystem (psammosere) caused by the removal of sediments by wind.

    _____ occur in partially vegetated dunefields or sandhills. _____ form when a patch of protective vegetation is lost, allowing strong winds to 'blow out' sand and form a depression.

Chapter 18. The Work of Wind and Deserts

a. 1509 Istanbul earthquake
b. Pothole
c. Blowouts
d. 1700 Cascadia earthquake

23. _____ in geology is a landform sunken or depressed below the surrounding area. _____s may be formed by various mechanisms, and may be referred to by a variety of technical terms.

- A basin may be any large sediment filled _____. In tectonics, it may refer specifically to a circular, syncline-like _____: a geologic basin; while in sedimentology, it may refer to an area thickly filled with sediment: sedimentary basin.

- A blowout is a _____ created by wind erosion typically in either a desert sand or dry soil (such as a post-glacial loess environment.)

- A graben is a down dropped and typically linear _____ or basin created by rifting in a region under tensional tectonic forces.

- An impact crater is a _____ created by an impact such as a meteorite crater.
- A pit crater is a _____ formed by a sinking, or caving in, of the ground surface lying over a void.
- A kettle is left behind when a piece of ice left behind in glacial deposits melts.

- A _____ may be an area of subsidence caused by the collapse of an underlying structure. Examples include sinkholes above caves in karst topography, or calderas.

a. Depression
b. Stratification
c. Platform
d. Drainage system

24. A _____ is a desert surface that is covered with closely packed, interlocking angular or rounded rock fragments of pebble and cobble size.

Several theories have been proposed for their formation. The more common theory is that they form by the gradual removal of the sand, dust and other fine grained material by the wind and intermittent rain leaving only the larger fragments behind.

a. 1700 Cascadia earthquake
b. Desert pavement
c. 1509 Istanbul earthquake
d. 1703 Genroku earthquake

25. _____ is a homogeneous, typically nonstratified, porous, friable, slightly coherent, often calcareous, fine-grained, silty, pale yellow or buff, windblown (aeolian) sediment. It generally occurs as a widespread blanket deposit that covers areas of hundreds of square kilometers and tens of meters thick. _____ often stands in either steep or vertical faces.

a. 1509 Istanbul earthquake
b. 1703 Genroku earthquake
c. 1700 Cascadia earthquake
d. Loess

26. A _____ dune is an arc-shaped sand ridge, comprising well-sorted sand. This type of dune possesses two 'horns' that face downwind, with the slip face (the downwind slope) at the angle of repose, or approximately 32 degrees. The upwind side is packed by the wind, and stands at about 15 degrees. Simple _____ dunes may stretch from meters to a hundred meters or so between the tips of the horns.

Chapter 18. The Work of Wind and Deserts

a. 1703 Genroku earthquake
b. 1509 Istanbul earthquake
c. Barchan
d. 1700 Cascadia earthquake

27. In geology, _____ refers to inclined sedimentary structures in a horizontal unit of rock. These tilted structures are deposits from bedforms such as ripples and dunes, and they indicate that the depositional environment contained a flowing fluid (typically, water or wind.) This is a case in geology when original depositional layering is tilted, and that the tilting is not a result of post-depositional deformation.

a. Perched coastline
b. Paralithic
c. Geopetal
d. Cross-bedding

28. An _____ is a large, relatively flat area of desert covered with wind-swept sand with little or no vegetative cover. The term takes its name from the Arabic word _____ , meaning 'dune field'. Strictly speaking, an _____ is defined as a desert area that contains more than 125 square kilometers of aeolian or wind-blown sand and where sand covers more than 20% of the surface.

a. AL 333
b. Erg
c. AASHTO Soil Classification System
d. AL 129-1

29. Radially symmetrical, _____ are pyramidal sand mounds with slipfaces on three or more arms that radiate from the high center of the mound. They tend to accumulate in areas with multidirectional wind regimes. _____ grow upward rather than laterally. They dominate the Grand Erg Oriental of the Sahara. In other deserts, they occur around the margins of the sand seas, particularly near topographic barriers. In the southeast Badain Jaran Desert of China, the _____ are up to 500 meters tall and may be the tallest dunes on Earth.

a. Star dunes
b. Loihi Seamount
c. Principle of inclusions and components
d. Pahoehoe lava

30. A _____ is flat or nearly flat land adjacent to a stream or river that experiences occasional or periodic flooding. It includes the floodway, which consists of the stream channel and adjacent areas that carry flood flows, and the flood fringe, which are areas covered by the flood, but which do not experience a strong current.

They generally contain unconsolidated sediments, often extending below the bed of the stream.

a. 1700 Cascadia earthquake
b. 1703 Genroku earthquake
c. Floodplain
d. 1509 Istanbul earthquake

31. A _____ is a glacial outwash plain formed of sediments deposited by meltwater at the terminus of a glacier.

_____ are found in glaciated areas, such as Svalbard, Kerguelen Islands, and Iceland. Glaciers and icecaps contain large amounts of silt and sediment, picked up as they erode the underlying rocks when they move slowly downhill, and at the snout of the glacier, meltwater can carry this sediment away from the glacier and deposit it on a broad plain.

a. Rogen moraine
b. Sandur
c. 1509 Istanbul earthquake
d. Monadnock

32. In physics, the _____ is an apparent deflection of moving objects when they are viewed from a rotating reference frame.

Newton's laws of motion govern the motion of an object in an inertial frame of reference. When transforming Newton's laws to a rotating frame of reference, the Coriolis force appears, along with the centrifugal force.

   a. 1509 Istanbul earthquake
   b. 1700 Cascadia earthquake
   c. 1703 Genroku earthquake
   d. Coriolis effect

33. Two important classifications of weathering processes exist -- physical and _____. Mechanical or physical weathering involves the breakdown of rocks and soils through direct contact with atmospheric conditions, such as heat, water, ice and pressure. The second classification, _____, involves the direct effect of atmospheric chemicals or biologically produced chemicals (also known as biological weathering) in the breakdown of rocks, soils and minerals.
   a. Physical weathering
   b. Frost disintegration
   c. 1509 Istanbul earthquake
   d. Chemical weathering

34. _____ can also be called frost shattering or frost-wedging. This type of weathering is common in mountain areas where the temperature is around freezing point. Frost induced weathering, although often attributed to the expansion of freezing water captured in cracks, is generally independent of the water-to-ice expansion. It has long been known that moist soils expand or frost heave upon freezing as a result of water migrating along from unfrozen areas via thin films to collect at growing ice lenses. This same phenomena occurs within pore spaces of rocks.
   a. Physical weathering
   b. 1509 Istanbul earthquake
   c. Weathering
   d. Frost disintegration

35. Two important classifications of weathering processes exist -- _____ and chemical weathering. Mechanical or _____ involves the breakdown of rocks and soils through direct contact with atmospheric conditions, such as heat, water, ice and pressure. The second classification, chemical weathering, involves the direct effect of atmospheric chemicals or biologically produced chemicals (also known as biological weathering) in the breakdown of rocks, soils and minerals.
   a. Physical weathering
   b. Weathering
   c. 1509 Istanbul earthquake
   d. Frost disintegration

36. _____ is the decomposition of Earth rocks, soils and their minerals through direct contact with the planet's atmosphere. _____ occurs in situ, or 'with no movement', and thus should not be confused with erosion, which involves the movement of rocks and minerals by agents such as water, ice, wind and gravity.

Two important classifications of _____ processes exist -- physical and chemical _____.

   a. Weathering
   b. Physical weathering
   c. Frost disintegration
   d. 1509 Istanbul earthquake

37. _____ are images created by removing part of a rock surface by incising, pecking, carving, and abrading. Outside North America, scholars often use terms such as 'carving', 'engraving', or other descriptions of the technique to refer to such images. _____ are found world-wide, and are often associated with prehistoric peoples.
   a. 1703 Genroku earthquake
   b. 1700 Cascadia earthquake
   c. 1509 Istanbul earthquake
   d. Petroglyphs

38. _____ is a term in archaeology for any man-made markings made on natural stone. They can be divided into: Petroglyphs in Val Camonica, Italy

- Petroglyphs - carvings into stone surfaces
- Pictographs - rock and cave paintings

In addition, petroforms and inukshuks are _____ made by aligning or piling natural stones. The stones themselves are used as large markings on the ground.

Buddhist stone carvings at Ili River, Kazakhstan

The term '_____' appears to have been used first used in about 1959: 'The _____ tells us little for, a certain human being, certain about marriage customs.', and has also been described as 'rock carvings', 'rock drawings', 'rock engravings', 'rock inscriptions', 'rock paintings', 'rock pictures', 'rock records' 'rock sculptures.,

Both petroglyphs and pictographs can be parietal, meaning on the walls of a cave or rock shelter, open-air meaning they are made on exposed natural outcrops or monument-based which are made on stones consciously deposited.

- a. 1703 Genroku earthquake
- b. 1700 Cascadia earthquake
- c. 1509 Istanbul earthquake
- d. Rock art

39. A _____ is a forest in which tree trunks have fossilized. That is, the wood in the trunks have turned into petrified wood, where organic cells have decomposed and are replaced by minerals, while preserving the structure of the wood.
- a. 1700 Cascadia earthquake
- b. Petrified Forest
- c. Phaneritic
- d. 1509 Istanbul earthquake

40. Uluru, also referred to as _____, is a large sandstone rock formation in the southern part of the Northern Territory, central Australia. It lies 335 km (208 mi) south west of the nearest large town, Alice Springs; 450 km (280 mi) by road. Kata Tjuta and Uluru are the two major features of the Uluru - Kata Tjuta National Park.

_____ is an inselberg, literally 'island mountain', an isolated remnant left after the slow erosion of an original mountain range. Uluru is also often referred to as a monolith, although this is a somewhat ambiguous term because of its multiple meanings, and thus a word generally avoided by geologists.

- a. AL 333
- b. AL 129-1
- c. AASHTO Soil Classification System
- d. Ayers Rock

41. _____ is water located beneath the ground surface in soil pore spaces and in the fractures of lithologic formations. A unit of rock or an unconsolidated deposit is called an aquifer when it can yield a usable quantity of water. The depth at which soil pore spaces or fractures and voids in rock become completely saturated with water is called the water table.
- a. 1509 Istanbul earthquake
- b. 1700 Cascadia earthquake
- c. Groundwater
- d. Depression focused recharge

Chapter 18. The Work of Wind and Deserts

42. _____ is the geomorphic process by which soil, regolith, and rock move downslope under the force of gravity. Types of _____ include creep, slides, flows, topples, and falls, each with its own characteristic features, and taking place over timescales from seconds to years. _____ occurs on both terrestrial and submarine slopes, and has been observed on Earth, Mars, and Venus.
   a. 1700 Cascadia earthquake
   b. 1509 Istanbul earthquake
   c. Soil liquefaction
   d. Mass wasting

43. A _____ or mudslide is the most rapid (up to 80 km/h, or 50 mph) and fluid type of downhill mass wasting. It is a rapid movement of a large mass of mud formed from loose earth and water. Similar terms are mudslide (not very liquid), mud stream, debris flow (e.g. in high mountains), j>ökulhlaup, and lahar
   a. 1509 Istanbul earthquake
   b. 1700 Cascadia earthquake
   c. 1703 Genroku earthquake
   d. Mudflow

44. The _____ is the epoch from 1.8 million to 11550 years BP covering the world's recent period of repeated glaciations. The _____ epoch follows the Pliocene epoch and is followed by the Holocene epoch. The _____ is the third epoch of the Neogene period or 6th epoch of the Cenozoic Era. The end of the _____ corresponds with the retreat of the last continental glacier. It also corresponds with the end of the Paleolithic age used in archaeology.
   a. Tyrrhenian
   b. Late Pleistocene
   c. Sicilian Stage
   d. Pleistocene

45. An _____ is a confined aquifer containing groundwater that will flow upward through a well without the need for pumping. Water may even reach the ground surface if the natural pressure is high enough, in which case the well is called a flowing artesian well. An aquifer provides the water for an artesian well.
   a. AASHTO Soil Classification System
   b. AL 333
   c. Artesian aquifer
   d. AL 129-1

46. The _____ is the zone of the ocean floor that separates the thin oceanic crust from thick continental crust. _____s constitute about 28% of the oceanic area.

The transition from continental to oceanic crust commonly occurs within the outer part of the margin, called continental rise.

   a. 1509 Istanbul earthquake
   b. Cuspate forelands
   c. Longshore drift
   d. Continental margin

47. _____ is the natural or artificial removal of surface and sub-surface water from an area. Many agricultural soils need _____ to improve production or to manage water supplies.

The earliest archaeological record of an advanced system of _____ comes from the Indus Valley Civilization from around 3100 BC in what is now Pakistan and North India.

   a. Drainage
   b. 1700 Cascadia earthquake
   c. 1509 Istanbul earthquake
   d. 1703 Genroku earthquake

Chapter 18. The Work of Wind and Deserts

48. In the earth sciences and geology sub-fields, a _____ or physical feature comprises a geomorphological unit, and is largely defined by its surface form and location in the landscape, as part of the terrain, and as such, is typically an element of topography. _____ elements also include seascape and oceanic waterbody interface features such as bays, peninsulas, seas and so forth, including sub-surface terrain features such as submersed mountain ranges, volcanoes, and the great ocean basins under the thin skin of water, for the whole earth is the province and domain of geology. This panorama in Great Smoky Mountains National Park has the readily identifiable physical features of a rolling plain, actually part of a broad valley, distant foothills, and a backdrop of the old much weathered Appalachian mountain range.

_____s are categorised by characteristic physical attributes such as elevation, slope, orientation, stratification, rock exposure, and soil type.

a. Landform
b. 1700 Cascadia earthquake
c. 1509 Istanbul earthquake
d. 1703 Genroku earthquake

49. An _____ is a fan-shaped deposit formed where a fast flowing stream flattens, slows, and spreads typically at the exit of a canyon onto a flatter plain. A convergence of neighboring fans into a single apron of deposits against a slope is called a bajada, or compound _____.

a. AL 333
b. AL 129-1
c. Alluvial fan
d. AASHTO Soil Classification System

50. _____ is a geologic term for a type of topography characterized by a series of separate and parallel mountain ranges with broad valleys interposed, extending over a more or less wide area. It is typified by the topography found in the Great Basin in the western United States, which is part of a larger regional topography known as the _____ Province. _____ topography results from crustal extension.

a. Slaty cleavage
b. Lithostatic pressure
c. Rill
d. Basin and Range

51. The _____ is a large geologic province which includes parts of the southwestern United States and northwestern Mexico, typified by basin and range topography.

The topography of the _____ is a result of crustal extension within this part of the North American Plate. The cause of this extension is as yet not fully understood, although several hypotheses have been offered. The crust here has been stretched up to 100% of its original width. In fact, the crust underneath the _____, especially under the Great Basin, is some of the thinnest in the world.

a. Basin and Range Province
b. Gawler craton
c. Musgrave Block
d. Great Artesian Basin

52. A _____ is a gently inclined erosional surface carved into bedrock. It is thinly covered with Fluvial gravel that has developed at the foot of mountains. It develops when running water erodes most of the mass of the mountain. It is typically a concave surface gently sloping away from mountainous desert areas.

a. Platform cover
b. Lake capture
c. Riegel
d. Pediment

Chapter 18. The Work of Wind and Deserts

53. A _____ is a dry or ephemeral lakebed, generally extending to the shore, or remnant of, an endorheic lake. Such flats consist of fine-grained sediments infused with alkali salts. _____s are also known as alkali flats, sabkhas, dry lakes or mud flats.

   a. 1700 Cascadia earthquake
   b. Playa
   c. 1703 Genroku earthquake
   d. 1509 Istanbul earthquake

54. A _____ or inselberg is an isolated rock hill, knob, ridge, or small mountain that rises abruptly from a gently sloping or virtually level surrounding plain. The term '_____' is usually used in the United States, whereas 'inselberg' is the more common international term. In southern and southern-central Africa, a similar formation of granite is known as a kopje (in fact a Dutch word) from the Afrikaans word: koppie.

_____ is an originally Native American term for an isolated hill or a lone mountain that has risen above the surrounding area, typically by surviving erosion.

   a. Sandur
   b. Rogen moraine
   c. 1509 Istanbul earthquake
   d. Monadnock

55. A _____ is an elevated area of land with a flat top and sides that are usually steep cliffs. It takes its name from its characteristic table-top shape. It is a characteristic landform of arid environments, particularly the southwestern United States.

_____s form usually in areas where horizontally layered rocks are uplifted by tectonic activity, but may form also in its absence.

_____s are formed by weathering and erosion. Variations in the ability of different types of rock to resist weathering and erosion cause the weaker types of rocks to be eroded away, leaving the more resistant types of rocks topographically higher relative to their surroundings. This process is called differential erosion.

   a. 1509 Istanbul earthquake
   b. Truncated spur
   c. Palustrine
   d. Mesa

56. _____ is a region of the Colorado Plateau characterized by a cluster of vast and iconic sandstone buttes, the largest reaching 1,000 ft (300 m) above the valley floor. It is located on the southern border of Utah with northern Arizona (around >>36>°59>'N 110>°6>'W'#20;/'#20;>36.983>°N 110.1>°W>'#20;/'#20;36.983; -110.1), near the Four Corners area. The valley lies within the range of the Navajo Nation Reservation, and is accessible from U.S. Highway 163.

   a. Paleorrota
   b. Monument Valley
   c. Thirtynine Mile volcanic field
   d. Rano Kau

Chapter 19. Shorelines and Shoreline Processes

1. In geology, sedimentary _____ describes the combination of physical, chemical and biological processes associated with the deposition of a particular type of sediment and, therefore, the rock types that will be formed after lithification, if the sediment is preserved in the rock record. In most cases the environments associated with particular rock types or associations of rock types can be matched to existing analogues. However, the further back in geological time sediments were deposited, the more likely that direct modern analogues are not available (e.g. banded iron formations.)
   - a. Depositional environment
   - b. 1703 Genroku earthquake
   - c. 1509 Istanbul earthquake
   - d. 1700 Cascadia earthquake

2. _____ is a geological process occurring when areas of submerged seafloor are exposed above the sea level. The opposite event, marine transgression, occurs when flooding from the sea covers previously exposed land.

   Evidence of _____ and transgression occurs throughout the fossil record, and these fluctuations are thought to have caused (or contributed to) several mass extinctions, among them the Permian-Triassic extinction event (250 million years ago) and Cretaceous-Tertiary extinction event (65 Ma.)
   - a. Marine regression
   - b. 1703 Genroku earthquake
   - c. 1509 Istanbul earthquake
   - d. 1700 Cascadia earthquake

3. _____ are waves that travel through the Earth or other elastic body, for example as the result of an earthquake, explosion, or some other process that imparts forces to the body. _____ are also continually excited on Earth by the incessant pounding of ocean waves (referred to as the microseism) and the wind. _____ are studied by seismologists, and measured by a seismograph, which records the output of a seismometer, or geophone.
   - a. Strong ground motion
   - b. Paleoliquefaction
   - c. Seismic waves
   - d. Seismic gap

4. _____ is a form of mass wasting event that occurs when loosely consolidated materials or rock layers move a short distance down a slope. The landmass and the surface it _____s upon is called a failure surface. When the movement occurs in soil, there is often a distinctive rotational movement to the mass, that cuts vertically through bedding planes (landslides take place along a bedding plane or fault). This rotational movement moves along a curved slip surface of regolith (the failure surface) which overlies bedrock. This results in internal deformation of the moving mass consisting chiefly of overturned folds called 'sheath folds.'
   - a. Topsoil
   - b. Soil
   - c. Slump
   - d. 1509 Istanbul earthquake

5. In geology, engineering, and surveying, _____ is the motion of a surface (usually, the Earth's surface) as it shifts downward relative to a datum such as sea-level. The opposite of _____ is uplift, which results in an increase in elevation. There are several types of _____.
   - a. 1700 Cascadia earthquake
   - b. 1509 Istanbul earthquake
   - c. Pothole
   - d. Subsidence

6. _____ are a distinctive type of rock often found in primordial sedimentary rocks. The structures consist of repeated thin layers of iron oxides, either magnetite or hematite, alternating with bands of iron-poor shale and chert. Some of the oldest known rock formations, formed around three thousand million years before present, include banded iron layers, and the banded layers are a common feature in sediments for much of the Earth's early history.
   - a. Sandstone
   - b. Diatomaceous earth
   - c. Coquina
   - d. Banded Iron Formations

Chapter 19. Shorelines and Shoreline Processes

7. The _____ is the zone of the ocean floor that separates the thin oceanic crust from thick continental crust. _____s constitute about 28% of the oceanic area.

The transition from continental to oceanic crust commonly occurs within the outer part of the margin, called continental rise.

   a. 1509 Istanbul earthquake
   b. Cuspate forelands
   c. Continental margin
   d. Longshore drift

8. _____ are the preserved remains or traces of animals, plants, and other organisms from the remote past. The totality of _____, both discovered and undiscovered, and their placement in fossiliferous rock formations and sedimentary layers (strata) is known as the fossil record. The study of _____ across geological time, how they were formed, and the evolutionary relationships between taxa (phylogeny) are some of the most important functions of the science of paleontology.
   a. 1703 Genroku earthquake
   b. Fossils
   c. 1509 Istanbul earthquake
   d. 1700 Cascadia earthquake

9. The _____ is a chronologic schema (or idealized model) relating stratigraphy to time that is used by geologists, paleontologists and other earth scientists to describe the timing and relationships between events that have occurred during the history of the Earth. The table of geologic time spans presented here agrees with the dates and nomenclature proposed by the International Commission on Stratigraphy, and uses the standard color codes of the United States Geological Survey.

Evidence from radiometric dating indicates that the Earth is about 4.570 billion years old.

   a. 1509 Istanbul earthquake
   b. 1700 Cascadia earthquake
   c. 1703 Genroku earthquake
   d. Geologic time scale

10. A _____ is a large, slow-moving mass of ice, formed from compacted layers of snow, that slowly deforms and flows in response to gravity and high pressure.

_____ ice is the largest reservoir of fresh water on Earth, and second only to oceans as the largest reservoir of total water.

   a. Little Ice Age
   b. Pacific Decadal Oscillation
   c. Greenhouse gases
   d. Glacier

11. A marine _____ is a geologic event during which sea level rises relative to the land and the shoreline moves toward higher ground, resulting in flooding. They can be caused either by the land sinking or the ocean basins filling with water (or decreasing in capacity.) Transgresssions and regressions may be caused by tectonic events such as orogenies, severe climate change such as ice ages or isostatic adjustments following removal of ice or sediment load.
   a. Hydraulic action
   b. Diagenesis
   c. Hydrothermal circulation
   d. Transgression

12. The _____ is the extended perimeter of each continent and associated coastal plain, and was part of the continent during the glacial periods, but is undersea during interglacial periods such as the current epoch by relatively shallow seas (known as shelf seas) and gulfs.

Chapter 19. Shorelines and Shoreline Processes

The continental rise is below the slope, but landward of the abyssal plains. Its gradient is intermediate between the slope and the shelf, on the order of 0.5-1°.

a. Surface runoff
b. Continental shelf
c. Mud
d. Continental slope

13. _____ is the geological process by which material is added to a landform or land mass. Fluids such as wind and water, as well as sediment gravity flows, transport previously eroded sediment, which, at the loss of enough kinetic energy in the fluid, is deposited, building up layers of sediment.

_____ occurs when the forces responsible for sediment transportation are no longer sufficient to overcome the forces of particle weight and friction, which resist motion.

a. Hydrothermal circulation
b. Hydraulic action
c. Stoping
d. Deposition

14. _____ is the removal of solids (sediment, soil, rock and other particles) in the natural environment. It usually occurs due to transport by wind, water, or ice; by down-slope creep of soil and other material under the force of gravity; or by living organisms, such as burrowing animals, in the case of bioerosion.

_____ is distinguished from weathering, which is the process of chemical or physical breakdown of the minerals in the rocks, although the two processes may occur concurrently.

a. AASHTO Soil Classification System
b. AL 333
c. AL 129-1
d. Erosion

15. In fluid dynamics, the _____ of a surface wave denotes the difference between the elevations of a crest and a neighbouring trough. _____ is a term used by mariners, as well as in coastal, ocean engineering and naval engineering.

At sea, the term significant _____ is used as a means to introduce a well-defined and standardized statistic to denote the characteristic height of the random waves in a sea state.

a. 1509 Istanbul earthquake
b. 1700 Cascadia earthquake
c. Wave base
d. Wave height

16. _____ is the number of occurrences of a repeating event per unit time. It is also referred to as temporal _____. The period is the duration of one cycle in a repeating event, so the period is the reciprocal of the _____.
a. 1703 Genroku earthquake
b. Frequency
c. 1509 Istanbul earthquake
d. 1700 Cascadia earthquake

17. A _____ column (or _____) is a column of rising air in the lower altitudes of the Earth's atmosphere. They are created by the uneven heating of the Earth's surface from solar radiation, and an example of convection. The Sun warms the ground, which in turn warms the air directly above it.

Chapter 19. Shorelines and Shoreline Processes 217

    a. 1703 Genroku earthquake
    b. 1700 Cascadia earthquake
    c. 1509 Istanbul earthquake
    d. Thermal

18. In geology, a _____ or _____ line is a planar fracture in rock in which the rock on one side of the fracture has moved with respect to the rock on the other side. Large _____ s within the Earth's crust are the result of differential or shear motion and active _____ zones are the causal locations of most earthquakes. Earthquakes are caused by energy release during rapid slippage along a _____.
    a. Cohesion
    b. Combe
    c. Fault
    d. Geothermal

19. A _____ is a geological phenomenon which includes a wide range of ground movement, such as rock falls, deep failure of slopes and shallow debris flows, which can occur in offshore, coastal and onshore environments. Although the action of gravity is the primary driving force for a _____ to occur, there are other contributing factors affecting the original slope stability. Typically, pre-conditional factors build up specific sub-surface conditions that make the area/slope prone to failure, whereas the actual _____ often requires a trigger before being released.
    a. 1700 Cascadia earthquake
    b. Soil liquefaction
    c. Landslide
    d. 1509 Istanbul earthquake

20. _____ is the geomorphic process by which soil, regolith, and rock move downslope under the force of gravity. Types of _____ include creep, slides, flows, topples, and falls, each with its own characteristic features, and taking place over timescales from seconds to years. _____ occurs on both terrestrial and submarine slopes, and has been observed on Earth, Mars, and Venus.
    a. Soil liquefaction
    b. 1509 Istanbul earthquake
    c. Mass wasting
    d. 1700 Cascadia earthquake

21. The _____ is a continental transform fault that runs a length of roughly 800 miles (1,300 km) through California in the United States. The fault's motion is right-lateral strike-slip (horizontal motion.) It forms the tectonic boundary between the Pacific Plate and the North American Plate.
    a. 1509 Istanbul earthquake
    b. 1700 Cascadia earthquake
    c. 1703 Genroku earthquake
    d. San Andreas fault

22. In materials science, _____ is a change in the shape or size of an object due to an applied force. This can be a result of tensile (pulling) forces, compressive (pushing) forces, shear, bending or torsion (twisting.) _____ is often described as strain.
    a. Melange
    b. Stack
    c. Combe
    d. Deformation

23. An _____ is the result of a sudden release of energy in the Earth's crust that creates seismic waves. They are recorded with a seismometer or the related and mostly obsolete Richter magnitude, with a magnitude 3 or lower _____ being mostly imperceptible and magnitude 7 causing serious damage over large areas.
    a. AL 333
    b. AASHTO Soil Classification System
    c. AL 129-1
    d. Earthquake

24. The _____ is the maximum depth at which a water wave's passage causes significant water motion. For water depths larger than the _____, bottom sediments are no longer stirred by the wave motion above.

Chapter 19. Shorelines and Shoreline Processes

In deep water, the water particles are moved in a circular orbital motion when a wave passes.

a. 1700 Cascadia earthquake
b. 1509 Istanbul earthquake
c. Wave height
d. Wave base

25. _____ are relatively large and spontaneous ocean surface waves that are a threat even to large ships and ocean liners. In oceanography, they are more precisely defined as waves whose height is more than twice the significant wave height, which is itself defined as the mean of the largest third of waves in a wave record. Therefore _____ are not necessarily the biggest waves found at sea; they are, rather, surprisingly large waves for a given sea state.

a. 1703 Genroku earthquake
b. 1700 Cascadia earthquake
c. 1509 Istanbul earthquake
d. Rogue waves

26. As ocean surface waves come closer to shore they break, forming the foamy, bubbly surface we call surf. The region of breaking waves defines the _____. After breaking in the _____, the waves (now reduced in height) continue to move in, and they run up onto the sloping front of the beach, forming an uprush of water called swash.

a. 1703 Genroku earthquake
b. 1509 Istanbul earthquake
c. 1700 Cascadia earthquake
d. Surf zone

27. _____, sometimes known as shore drift, is a geological process by which sediments such as sand or other materials, move along a beach shore. It uses the process of swash to push the material up the beach and backwash down the beach; until it reaches a groyne or another obstacle.

Where waves approach the coastline at an angle, when they break their swash pushes beach material up the beach at the same angle.

a. 1509 Istanbul earthquake
b. Swash
c. Cuspate forelands
d. Longshore drift

28. The _____, usually referred to as the Moho, is the boundary between the Earth's crust and the mantle. The Moho serves to separate both oceanic crust and continental crust from underlying mantle. The Moho mostly lies entirely within the lithosphere; only beneath mid-ocean ridges does it define the lithosphere-asthenosphere boundary.

a. Copperbelt Province
b. Gorda Ridge
c. Panthalassa
d. Mohorovičić discontinuity

29. A _____ or sandbar is a somewhat linear landform within or extending into a body of water, typically composed of sand, silt or small pebbles. A bar is characteristically long and narrow and develops where a stream or ocean current promotes deposition of granular material, resulting in localized shallowing of the water. Bars can appear in the sea, in a lake, or in a river.

The term _____ can be applied to larger geological units that form off a coastline as part of the process of coastal erosion. These include spits and baymouth bars that form across the front of embayments and rias. A tombolo is a bar that forms an isthmus between an island or offshore rock and a mainland shore.

Chapter 19. Shorelines and Shoreline Processes 219

    a. 1703 Genroku earthquake
    b. 1700 Cascadia earthquake
    c. 1509 Istanbul earthquake
    d. Shoal

30. _____ is a common extrusive volcanic rock. It is usually grey to black and fine-grained due to rapid cooling of lava at the surface of a planet. It may be porphyritic containing larger crystals in a fine matrix, or vesicular, or frothy scoria.
    a. Basalt
    b. 1703 Genroku earthquake
    c. 1509 Istanbul earthquake
    d. 1700 Cascadia earthquake

31. The _____ zone is the area that is exposed to the air at low tide and submerged at high tide, for example, the area between tide marks. This area can include many different types of habitats, including steep rocky cliffs, sandy beaches, or wetlands The area can be a narrow strip, as in Pacific islands that have only a narrow tidal range, or can include many meters of shoreline where shallow beach slope interacts with high tidal excursion.
    a. Eutrophication
    b. Upwelling
    c. Intertidal
    d. Overland flow

32. _____ is rock that is of a specific particle size range. Specifically, it is any loose rock that is larger than two millimeters (2mm) in its largest dimension (about 1/12 of an inch) and no more than 64 millimeters (about 2.5 inches.) The next smaller size class in geology is sand, which is >0.0625 mm to 2 mm in size.
    a. 1703 Genroku earthquake
    b. 1700 Cascadia earthquake
    c. 1509 Istanbul earthquake
    d. Gravel

33. _____ is the second most abundant mineral in the Earth's continental crust . It is made up of a framework of silicon-oxygen tetrahedra SiO_4, with each silicon shared between two oxygens to give the overall formula SiO_2. _____ has a hardness of 7 on the Mohs scale and a density of 2.65 g/cmÂ³.
    a. Shocked quartz
    b. 1700 Cascadia earthquake
    c. 1509 Istanbul earthquake
    d. Quartz

34. _____ is a naturally occurring granular material composed of finely divided rock and mineral particles.

As the term is used by geologists, _____ particles range in diameter from 0.0625 (or $>^1\!/_{16}$ mm, or 62.5 micrometers) to 2 millimeters. An individual particle in this range size is termed a _____ grain.

    a. 1509 Istanbul earthquake
    b. 1700 Cascadia earthquake
    c. 1703 Genroku earthquake
    d. Sand

35. _____ is the decomposition of Earth rocks, soils and their minerals through direct contact with the planet's atmosphere. _____ occurs in situ, or 'with no movement', and thus should not be confused with erosion, which involves the movement of rocks and minerals by agents such as water, ice, wind and gravity.

Two important classifications of _____ processes exist -- physical and chemical _____.

    a. Frost disintegration
    b. Weathering
    c. Physical weathering
    d. 1509 Istanbul earthquake

Chapter 19. Shorelines and Shoreline Processes

36. In geology, _____ is transported rock debris overlying the solid bedrock. The term is also sometimes refers to organic debris so-transported. In the largest sense, it refers to the material left behind by retreating continental glaciers.
    a. Geostrophic current
    b. Detritus
    c. Contact metamorphism
    d. Drift

37. A _____ is a mountain rising from the ocean seafloor that does not reach to the water's surface (sea level), and thus is not an island. These are typically formed from extinct volcanoes, that rise abruptly and are usually found rising from a seafloor of 1,000-4,000 meters depth. They are defined by oceanographers as independent features that rise to at least 1,000 meters above the seafloor.
    a. 1700 Cascadia earthquake
    b. 1509 Istanbul earthquake
    c. 1703 Genroku earthquake
    d. Seamount

38. A _____ or sometimes ayre is a deposition landform in which an island is attached to the mainland by a narrow piece of land such as a spit or bar. They usually form because the island causes wave refraction, depositing sand and shingle moved by longshore drift in each direction around the island where the waves meet. Eustatic sea level rise may also contribute to accretion as material is pushed up with rising sea levels.
    a. 1703 Genroku earthquake
    b. Tombolo
    c. 1700 Cascadia earthquake
    d. 1509 Istanbul earthquake

39. _____ is a naturally occurring glass formed as an extrusive igneous rock. It is produced when felsic lava extruded from a volcano cools without crystal growth. _____ is commonly found within the margins of rhyolitic lava flows known as _____ flows, where the chemical composition (high silica content) induces a high viscosity and polymerization degree of the lava.
    a. AL 129-1
    b. AASHTO Soil Classification System
    c. AL 333
    d. Obsidian

40. In geography and geology, a _____ is a significant vertical, or near vertical, rock exposure. _____s are formed as erosion landforms due to the processes of erosion and weathering that produce them. _____s are common on coasts, in mountainous areas, escarpments and along rivers. _____s are usually formed by rock that is resistant to erosion and weathering. Sedimentary rocks are most likely to form sandstone, limestone, chalk, and dolomite. Igneous rocks, such as granite and basalt also often form _____s.
    a. 1703 Genroku earthquake
    b. 1700 Cascadia earthquake
    c. 1509 Istanbul earthquake
    d. Cliff

41. _____ is mechanical scraping of a rock surface by friction between rocks and moving particles during their transport in wind, glacier, waves, gravity or running water, after friction, the moving particles dislodge loose and weak debris from the side of the rock, these particles can be dissolved in the water source.

The intensity of _____ depends on the hardness, concentration, velocity and mass of moving particles.

A virtually smooth marine platform cut by the ocean waves at a coastline.

    a. Abrasion
    b. AL 129-1
    c. AL 333
    d. AASHTO Soil Classification System

42. _____ is a form of mechanical weathering caused by the force of moving water currents rushing into a crack in the rockface. The water compresses the air in the crack, pushing it right to the back. As the wave retreats, the highly pressurised air is suddenly released with explosive force, capable of chipping away the rockface over time.
  a. Mid-ocean ridge
  b. Deposition
  c. Hydrothermal circulation
  d. Hydraulic action

43. A _____, or shore platform is the narrow flat area often seen at the base of a sea cliff or along a large lake shore caused by the action of the waves. It forms after destructive waves hit against the cliff face, causing undercutting between the high and low water marks, mainly as a result of corrasion and hydraulic power, creating a wave-cut notch. This notch then enlarges into a cave. The waves undermine this portion until the roof of the cave cannot hold due to the pressure and freeze-thaw weathering acting on it, and collapses, resulting in the cliff retreating landward.
  a. Wave-cut platform
  b. Sclavia craton
  c. Cap carbonates
  d. Rill

44. In geology, a _____ is a continental area covered by relatively flat or gently tilted, mainly sedimentary strata, which overlie a basement of consolidated igneous or metamorphic rocks of an earlier deformation. They as well as, shields and the basement rocks together constitute cratons.

It is also common practice to use the term _____ as a very general term for a sequence of shallow water carbonate _____.

  a. Texture
  b. Streak
  c. Nodule
  d. Platform

45. A _____ is a natural formation (or landform) where a rock arch forms, with a natural passageway through underneath. Most _____es form as a narrow ridge, walled by cliffs, become narrower from erosion, with a softer rock stratum under the cliff-forming stratum gradually eroding out until the rock shelters thus formed meet underneath the ridge, thus forming the arch. They commonly form where cliffs are subject to erosion from the sea, rivers or weathering (sub-aerial processes); the processes 'find' weaknesses in rocks and work on them, making them bigger until they break through.
  a. 1700 Cascadia earthquake
  b. 1509 Istanbul earthquake
  c. 1703 Genroku earthquake
  d. Natural arch

46. A _____ is a geological landform consisting of a steep and often vertical column or columns of rock in the sea near a coast. They are formed when part of a headland is eroded by hydraulic action, which is the force of the sea or water crashing against the rock. The force of the water weakens cracks in the headland, causing them to later collapse, forming free-standing _____s and even a small island.
  a. Stratification
  b. Geothermal
  c. Combe
  d. Stack

47. _____ is any particulate matter that can be transported by fluid flow, and which eventually is deposited.

They are most often transported by water (fluvial processes) transported by wind (aeolian processes) and glaciers. Beach sands and river channel deposits are examples of fluvial transport and deposition, though _____ also often settles out of slow-moving or standing water in lakes and oceans.

Chapter 19. Shoreline and Shoreline Processes

    a. Quick clay
    c. Bovey Beds
    b. Sediment
    d. Salt glacier

48. A _____ is a steep-sided valley on the sea floor of the continental slope. Many _____s are found as extensions to large rivers; however there are many that have no such association. Canyons cutting the continental slopes have been found at depths greater than 2 km below sea level.
    a. 1509 Istanbul earthquake
    c. 1703 Genroku earthquake
    b. 1700 Cascadia earthquake
    d. Submarine canyon

49. The terms _____ and icehouse Earth refer to the prevailing global climate on a timescale of millions of years.

During a _____ Earth period, the planet's atmosphere contains sufficient _____ gases such as carbon dioxide and methane for ice to be entirely absent from the planet's surface.

During icehouse periods, glaciers are present in fluctuating amounts; variations in the Earth's orbit may result in many ice ages, glacials, and interglacials.

    a. Greenhouse
    c. 1509 Istanbul earthquake
    b. 1700 Cascadia earthquake
    d. 1703 Genroku earthquake

50. The general term '_____' or, more precisely, 'glacial age' denotes a geological period of long-term reduction in the temperature of the Earth's surface and atmosphere, resulting in an expansion of continental ice sheets, polar ice sheets and alpine glaciers. Within a long-term _____, individual pulses of extra cold climate are termed 'glaciations'. Glaciologically, _____ implies the presence of extensive ice sheets in the northern and southern hemispheres; by this definition we are still in an _____.
    a. AL 333
    c. AL 129-1
    b. AASHTO Soil Classification System
    d. Ice Age

51. _____ refers to natural mountain building, and may be studied as a tectonic structural event, (b) as a geographical event, and (c) a chronological event. Orogenic events (a) cause distinctive structural phenomena and related tectonic activity, (b) affect certain regions of rocks and crust, and (c) happen within a specific period of time.
    a. Orogenesis
    c. Alice Springs Orogeny
    b. Antler orogeny
    d. Orogeny

52. _____ refers to the process by which a sediment progressively loses its porosity due to the effects of loading. This forms part of the process of lithification. When a layer of sediment is originally deposited, it contains an open framework of particles with the pore space being usually filled with water.
    a. Submersion
    c. Cleavage
    b. Compaction
    d. Depression

53. The _____ is the epoch from 1.8 million to 11550 years BP covering the world's recent period of repeated glaciations. The _____ epoch follows the Pliocene epoch and is followed by the Holocene epoch. The _____ is the third epoch of the Neogene period or 6th epoch of the Cenozoic Era. The end of the _____ corresponds with the retreat of the last continental glacier. It also corresponds with the end of the Paleolithic age used in archaeology.

a. Pleistocene
c. Late Pleistocene
b. Sicilian Stage
d. Tyrrhenian

54. _____ is a term used in geology to refer to the state of gravitational equilibrium between the earth's lithosphere and asthenosphere such that the tectonic plates 'float' at an elevation which depends on their thickness and density. This concept is invoked to explain how different topographic heights can exist at the Earth's surface. When a certain area of lithosphere reaches the state of _____, it is said to be in isostatic equilibrium.

a. Orientation Tensor
c. Isograd
b. Economic geology
d. Isostasy

Chapter 20. Physical Geology in Perspective

1. _____ is molten rock expelled by a volcano during eruption. When first expelled from a volcanic vent, it is a liquid at temperatures from 700 >°C to 1,200 >°C (1,300 >°F to 2,200 >°F.) Although _____ is quite viscous, with about 100,000 times the viscosity of water, it can flow great distances before cooling and solidifying, because of both its thixotropic and shear thinning properties.
   a. Pumice
   b. Pyroclastic flow
   c. Cinder
   d. Lava

2. An _____ is the result of a sudden release of energy in the Earth's crust that creates seismic waves. They are recorded with a seismometer or the related and mostly obsolete Richter magnitude, with a magnitude 3 or lower _____ being mostly imperceptible and magnitude 7 causing serious damage over large areas.
   a. AASHTO Soil Classification System
   b. AL 129-1
   c. AL 333
   d. Earthquake

3. A _____ is a geological phenomenon which includes a wide range of ground movement, such as rock falls, deep failure of slopes and shallow debris flows, which can occur in offshore, coastal and onshore environments. Although the action of gravity is the primary driving force for a _____ to occur, there are other contributing factors affecting the original slope stability. Typically, pre-conditional factors build up specific sub-surface conditions that make the area/slope prone to failure, whereas the actual _____ often requires a trigger before being released.
   a. 1700 Cascadia earthquake
   b. Landslide
   c. Soil liquefaction
   d. 1509 Istanbul earthquake

4. _____ is the geomorphic process by which soil, regolith, and rock move downslope under the force of gravity. Types of _____ include creep, slides, flows, topples, and falls, each with its own characteristic features, and taking place over timescales from seconds to years. _____ occurs on both terrestrial and submarine slopes, and has been observed on Earth, Mars, and Venus.
   a. Soil liquefaction
   b. 1509 Istanbul earthquake
   c. 1700 Cascadia earthquake
   d. Mass wasting

5. _____ is the change in population over time, and can be quantified as the change in the number of individuals in a population using 'per unit time' for measurement. The term _____ can technically refer to any species, but almost always refers to humans, and it is often used informally for the more specific demographic term _____ rate , and is often used to refer specifically to the growth of the population of the world.

Simple models of _____ include the Malthusian Growth Model and the logistic model.

   a. 1703 Genroku earthquake
   b. Population growth
   c. 1509 Istanbul earthquake
   d. 1700 Cascadia earthquake

6. _____ is a chemical element with symbol Rn and atomic number 86. _____ is a colorless, odorless, tasteless, naturally occurring, radioactive noble gas that is formed from the decay of radium. It is one of the heaviest substances that remains a gas under normal conditions and is considered to be a health hazard.
   a. 1700 Cascadia earthquake
   b. 1703 Genroku earthquake
   c. Radon
   d. 1509 Istanbul earthquake

7. _____ is the naturally occurring, unconsolidated or loose covering on the Earth's surface. _____ is composed of particles of broken rock that have been altered by chemical, biological and environmental processes including weathering and erosion. _____ is different from its parent rock(s) source(s), altered by interactions between the lithosphere, hydrosphere, atmosphere, and the biosphere.

a. 1509 Istanbul earthquake
b. Topsoil
c. Slump
d. Soil

8. The _____ is the zone of the ocean floor that separates the thin oceanic crust from thick continental crust. _____s constitute about 28% of the oceanic area.

The transition from continental to oceanic crust commonly occurs within the outer part of the margin, called continental rise.

a. Cuspate forelands
b. Longshore drift
c. 1509 Istanbul earthquake
d. Continental margin

9. The _____ is a chronologic schema (or idealized model) relating stratigraphy to time that is used by geologists, paleontologists and other earth scientists to describe the timing and relationships between events that have occurred during the history of the Earth. The table of geologic time spans presented here agrees with the dates and nomenclature proposed by the International Commission on Stratigraphy, and uses the standard color codes of the United States Geological Survey.

Evidence from radiometric dating indicates that the Earth is about 4.570 billion years old.

a. Geologic time scale
b. 1700 Cascadia earthquake
c. 1509 Istanbul earthquake
d. 1703 Genroku earthquake

10. In organic chemistry, a _____ is an organic compound consisting entirely of hydrogen and carbon. With relation to chemical terminology, aromatic _____s or arenes, alkanes, alkenes and alkyne-based compounds composed entirely of carbon or hydrogen are referred to as 'pure' _____s, whereas other _____s with bonded compounds or impurities of sulfur or nitrogen, are referred to as 'impure', and remain somewhat erroneously referred to as _____s.

_____s are referred to as consisting of a 'backbone' or 'skeleton' composed entirely of carbon and hydrogen and other bonded compounds, and have a functional group that generally facilitates combustion.

a. Hydrocarbon
b. 1703 Genroku earthquake
c. 1509 Istanbul earthquake
d. 1700 Cascadia earthquake

11. _____ are rocks and minerals from which metallic iron can be economically extracted. The ores are usually rich in iron oxides and vary in color from dark grey, bright yellow, deep purple, to rusty red. The iron itself is usually found in the form of magnetite (Fe_3O_4), haematite (Fe_2O_3), goethite, limonite or siderite.

a. Ore genesis
b. AASHTO Soil Classification System
c. Ore
d. Iron ores

12. A _____ is a sand- to boulder-sized particle of debris in the Solar System. The visible path of a _____ that enters Earth's (or another body's) atmosphere is called a meteor, or commonly a 'shooting star' or 'falling star.' If a _____ reaches the ground, it is then called a meteorite. Many meteors are part of a meteor shower.

a. 1509 Istanbul earthquake
b. 1700 Cascadia earthquake
c. 1703 Genroku earthquake
d. Meteoroid

13. _____ or phosphorite is a general description applied to several kinds of rock which contain significant concentrations of phosphate minerals, which are minerals that contain the phosphate ion in their chemical structure.

Many kinds of rock contain mineral components containing phosphate or other phosphorus compounds in small amounts. However, rocks which contain phosphate in quantity and concentration which are economic to mine as ore for their phosphate content are not particularly common.

a. Phosphate rock
b. Diapir
c. Slyne-Erris Trough
d. Skarn

14. _____s, sometimes called minor planets or planetoids, are small Solar System bodies in orbit around the Sun, especially in the inner Solar System; they are smaller than planets but larger than meteoroids. The term '_____' has historically been applied primarily to bodies in the inner Solar System since the outer Solar System was poorly known when it came into common usage. The distinction between _____s and comets is made on visual appearance: Comets show a perceptible coma while _____s do not.

a. AL 333
b. AL 129-1
c. AASHTO Soil Classification System
d. Asteroid

15. The _____ is the extended perimeter of each continent and associated coastal plain, and was part of the continent during the glacial periods, but is undersea during interglacial periods such as the current epoch by relatively shallow seas (known as shelf seas) and gulfs.

The continental rise is below the slope, but landward of the abyssal plains. Its gradient is intermediate between the slope and the shelf, on the order of 0.5-1°.

a. Mud
b. Continental slope
c. Continental shelf
d. Surface runoff

16. An _____ is a type of rock that contains minerals such as gemstones and metals that can be extracted through mining and refined for use. Samples of _____ in the form of exceptionally beautiful crystals, exotic layering visible when sectioned or polished or metallic presentations such as large nuggets or crystalline formations of metals such as gold or copper may command a value far beyond their value as mere _____ or raw metal for subsequent reduction to utilitarian purposes.

The grade or concentration of an _____ mineral, or metal, as well as its form of occurrence, will directly affect the costs associated with mining the _____.

a. AASHTO Soil Classification System
b. Ore genesis
c. Iron ores
d. Ore

17. _____ is a naturally occurring granular material composed of finely divided rock and mineral particles.

As the term is used by geologists, _____ particles range in diameter from 0.0625 (or >$^1\!/_{16}$ mm, or 62.5 micrometers) to 2 millimeters. An individual particle in this range size is termed a _____ grain.

a. 1700 Cascadia earthquake
b. 1509 Istanbul earthquake
c. 1703 Genroku earthquake
d. Sand

18. The term _____ can be used to describe both the conduct of a survey for geological purposes and an institution holding geological information.

A _____ is the systematic investigation of the subsurface of a given piece of ground for the purpose of creating a geological map or model. A _____ employs techniques from the traditional walk-over survey, studying outcrops and landforms, to intrusive methods, such as hand augering and machine driven boreholes, to the use of geophysical techniques and remote sensing methods, such as aerial photography and satellite imagery.

a. Geological Survey
b. Paralithic
c. Leaverite
d. Reading Prong

19. A _____ is a type of map characterized by large-scale detail and quantitative representation of relief, usually using contour lines in modern mapping, but historically using a variety of methods. Traditional definitions require a _____ to show both natural and man-made features.

The Canadian Centre for Topographic Information provides this definition of a _____:

Other authors define _____s by contrasting them with another type of map; they are distinguished from smaller-scale 'chorographic maps' that cover large regions, 'planimetric maps' that do not show elevations, and 'thematic maps' that focus on specific topics.

a. 1509 Istanbul earthquake
b. 1703 Genroku earthquake
c. Topographic map
d. 1700 Cascadia earthquake

20. A meridian is an imaginary line on the Earth's surface from the North Pole to the South Pole that connects all locations with a given longitude. Each is half of a great circle on the Earth's surface. A _____ is the principal north-south line used for survey control in a large region.

a. Principal meridian
b. 1509 Istanbul earthquake
c. 1703 Genroku earthquake
d. 1700 Cascadia earthquake

Chapter 1
1. d	2. d	3. c	4. d	5. c	6. a	7. c	8. b	9. b	10. d
11. c	12. d	13. d	14. d	15. c	16. a	17. d	18. d	19. a	20. b
21. d	22. d	23. c	24. a	25. a	26. d	27. d	28. d	29. d	30. b
31. b	32. d	33. c	34. d	35. d	36. a	37. b	38. b	39. d	40. d
41. a	42. d	43. a	44. d	45. d	46. a	47. d	48. d	49. a	

Chapter 2
1. d	2. a	3. a	4. c	5. d	6. d	7. c	8. d	9. b	10. d
11. d	12. d	13. a	14. c	15. a	16. d	17. a	18. c	19. d	20. c
21. a	22. d	23. a	24. a	25. a	26. a	27. c	28. d	29. d	30. d
31. b	32. b	33. a	34. a	35. c	36. c	37. a	38. d	39. a	40. b
41. b	42. b	43. a	44. a	45. a	46. d	47. b	48. b	49. d	50. d
51. b	52. d	53. d	54. a	55. c	56. a	57. d	58. b	59. d	60. d
61. a	62. c	63. c	64. d	65. b	66. c	67. a	68. c	69. d	70. d
71. b	72. c	73. d	74. a	75. d					

Chapter 3
1. d	2. b	3. d	4. b	5. a	6. c	7. d	8. d	9. a	10. c
11. a	12. d	13. d	14. d	15. c	16. c	17. b	18. d	19. a	20. d
21. d	22. d	23. d	24. d	25. a	26. a	27. d	28. a	29. c	30. d
31. d	32. c	33. d	34. d	35. c	36. a	37. a	38. a	39. b	40. d
41. c	42. a	43. c	44. b	45. b	46. a	47. a	48. d	49. d	50. d
51. b	52. a	53. d	54. c	55. b	56. d	57. a	58. d	59. a	60. b
61. d	62. d	63. d	64. c	65. c	66. b	67. d			

Chapter 4
1. b	2. d	3. d	4. a	5. d	6. b	7. c	8. d	9. d	10. c
11. b	12. b	13. d	14. b	15. c	16. a	17. d	18. a	19. c	20. a
21. d	22. d	23. d	24. a	25. c	26. d	27. d	28. d	29. a	30. c
31. c	32. a	33. d	34. d	35. c	36. c	37. a	38. b	39. d	40. b
41. b	42. d	43. b	44. d	45. d	46. c	47. d	48. d	49. d	50. d
51. d	52. d	53. a	54. d	55. a	56. b	57. a	58. d	59. a	60. d
61. b	62. d	63. a	64. c						

Chapter 5
1. d	2. b	3. b	4. d	5. b	6. d	7. d	8. c	9. b	10. d
11. d	12. d	13. a	14. d	15. a	16. d	17. d	18. d	19. c	20. d
21. a	22. c	23. d	24. c	25. b	26. d	27. b	28. a	29. c	30. d
31. d	32. a	33. b	34. b	35. c	36. d	37. d	38. d	39. c	40. d
41. d	42. a	43. b	44. d	45. d	46. d	47. d	48. d	49. d	50. d
51. a	52. c	53. d	54. d	55. d	56. d	57. d	58. c	59. b	60. d
61. d	62. c	63. d	64. c	65. d	66. c	67. c	68. b		

ANSWER KEY

Chapter 6
1. b	2. c	3. b	4. c	5. d	6. d	7. d	8. d	9. c	10. b
11. d	12. c	13. b	14. d	15. d	16. b	17. a	18. a	19. d	20. d
21. d	22. d	23. c	24. b	25. c	26. d	27. d	28. d	29. b	30. a
31. d	32. a	33. c	34. b	35. c	36. d	37. d	38. d	39. d	40. d
41. c	42. d	43. b	44. c	45. d	46. c	47. a	48. d	49. b	50. a
51. c	52. d	53. b	54. b	55. a	56. c	57. c	58. d	59. d	60. c
61. d	62. c	63. a	64. d	65. d	66. c	67. d	68. d	69. d	70. d
71. d	72. a	73. b	74. d	75. d	76. c	77. b	78. c	79. d	80. d
81. d	82. d	83. b	84. a	85. b	86. d	87. d	88. a	89. b	90. c
91. c	92. d	93. c	94. b	95. d	96. d	97. d	98. c	99. a	100. b

Chapter 7
1. d	2. d	3. d	4. c	5. d	6. a	7. c	8. d	9. d	10. d
11. c	12. d	13. d	14. d	15. c	16. d	17. c	18. b	19. c	20. c
21. c	22. d	23. d	24. d	25. c	26. b	27. d	28. d	29. d	30. d
31. b	32. b	33. d	34. d	35. b	36. d	37. c	38. c	39. d	40. d
41. b	42. d	43. d	44. a	45. d	46. d	47. b	48. d	49. d	50. b
51. b	52. d	53. d	54. d	55. b	56. d	57. c	58. b	59. b	60. d
61. d	62. b	63. a	64. d	65. d	66. a	67. d	68. c	69. d	70. d

Chapter 8
1. b	2. d	3. d	4. d	5. d	6. d	7. c	8. a	9. c	10. c
11. d	12. b	13. c	14. d	15. d	16. a	17. d	18. d	19. d	20. d
21. b	22. d	23. b	24. c	25. b	26. a	27. d	28. d	29. d	30. b
31. b	32. d	33. d	34. d	35. a	36. d	37. c	38. d	39. a	40. d
41. d	42. d	43. a	44. c	45. a	46. d	47. d	48. c	49. d	50. d
51. d									

Chapter 9
1. b	2. b	3. d	4. d	5. b	6. d	7. d	8. d	9. d	10. d
11. d	12. d	13. a	14. a	15. a	16. c	17. b	18. d	19. b	20. d
21. b	22. d	23. a	24. d	25. d	26. b	27. a	28. a	29. d	30. d
31. a	32. d	33. d	34. d	35. d	36. a	37. d	38. b	39. a	40. b

Chapter 10
1. a	2. a	3. b	4. d	5. b	6. d	7. c	8. b	9. d	10. c
11. d	12. d	13. b	14. d	15. c	16. d	17. b	18. d	19. c	20. b
21. d	22. c	23. a	24. d	25. d	26. d	27. d	28. b	29. b	30. a
31. a	32. d	33. d	34. b	35. d	36. d	37. b	38. a	39. d	40. d
41. c	42. b	43. d	44. d	45. d					

Chapter 11

1. b	2. c	3. d	4. d	5. a	6. d	7. b	8. d	9. d	10. c
11. c	12. d	13. d	14. d	15. a	16. a	17. a	18. d	19. a	20. c
21. d	22. b	23. d	24. c	25. b	26. d	27. d	28. d	29. d	30. d
31. d	32. d	33. a	34. a	35. c	36. c	37. d	38. d	39. d	40. a
41. b	42. d	43. a	44. a	45. d	46. d	47. a	48. c	49. d	50. d
51. c	52. d	53. d	54. c	55. c	56. b	57. d	58. d	59. d	60. d
61. d	62. d	63. b	64. d	65. d	66. d	67. d	68. b	69. a	70. c
71. b	72. d	73. a	74. d						

Chapter 12

1. b	2. d	3. d	4. d	5. b	6. b	7. a	8. c	9. d	10. b
11. d	12. d	13. b	14. c	15. c	16. b	17. b	18. d	19. a	20. c
21. c	22. a	23. b	24. d	25. c	26. a	27. d	28. a	29. b	30. c
31. d	32. d	33. c	34. c	35. d	36. a	37. d	38. b	39. c	40. d
41. d	42. d	43. d	44. c	45. d	46. a	47. d	48. d	49. b	50. d
51. d	52. c	53. d	54. a	55. a	56. c	57. c	58. d	59. c	60. b
61. d	62. c	63. a	64. b	65. a	66. d	67. d	68. d	69. d	70. c
71. d	72. d	73. d	74. b	75. d	76. b	77. d	78. d	79. b	80. b
81. d									

Chapter 13

1. b	2. c	3. d	4. d	5. c	6. a	7. a	8. c	9. d	10. c
11. a	12. d	13. c	14. a	15. d	16. c	17. d	18. d	19. a	20. a
21. b	22. d	23. a	24. d	25. d	26. d	27. d	28. b	29. b	30. d
31. d	32. a	33. a	34. a	35. c	36. d	37. c	38. c	39. c	40. d
41. d	42. c	43. b	44. d	45. b	46. b	47. d	48. d	49. d	50. d
51. a	52. b	53. d	54. d	55. d	56. b	57. d	58. d	59. c	60. d
61. b	62. b	63. d	64. a	65. d	66. d	67. d	68. d	69. d	70. d
71. d	72. d	73. b	74. d	75. d	76. a	77. d	78. d	79. b	80. d
81. c	82. d	83. d	84. d						

Chapter 14

1. d	2. d	3. d	4. b	5. d	6. a	7. a	8. a	9. a	10. c
11. d	12. b	13. d	14. a	15. d	16. c	17. d	18. d	19. d	20. c
21. a	22. b	23. a	24. a	25. a	26. c	27. d	28. d	29. b	30. c
31. d	32. b	33. c	34. d	35. c					

ANSWER KEY

Chapter 15

1. d	2. b	3. d	4. d	5. c	6. d	7. a	8. d	9. a	10. b
11. d	12. b	13. d	14. d	15. d	16. b	17. b	18. d	19. a	20. d
21. d	22. d	23. b	24. d	25. b	26. d	27. a	28. c	29. a	30. d
31. d	32. b	33. a	34. c	35. d	36. a	37. d	38. b	39. d	40. d
41. c	42. d	43. d	44. d	45. d	46. d	47. c	48. a	49. d	50. d
51. a	52. d	53. c	54. c	55. a	56. d	57. d			

Chapter 16

1. d	2. b	3. d	4. b	5. d	6. d	7. a	8. a	9. c	10. d
11. b	12. b	13. b	14. c	15. b	16. d	17. d	18. d	19. d	20. a
21. a	22. c	23. a	24. c	25. d	26. b	27. d	28. b	29. b	30. d
31. d	32. c	33. d	34. a	35. a	36. a	37. a	38. a	39. d	40. b
41. c	42. d	43. d	44. c	45. d	46. d	47. d	48. b	49. a	50. c
51. b	52. b	53. d	54. b	55. d	56. d				

Chapter 17

1. b	2. c	3. d	4. d	5. d	6. d	7. d	8. d	9. d	10. a
11. d	12. d	13. d	14. a	15. d	16. d	17. d	18. d	19. c	20. a
21. c	22. d	23. d	24. c	25. a	26. c	27. d	28. c	29. c	30. c
31. d	32. d	33. b	34. c	35. d	36. a	37. d	38. d	39. c	40. a
41. d	42. b	43. d	44. c	45. c	46. d	47. b	48. a	49. d	50. c
51. d	52. a	53. d	54. b	55. b	56. b	57. a	58. c	59. d	60. d
61. d	62. d	63. a	64. d	65. c	66. d	67. a	68. c	69. a	70. a

Chapter 18

1. d	2. a	3. d	4. c	5. d	6. d	7. d	8. d	9. a	10. c
11. d	12. d	13. d	14. d	15. d	16. b	17. d	18. a	19. a	20. b
21. b	22. c	23. a	24. b	25. d	26. c	27. d	28. b	29. a	30. c
31. b	32. d	33. d	34. d	35. a	36. a	37. d	38. d	39. b	40. d
41. c	42. d	43. d	44. d	45. c	46. d	47. a	48. a	49. c	50. d
51. a	52. d	53. b	54. d	55. d	56. b				

Chapter 19

1. a	2. a	3. c	4. c	5. d	6. d	7. c	8. b	9. d	10. d
11. d	12. b	13. d	14. d	15. d	16. b	17. d	18. c	19. c	20. c
21. d	22. d	23. d	24. d	25. d	26. d	27. d	28. d	29. d	30. a
31. c	32. d	33. d	34. d	35. b	36. d	37. d	38. b	39. d	40. d
41. a	42. d	43. a	44. d	45. d	46. d	47. b	48. d	49. a	50. d
51. d	52. b	53. a	54. d						

Chapter 20

1. d	2. d	3. b	4. d	5. b	6. c	7. d	8. d	9. a	10. a
11. d	12. d	13. a	14. d	15. c	16. d	17. d	18. a	19. c	20. a